PUPPY
COACH

SET THEM UP TO SUCCEED

A COMPLETE GUIDE
TO RAISING A PUPPY

JO CROFT MA

Matador
9 Priory Business Park,
Wistow Road, Kibworth Beauchamp,
Leicestershire. LE8 0RX
Tel: 0116 279 2299
Email: books@troubador.co.uk
Web: www.troubador.co.uk/matador
Twitter: @matadorbooks

ISBN 978 1788037 228

British Library Cataloguing in Publication Data.
A catalogue record for this book is available from the British Library.

Printed by CPI Ltd, Croyden, London
Typeset in 11pt Gill Sans by Troubador Publishing Ltd, Leicester, UK

Matador is an imprint of Troubador Publishing Ltd

For Olivia and Max.
"Always follow your dreams."

CONTENTS

ACKNOWLEDGEMENTS

A special thank you to my husband James for his trust, patience and involvement in the Puppy Coach project. His intolerance of my negativity was appreciated even if it didn't appear so at times! Olivia and Max for giving me the determination to succeed. Mum, you are and will always be my inspiration, and thank you to my dad for giving me an immeasurable strength of character, motivation and determination to never give in. You are always in my thoughts.

To Merlin, Marley and Hogan, Jake and Sheba and all of the dogs I have worked with physically and mentally. You remind me just how amazing dogs are but also encouraged me to dig deep and challenge my own thoughts and opinions. You have taught me never to take anything for granted, to observe and listen before acting and to always have self-belief. I will continue to strive to educate and ensure the dog remains the loyal, adaptive man's best friend we want and need them to be.

Finally, a huge and heartfelt thank you to Jenny, without her I would not have had an opportunity to achieve this dream. Her belief and trust in my ability kept me going through the most challenging times. I hope this makes you proud.

BIOGRAPHY

Jo has a lifetime of diverse experience working with dogs both professionally and personally. 17 years as a qualified veterinary nurse sparked a specialist interest in canine behaviour and the start of a successful behaviour consultancy company. Jo has rehabilitated thousands of troubled dogs and successfully integrates new puppies into family homes. Academically Jo has a master's degree in Canine Psychology and Training, passing with a distinction and is a member of two leading canine behaviour associations: The Canine and Feline Behaviour Association and the Guild of Dog Trainers.

"Be part of the Puppy Coach community and set your puppy up for success."

www.PuppyCoach.com

INTRODUCTION

Welcome to a world full of joy and one of the best learning experiences you will ever have, sharing your life with one of the most amenable, trusting and loyal species on the planet. My role is to arm you with all the knowledge you'll need to ensure you raise your new puppy in the right way, preparing them to handle a domestic life and guiding them to become an adult dog you can be proud of.

It has taken a little time for me to consider that other people will want to hear what I have to say. I have been humbled by the canine species on many occasions but I would like to think my lifetime interacting with dogs in a variety of situations, professionally and personally, has stood me in good stead to share what I have learnt to date. I will continue to learn and be open to the opinions and ideas of others, our individual experiences will all deliver valuable lessons.

My journey began with a lengthy career working with animals from the age of 11. We weren't able to have dogs in our family due to the men of the house having asthma attacks if any hint of fur was evident in a 10 mile radius. So my canine kicks came from a little dog walking business earning 20p per half an hour walk, rain or shine and weekends and evenings spent at the local horse yard with horses, dogs, chickens, cats and some rather terrifying geese. My career choice never wavered. I went on to enjoy 17 years as a qualified Veterinary Nurse in practice where I was privileged to meet some of the most tolerant, inspiring animals and humans. It was during this time that I was to finally get my own dog. The Labrador had been my dream dog for as long as I could remember so once the decision was made, Merlin, my beautiful black male working Labrador retriever arrived just a few weeks later.

Aside from checking that my chosen breeder was registered with the Kennel Club, I pretty much did everything else wrong. Merlin slept in my bed, travelled on the front seat of my car and ate like a king even when I only had a jacket potato left in my kitchen. He came to work with me every day, accompanied me on my intense long distance runs in the dark, was welcome in everyone's home and quite frankly became my best friend and soul mate.

To this day I retain a level of guilt for the emotional stress I put him through. It was a tricky period in my life personally and Merlin did a fine job as my emotional crutch. Something I am not proud of today.

Merlin suffered beyond belief with atopy and food allergies, conditions that are prevalent in the breed. Specialist after specialist offered little support in the way of improving his symptoms but working in the veterinary world meant I had access to some knowledgeable people and with guidance I found a means of managing him. Little did I know at the time that I would go on to help dogs like Merlin with their allergies using my behaviour modification techniques to remove stress and balance their lives. The scratch-itch cycle is caused by a release of histamine and this process is triggered in the presence of stress chemicals. On reflection I now feel my emotional dramas potentially added to his symptoms, as the physical and emotional bond I had with Merlin was so close he would most definitely have been susceptible.

Merlin in his prime – the perfect teacher!

That said, this bond was the catalyst for all I know about dogs today. Merlin could manage an unruly dog like no other as he knew when to convert to play, when to stand his ground and when to ignore. His body language cues were intense and I observed and have copied his approach in many situations. Ultimately he taught me an invaluable skill in how to control the energy in any scenario, allowing subtle communication and breathing space or time to think for every individual. So from here my interest in canine behaviour began to develop, dogs were so much more than human companions and I became fascinated by their evolution and ability to fit in to our complicated world.

This fascination wouldn't stay untouched for long, so driven by a desire to pass on my knowledge to others and help the increasing numbers of troubled dogs, I took the leap into a new career path. I was propelled into a world of constant learning, changes in dynamics, interesting lifestyles and heartbreaking stories. I ventured off on my own to specialise in one of my greatest loves, helping dogs to thrive socially in domestic environments, living happily with humans just as they should be. I could never have gained the knowledge or confidence I have today without the help of my gorgeous boy. He really was a dog in a million.

In the early days there were countless times I sat outside a client's house chewing my fingernails, anticipating what was ahead and wondering if I would be competent enough to pass on my knowledge in a viable format. Merlin always retained his calm, confident energy even in the midst of an owner meltdown!

All of the dogs I saw during this early period were taken out for a walk to meet Merlin and he allowed me to understand if I had read them correctly. His response to aggressive or reactive cases in particular would help me decide where their coping threshold failed and provided guidance on the deep rooted triggers in some of the most complex cases. I trusted his judgement and took his lead. This period of learning was tough on my confidence, I knew my dogs but educating my owners was a whole different challenge and human psychology was definitely high on my list of things to learn!

When Merlin passed away in 2010 I had already retired him for a much quieter life, but his legacy lives on in all the dogs he has helped, the knowledge I gained and the beautiful memories we created together. Rest in peace special boy.

I am now no longer that jibbering new therapist but instead I respect how privileged I am to be in a position to make changes to people's lives that I would never have thought possible, just by reconnecting them with their dog on the right platform. My canine consultancy has now been successfully running since 2005. After a variety of informative academic courses I achieved a master's degree in Canine Psychology and Training, passing with a distinction in 2015. My project on canine anxiety and human emotion encapsulated my prior learning, opinions and observations and became a catalyst for a variety of new ventures – Puppy Coach being the first.

Puppy Coach consists of an online and bespoke series of films available at www.PuppyCoach.com in conjunction with this book. It is designed to guide every new dog owner through the highs and lows of the introduction, training and development of a new puppy and his or her integration into family life.

Hogan as a 4 week old puppy.

I am frequently asked simple questions such as "How do I stop my dog barking at the front door?", "What can I do as my dog never comes back when I call?"; the list is endless. My frustration comes when I try to explain that there is no 'quick fix' answer or simple solutions when it comes to dogs. In a world of fast service, throw away and replaceable objects I feel the essence of the dog is being lost. They speak a different language to us and each and every one is individual. There isn't a text book available that will describe your dog completely, they are as unique as we are, but this book and accompanying videos are designed to give you focal points, educate you to meet your dog's needs and understand their expectations to build a heathy, happy relationship.

The advice provides an abundance of professional guidance, delivering thought provoking evidence on the importance of raising a well-trained puppy. It is a window into the reality of puppy ownership from the early puppy days up to and including the onset of adolescence, through the eyes of myself and my new puppy Labrador Hogan, who had big shoes to fill! The entire project is designed to shed light on how and where problems arise. I use my first hand experiences to portray a realistic perspective on managing a new puppy and ultimately the adult dog.

This book is designed to stand alone and provide a text version of all of the content within the films, also providing you with further information and depth of knowledge.

A break from filming with cameraman Sal Ormandji.

Hogan's development was extremely fast in the early weeks and you, as a new puppy owner, will experience this too. While your relationship is new and exciting, it is important to recognise that from the first minute you interact with your puppy, you are shaping their behaviour for the rest of their lives.

During the filming we tried to capture all the key aspects of Hogan's early life, my management of his behaviour, his basic training and development of our relationship. The subjects were dealt with individually and so Hogan was inevitably at different life stages throughout. Much of what was covered began as soon as Hogan arrived with us, even if you see Hogan as an older puppy on film. This book serves as a more detailed account of the experience. The films are listed in order of how we shot and edited them but you will be able to view any film or read any chapter in which ever order you prefer and it will be relevant.

There have been many times where I have reflected on Hogan's early weeks and felt the true 'puppy period' was way too short, this time really does fly by and so it is worth investing as much knowledge, care and attention to your puppy to ensure you give them the best start.

CHAPTER 1

What to Expect from your Learning Journey

Training Methods

All the methods used throughout the series focus on positively reinforcing good, desirable behaviours in your puppy.

I am often asked how I achieve my results. Clients want a clear explanation of this prior to any booking and rightly so. I work with one rule and that is to open up an effective line of communication with every dog or puppy I meet. This is always achieved by observing the dog's communication and their response to my chosen behaviours. I do not arrive at a consultation looking to adopt a dictatorial attitude to my clients or put unnecessary pressure on their dog to make it conform.

I do however want to reach a successful result and keep a happy dog in a happy home so I strive to create calm and rebalance the relationship between dog and owner using a structured approach via a behaviour program and educating my owners. I would like to consider that most of my clients view me as somebody they can trust and rely on to help them develop or change their relationship with their dog.

An unruly, badly behaved puppy or adult dog really can cause family stress. There has been more than one case where my client's personal relationships are suffering because of a difference of opinion on how to manage the dog. Divorce is just not a solution, so getting two individuals on the same page is often trickier than treating the dog!

When educating your puppy make sure that all members of the family are on board with a consistent approach, even if perceptions are different the puppy will still need the same guidance if it is to learn from different handlers.

People, whether they are trainers, handlers or owners will always have their own opinions based on personal learning and experience. I pride myself in being open to everyone's opinions; no matter how experienced we are, we should all be open to learning.

We are dealing with the brain of another species and each one is as individual as we are, what works for one won't work for another, so having lots of tools in your box is essential! I have had to move goal posts and change direction with many puppies depending on what they deliver and I learnt this lesson the hard way with my own dog Marley, who you will meet later.

I prefer to teach a concept of understanding and provide my clients with tools and education to help them make their own decisions, this is the most effective means of training.

It is also important to recognise your own limitations. Patience in people is varied and usually low so you will be provided with consistent and clear management techniques beneficial to your puppy and you throughout.

In order to develop your puppy successfully you shouldn't just focus on one means of management. To solely give treats every time your puppy meets your expectation could be damaging. If you compare this to how we manage children, we don't offer treats just to stop a child having a tantrum in a public place. So you wouldn't give treats just because your puppy happens to walk past another dog or person without jumping up!

It is more beneficial to provide the treat as a goal for positive behaviour and remove the treat if the goal is not achieved. Therefore, creating a consequence for the individual's actions, if they fail to follow direction.

A treat may take many different forms for a child and this is also the case for your puppy.

Dogs love to please people; this is why they have become such fantastic family pets. With this in mind it is likely you can utilise the time spent with you as one of the rewards for your puppy's positive behaviour.

This is only achievable if you work to create your balanced relationship. Otherwise you may find your only means of control is your treat! This will set you, as an owner, up to fail in so many situations.

Treats will take a firm back seat to events such as play with another dog, chasing wildlife or interrupting the local boys football team! The piece of cheese you are frantically waving will become a dark and distant memory in most of these cases along with your reputation as a responsible dog owner!

If you think logically about how you manage a child, or for that matter any fellow human being who you may be educating or working with, you are following some simple but clear steps. Maybe without even realising you are doing so, as follows:

- Communicating with them on their level
- Remaining calm and clear throughout
- Setting a boundary for your tolerance
- Being clear with your expectation
- Encouraging good behaviour
- Providing a reward when the goal is achieved
- Having the ability to provide a consequence if the goal is not achieved therefore, encouraging the individual to perform the positive behaviour
- Having the ability to repeat this process with success

We can apply exactly the same rationale to how we manage our puppy.

My focus is always to set the puppy up for success as this builds their confidence and most importantly their trust in you as an owner. It also creates a platform for authority and direction without the need for frustration or anger if things don't go to plan. You will always have an 'end stage', where you will put some distance between yourself and your puppy giving you both room to calm down, or you will have encouraged a successful result. You will work efficiently to reach the latter!

I never teach my clients to tell a puppy off or punish them, this would mean coping strategies have failed and the puppy has been allowed to display normal dog behaviour in a negative way. However, the puppy can be taught that the negative behaviour still has a consequence, you will communicate your dislike in the form of removal from the situation, clearly and firmly and without discussion.

Never use your voice in these instances and never act in an overly challenging or physical manner. This will only heighten the situation and result in a more severe negative response, developing in the form of aggression and/or fear.

I am definitely not perfect so making mistakes is as normal for me as it is everyone else, especially when you have two small children running around and another dog. Realising where you have gone wrong takes time and patience but it will help you develop a better relationship with your puppy if you can identify where you need to improve. Your puppy will be very forgiving so you may not know things are going wrong until it's too late.

If in doubt, adopt an aloof attitude, remove all human emotion and think about the problem you are facing with a very black and white attitude.

Dogs don't do grey areas or complex human emotion such as guilt, sympathy and jealousy. They are all about survival and will focus on resources that provide them the security to achieve this. You need to be their primary resource!

If you are viewed as an equal or lower ranking individual, you will make yourself and your family a target for constant challenges and this is not conducive to a harmonious relationship. This is where your new attitude should begin to develop. THINK DOG and you will go far!

So to recap. This form of management is achieved by following the same guidelines you would use to manage any situation with a human. As follows:

- Provide your puppy with clear direction
- Set boundaries for their physical environment
- Communicate with your body language
- Stay calm and clear
- Be realistic with your expectations
- Provide a goal (this may be food, praise, toy or just to join a social space)
- If they still fail, then remove the goal
- If the behaviour continues remove the puppy
- Stay calm and consistent throughout

You must always remember that your puppy will be lost in your world to begin with, you need to act as the individual who will guide them around each stage of social interaction. Do not set your puppy up to fail by over exposing them too quickly without controls and guidance being in place.

Your puppy's socialisation is one of the most important aspects of their development but you can easily over socialise, so set a plan for this and ensure you are observing the body language of your puppy to gauge whether they are comfortable or not.

Observing your puppy's body language around children will help you understand what they are able to cope with. This is a very relaxed 4 week old Hogan with our little boy.

Avoid simple mistakes like picking your puppy up and carrying them to the front door every time someone visits, this will be challenging for your puppy and you will be distracted so it isn't a great time to allow your puppy to learn positive interaction. Deal with guest arrival in a sensitive and careful manner.

Approach all social scenarios the same, keep it simple and calm, always ensure there is physical space between your puppy and social situation. Your puppy should be able to hear, see and smell but not touch! Baby gates are brilliant for this as is a carefully placed crate. Your guests should be respectful of your direction.

To put this in place it is advisable to take your puppy to their crate or down time area prior to the arrival or departure of any guest and during any level of high activity in your home.

You should not expect your puppy to cope with the complex nature of human behaviour and giving them some physical space to observe this will really help their understanding and early learning.

I encourage people to treat new puppies as you would the arrival of a new human baby. I would never dream of reaching out and touching a stranger's new baby in a pram and I therefore expect the same courtesy when I'm out with my puppy. Sadly, this isn't realistic and a puppy will always evoke a response from passers by.

Here is Kerry, my live consult client (chapters 25 and 26), with her puppy Willis and Hogan practising perfect control. Hogan is 6 months here.

Just remember if your puppy jumps up every time they are greeted by someone, this will result in a response or reward, the passer by is actually training your puppy to jump up on everyone. This may be cute when they are small but having a 40kg muddy Labrador or such like flatten random strangers is not only socially unacceptable but it is also dangerous!

Don't set yourself up for failure. I spent the first 3 months of Hogan's little life asking everyone not to talk to him but to speak to me instead when we were out. Adopting an 'it's all about me' attitude is not always easy but it's something that you really need to address to avoid things going wrong from the start.

Hogan has never learnt that people are exciting out on a walk. The only reward he routinely received was from me, for sitting while I had a conversation. I did let the occasional person greet him, under direction and this helped with his social interaction.

You, as an owner have a responsibility to protect your puppy now before they have their own way of dealing with passers by later on!

Throughout this book you will be guided to manage your puppy's behaviour by observing their body language, learning to recognise stress indicators and developing a solid relationship.

You will be taught how to respond to poor behaviour by removing the puppy to a simple boundary line to create calm before re-introducing them.

Finally, you will be educated in understanding what motivates your puppy rather than just teaching them responses to a variety of human spoken words.

Hogan with his pal Buddy on a walk at 11 weeks.

Training Motivation

To support your puppy's learning it is important that you find something that motivates them in order to be able to reinforce their positive behaviours and develop their learning ability.

Instigating toy-focused play with Marley during the PuppyCoach.com filming.

This doesn't have to be food; in fact, some dogs don't always respond well to food. I have witnessed many a struggling owner turn up to a puppy training class only to find their puppy is more interested in what the heating pipes do than any piece of sausage or even chopped liver!

There can be many reasons for this, firstly if a puppy is in a heightened state the focus will not be on eating and there will be no natural motivation for food. This also applies to a very nervous or fearful puppy. Anxiety is to blame here, how you manage the whole scenario needs to be addressed.

Ultimately dogs that are not motivated by food would die in the wild so it should be recognised as a problem with a deeper meaning if you have this issue in training.

I often use high prize food to gauge how stressed my adult dog behaviour cases are in a particular situation. It can sometimes appear that a dog is coping but if a usually 'food motivated' dog is refusing to take a treat then all is not well.

Some breeds of dog are generally less motivated by food and you will often find this with whippets and greyhounds, again because they are generally of a more nervous disposition. You can always try and deliver the puppy's main meal during their training session and if you establish this pattern early, the transition to associating food along with your direction and positive commands should be smooth.

Finally, your puppy may just not be hungry. Over feeding is likely when they are very young as you will have been encouraged to feed 3-4 meals per day. It is very easy to ensure your puppy never has an empty tummy feeding this way, so again, why not make one of the meals focused around hand feeding during training. This will also help cement your positive relationship.

If you still can't win this battle then find something else that works for your puppy, you can use various different toys (squeaky if necessary), praise or ball games. Set this up at home before trying to make it work in a more stimulating environment. It is my opinion that this is often much harder than trying to work through with the food motivator as you have to associate a toy rather than work with something that's already associated positively for your puppy as a survival tool!

A Personal Perspective

I can speak from the heart when I say that I had to battle my emotional connection with Hogan throughout his early months to ensure he had only clear and positive direction to learn from. Allowing the true love and adoration I have for him to take over would have left me creating grey areas of leadership that would have been hard to recover from.

Instead I channelled this into 'attention giving' time, focused around rewarding a calm down stay or short period sat next to me on the floor of our living room, on my terms.

Caught in the act giving Hogan a quick squeeze.

His true puppy period lasted only just a few weeks, from then on he established himself and worked out where all his boundaries lay, ensuring he tested the strength of every one of them over time!

The point here is to make sure you never allow your puppy full access to your entire home without guidance from you, they thrive off clear direction and do well when they understand some areas are out of bounds!

My motivation for Puppy Coach is to deliver a 'real' and personal approach to training a puppy while juggling family life. It takes time, patience and an abundance of understanding to develop and teach a much loved family pet the rules of human life, put the work in during the first year and you will be rewarded for life.

Hogan and the Film Crew!

Hogan arrived with us at the age of 8 weeks. We began filming the Puppy Coach series two weeks later so he was 10 weeks old in the first film. This was essential time required for him to settle and a develop a relationship with both me and my family without the added distraction of a camera crew.

One of Hogan's first experiences on camera.

I advise that you adopt the same mentality for the arrival of your new puppy. Establishing routines and effectively going through the 'getting to know you' period is important social time, you will never get this back so keep your distractions to a minimum. Likewise, if you have taken time off work to settle your puppy but intend to return, make sure you establish early on what will be your normal routine.

If you are intending to be away from home for several hours then begin this routine by ignoring your puppy for short periods while you are home, then building on their tolerance of solitary time over the period you are off.

It will be damaging for your puppy if you devote all your time to them while you are away from work but then suddenly disappear daily for hours when you return, cutting your contact time dramatically. Again consider setting your puppy up for success!

Puppy Coach Task

At the end of each of the chapters (and films) you will be given a task to complete which will help you document your personal progress while you raise your well-mannered Puppy Coach puppy.

Your first task is…

Document your motivation for acquiring a puppy. Make a note on areas where you feel a dog will benefit your life and how much of this can be attributed to emotional support.

This will help you address the needs of the dog and also ensure you start off on the right foot in protecting them from high energy in your social environment.

CHAPTER 2

Focus on Owner Education

During my consultations I am always aware that the successful integration of a puppy is based not only on understanding the puppy but having the ability to educate the owner ensuring they are able to apply the techniques and knowledge required. This knowledge empowered me to find ways of educating, understanding human characters and personality traits and assessing the best way of delivering advice. This book takes into account all of these factors and aims to provide comprehensive, clear direction to empower each and every reader. My motivation for Puppy Coach is immeasurable but a few areas stand out as being instrumental in its development.

Motivation for Puppy Coach

The background to my motivation for Puppy Coach evolved as a result of two incidents with dogs who I had been called out to assess and rehabilitate. The result from each visit was two separate, sustained attacks from different dogs, occurring due to misinformation and owner denial, something I had never experienced to this degree before.

Early in 2014 I sustained the first dog attack whilst attending a family home. This took place on the doorstep of the owner's house. I had rung the front door bell and as the door opened I was greeted with a dog in full on 'attack mode'. He subsequently delivered a full thickness bite to one of my arms, breaking my watch strap and then continued by 'ragging' my opposing elbow!

Fortunately, I had asked the owner to attach a lead to the dog's collar so they were able to eventually pull him off me before I sustained further injury.

Despite my injuries, I subsequently spent the following two hours assessing and working with the dog before taking myself off to A&E!

My conclusion was the dog was overly stressed, lacking in appropriate mental and physical stimulation, poorly socialised and living in an empowered role in the home. A recipe for disaster but no longer an isolated incident as this was becoming normal for many of my clients requesting help.

This attack led me to question the safety of my work, but more importantly the perception of dog behaviour by the general public. After all, I could have just been a child approaching the door to ask for his ball back – the owners may have been facing a very different scenario.

Discussion with the client revealed that the dog had very little external social time, he was difficult to manage and so spent most days laid by the front door and of an evening he slept in his owner's bed. Although the dog's welfare was a concern, these clients needed support not criticism and I did my best to offer that.

It really was not surprising at the level of misunderstanding this dog had developed towards the ownership of household territory, nor was it surprising that I became the focus for his immense frustration as I triggered stimulation and hyperactivity around the area he was clearly guarding.

I am in no doubt that the client loved their dog and felt they were giving him the best life possible, but it does raise the question… at what point does 'loving an animal' make it acceptable to house them inside four walls with nothing to do all day. Socially this appears to be on the increase as a worrying trend develops towards the humanising of this amazing species.

I will refrain from giving further details about the breed as I don't feel it is relevant. This was the result of a circumstance. The owners were definitely out of their depth with the capability of this dog, making its presence in a domestic home dangerous.

This attack was to be followed later in the year by a second incident. This was much more severe and almost ended my career working with dogs. I struggle to think that the clients in question intentionally withheld important information about their dogs behaviour, I prefer therefore to consider that they were in denial and chose to ignore the severity of the problem in the hope that I would make it go away.

I will always strive to calm a hyper, excitable dog before engaging with it and this dog was no exception. However, it was clear that this dog was extremely confident in its behaviour as you would expect from a large, powerful animal on its own territory. He had also been given every marker of authority and was taking the lead role in the home. Greeting guests at the front door, being overly boisterous while in a social space, sleeping on and guarding the owners bed and generally acting in a very unbalanced manner.

Taking calm control of any dog is a positive in pretty much all households. In fact, I would suggest that the dogs I visit welcome an opportunity to follow clear, positive guidance and have their natural expectations met. However, there are a handful of dogs who retain such dominant traits that they will not accept authority from any individual, including their owners. This appeared to be such a case.

Taking control of the dog was successful but the calm was tainted with an energy that I can only describe as spine tingling. Suffice to say I was not comfortable sharing the same space as this dog, here is where your 'gut instinct' kicks in. You either listen to it or apply professional stupidity and 'power on,' striving to make this dog's relationship with its owner better, to improve things for all. The choice I made was to become one that I initially regretted but later recognised the positive, as it was the trigger for the development of Puppy Coach and all it strives to achieve.

So I stayed at the house and worked solidly to educate the dog's owner and set new boundaries for the dog to work to. My niggling gut ensured I worked at a distance and predominantly directed the owner through a series of handling techniques and the implementation of boundary control. The consult went well but the dog didn't take his eyes off me. We were working with a level of respect for each other's personal space, this was very much 'his' space and he didn't welcome the sudden owner control that occurred with my direction.

Once the rehabilitation plan was in place and all was settled I got ready to leave. I should point out that I had asked the client several times as to whether the dog had ever been aggressive, to which the reply was a firm 'No'.

Apparently he was only walked in a muzzle as he had a dislike for small furry creatures and the blinds at the window of their living room were closed due to nosey neighbours, not because he guarded the front of the house! Listening to an owner can be hugely valuable but I will never again question my gut instinct over what I am being told.

My intended exit from the house meant that I turned my body language away from the dog in order to leave, this provided an opportunity for the dog to react (the minute you turn your back on a dog of this nature, you become prey!) He seized the opportunity and I sustained two separate full thickness bites to my hand and leg. Currently, 18 months after the event my physical injuries are still visible. I believe I was spared the 'red mist' behaviour as I did not react in any way. This included not breathing, speaking or moving! I am very happy that this was my instinctive response as anything else would have resulted in a much more serious outcome! Feeling the power of a 45kg dog and its jaws on your body is one of the most terrifying things I have ever had to face.

The whole incident provided a massive learning experience that was to change and re-shape my approach to professional canine rehabilitation. We are human and expect our lives and that of other species to conform to our way of thinking but this was a very real reminder of how fragile life is and how very vulnerable we are against animal instinct.

With regards the outcome of the dog, sadly there are occasions where a dog's behaviour is not salvageable, whether this is due to genetics or the fact that it is just too embedded. An assessment of many factors which included the dog's age, lifestyle and social learning alongside the behaviour exhibited, concluded this dog was unsafe in a domestic environment and rehabilitation was not deemed viable. I have a moral and legal obligation to assess and advise on whether it is safe to apply a treatment program within the dog's current home environment. This dog was just not suitable. The clients chose to keep the dog under restriction guidelines.

I became concerned at the direction our social relationship with dogs was going but I also wanted something positive to come from my experiences. This will provide a depth of understanding for why I focus on educating a control of your emotional led behaviours throughout.

I am truly worried for the sustained safe survival of the canine species as a companion animal. If the continued path of humanising the dog, dressing them up, referring to them as human babies and showering them with emotion is to continue, so will the rise in human and dog to dog aggression. It is worth pointing out that when I first entered veterinary medicine the canine behaviour profession didn't exist. We were familiar with the dog training imposed by classic leaders in the field at the time, such as Barbara Woodhouse, but training dogs to conform to our requirements was the only goal here. Studying the behaviour of dogs and educating the public has become a necessity of much more recent years.

I would like to stress that in all the time I have worked with dogs I had never been in the unfortunate position of sustaining a dog bite or attack such as these ever, despite handling some serious aggression cases.

A normal dog will do everything it can to avoid an aggressive altercation, unless there is an underlying genetic motivation or a serious management/ communication problem that has embedded a confident aggressive response.

Sadly, dogs can and do bite and so you need to be aware of how to avoid this at all costs and more importantly how to avoid your puppy resorting to aggression to make themselves understood. However, if you correctly set up your puppy, take the time to recognise communication and stress indicators, while providing them with their basic needs, there is no reason why you should ever have to face aggression.

Dogs of this calibre are rare and attacks occurred because the owners chose to follow human emotional perception of a situation, rather than addressing the severity of it and implementing safety procedures. This at the very least would have set the dog up for a more successful outcome.

Years working with and owning dogs has led me to recognise how much of their communication focuses on energy. They are completely receptive and sensitive to the energy around them and utilise different levels of energy to communicate with other dogs and humans. An awareness of a dog's energy enables you to stay safe in their company. What has become apparent is that the majority of cases I see are led by the dog's insecurity and anxiety responses, as a result high and unbalanced energy is a common observation. This coupled with the cross-breeding of our finely-tuned pedigree dogs to produce breeds such as the Cavapoo, Labradoodle, Cockerpoo and my own dog Marley, a Goldendoodle, seems to have given a genetic element as a consideration for this too.

I have included Marley's story within this chapter as I feel he gave me the biggest learning curve of my career and huge motivation for Puppy Coach. He provided me with an opportunity to truly appreciate the difficulties faced by my clients as they work through a behaviour program to balance their dogs and maintain a solid positive relationship when behaviour issues are present.

I also feel his story is not isolated and that there are many people struggling with the fallout from pedigree crossbreeding. If you are sitting there with your newly purchased pedigree cross you may initially be a little alarmed when you read about the struggles Marley faced. I feel it is important to raise awareness and also give direction on how to manage your puppy correctly if you find yourself with an unbalanced ball of fluff!

Marley's Story

Marley has provided me with an immense understanding of what it's like to manage, train and rehabilitate a 'confused' dog. A confused dog is frustrated, intolerant and reactive and takes anxiety to a whole new level.

Marley on one of his many holidays to sunny Cornwall.

His story is complex and long but a fair amount of my own self-control, patience and focused puppy exercises have all developed as a result of working with this special boy.

In March 2010 I received a phone call from a lovely family who had just brought home their Goldendoodle puppy 'Marwood'. There wasn't anything particularly unusual about the conversation, they were struggling with the normal puppy behaviour problems – mouthing, jumping up and vocal issues – that many new puppy owners experience. Little did I know that this would be the beginning of a huge professional life lesson!

The originally named 'Marwood' was 10 weeks old at this point so I was keen to see them as soon as possible to ensure any changes were made in the valuable critical learning period. I booked my usual two hour initial puppy consult with them with a view to addressing all their concerns, under normal circumstances this would be adequate time.

Marley as an adult has grown to be a lovely dog and has bonded well with Hogan.

Early History

The Goldendoodle is sometimes referred to as one of the 'designer' breeds. Marley was the first of his kind that I had been asked to assess at the time.

The UK was flooded with Labradoodles but Goldendoodle's were rare. Marley happens to be the 2nd generation of this 50/50 mix of Golden Retriever and Standard Poodle, so his parents were both Goldendoodles. The fine working retriever genes and hunting instinct of the poodle were a long way back.

It wouldn't take much to recognise that the instinctive behaviour of this dog would be hindered and therefore he would possibly require a higher level of control than some!

Marley was bred in Scotland by a really lovely family who had ticked all the right boxes with regards early handling and socialisation and had basically bred with the best of intentions. His new owners had flown up to Scotland on two occasions to visit prior to actually bringing him home. I was content with the fact this Goldendoodle puppy had a great start in life with regard to being introduced to many social scenarios he would experience as an adult dog.

Marley is now in his developed adult years and over this time there has been huge progress in breeding programs and lessons learnt. Many good breeders are now considering the calibre and breed traits of the dogs they are putting together. This has resulted in an improvement in the behaviour of the breed overall. Since writing the first edition of this book I have now had the pleasure of meeting dedicated, knowledgable doodle breeders. Their dogs have been fun, social and well behaved, something that I have been really encouraged to see.

That said, my story with Marley continues in this book as the foundations I created in supporting him through his young years have stood me well. I used my experiences to develop many coping strategies and management tools which I now regularly pass on to clients. Finding a happy balance of positive interaction to build confidence and trust alongside management of his ability to cope with stimulation was challenging. He provided me with the raw learning of what it's really like to manage a highly strung, tricky character and most importantly he has given me many years afterwards of pleasure, laughs and proud moments which has made all the hard work just that little bit more worthwhile.

My Opinion

I purposefully haven't researched the opinions of others on pedigree mixed breeds prior to writing this account, although I am aware there are many and the opinions are as diverse as the breed itself! When it comes to Marley he is unique and I consider myself an authority on him and only him. There are variants in dogs with similar breeding as you would expect, these guys are individuals with many things that may affect their adult behaviour.

The Highs and Lows

Marley's story is tricky to write as it means I have to reflect on and revisit my relationship with him as a whole, highlighting feelings of failure alongside elation.

He totally showed me up during his puppy consult, straightforward he was not! In fact every time I managed to get his biting, high energy and general bad manners under control he sent me something worse to deal with.

I am not too proud to say that there wasn't one thing I actually did during the consultation that he responded well to. I had quickly realised that unless I was content to get my fingers bitten then treats were a no go, correct use of his crate resulted in so much barking I couldn't even hear myself speak, his poor owner was just speechless as she watched in horror as this mini beast seemed to run as many rings around me as he did her!

My puppy consults were usually enjoyable and hugely rewarding and that included my experience with some really difficult dogs. I was used to challenging situations dealing with large breeds who were biting people, dogs pulling their owners off their feet and serious high level separation anxiety cases. Surely this 10 week old terror would be no match for me… how wrong I was!

Marley at 4 months – a picture of perfection.

I did manage to regain my composure during the consult and at least prove to my client that I knew what I was doing, but I had the feeling things wouldn't go to plan when I left.

We changed his food to a more natural diet and set a behaviour modification program in place with a focus on leadership and calm control.

The children in the house had been using water sprays to keep him from biting them so we removed those and attached a lead to his collar in the house so his owner had more ability to physically control him.

Nothing worked and a week later I offered to take him for free so he could live with us and I would have a better understanding of what was going on, not something I would normally have to do. I felt I needed time with this little puppy, plus I don't do failure!

I had a mission to put him through his paces and work out why he was so reactive. He spent four days with us and didn't put a foot wrong. He slept downstairs in the kitchen overnight without making a sound, walked to heel, started learning recall, sit and down stays and appeared to be the perfect puppy. So I delivered him back to his owners extremely happy with all that we had achieved.

Within a few hours the delinquent had returned and I received a phone call to say that he had bitten his owner through her heel quite badly. I could hear him barking so excessively in the background that I said I would go and collect him.

This is absolutely no reflection on this family. They were truly lovely and did everything they could to cope. When I later experienced the darker side of my boy I was to sympathise hugely with their plight.

Cutting a long story short we ended up taking him on. We didn't want another dog at the time but I just had a feeling things wouldn't go well for Marley if he had been re-homed to another poor, unsuspecting household.

Our Journey Begins

By now two weeks had passed and Marley was on his third home in as many weeks. I was hopeful that technically we were still within the critical early learning period so establishing new routines and embedding desirable behaviour should be fairly straightforward. We changed his name to Marley just because it was a little less formal than Marwood but not too tricky for him to get to grips with.

I haven't documented the exact path of social learning and training that I put Marley through as I was too busy physically managing him. Suffice to say things started well, he integrated into our home and my professional environment smoothly and with Merlin, my Labrador at the time, running a tight ship there was little opportunity for him to push boundaries. That was until he reached 16 weeks and then things were to change.

I had recognised that Marley required a huge amount of clear direction and it was impossible for me to lower my authority in any way. I still describe him as a boiling pot that needs a lid, even now. On one occasion I let him come up on the sofa for a quick cuddle, before I knew it he was sitting on the back of the sofa with his head on top of mine. I never did that again!

He also failed to cope in our living room, choosing to spend the majority of his time in the kitchen. If invited in to be with us he would pace around the room walking figures of eight until I directed him into a down, even then he would fidget and appear uncomfortable.

I basically couldn't switch off at all and found myself second guessing his behaviour and 'thinking dog' far too often.

I guess a flood of testosterone was an added complication and this hormone served to ramp up Marley's quest for authority. So I was about to be tested by my own dog more than any other I had ever dealt with.

So we had generally good manners socially around possessions, attention and social interaction. His food manners were spot on but treat training was a no go, the mere sight of a treat sent him wild, as did any high level praise. Calm, quiet and soft was the required level of vocal praise. Get this wrong or show a bit too much exuberance and a 15kg Goldendoodle would land on your head in a heartbeat!

Posing in the wind at Lands End.

We were making good progress until breakfast one morning. Placing his food bowl on the floor while he waited patiently was the norm and something he picked up pretty quickly, this was conducted as usual.

This particular day, I bent down to pick up a pair of shoes reasonably near his bowl. As I did so he spun round and directed a bite at my face. Finely tuned reflexes from my years as a vet nurse allowed me to deflect his attack and launch him through the open back door.

Hardly what you would expect from a dog behaviourist but in this instance self-preservation kicked in! My response and timing made an impact that would begin Marley's learning journey in a domestic environment, creating a new awareness of human boundaries.

So apparently my fluffy pooch had another side to him and probably one of the most difficult behaviour problems to address. He had never had food taken from him or had to struggle to feed as a puppy in the litter so in the absence of learnt behaviour this had to be genetically motivated or in simple terms, part of his character and personality.

After this incident, Marley was really cautious near me around food, I should point out it didn't affect any other area of our relationship and this really serves to underpin the fact that dogs 'live in the moment' and 'learn by association.'

I spent the following six weeks placing his food down and then adding food to his bowl while he ate, to re-establish our relationship. He spent most of this time displaying discomfort at my presence during this exercise, but ultimately dealt with it and we have never looked back. So much so that four years later our kids deliver him his food and treats under my direction and it's been a fantastic way of establishing their relationship. This incident would not act as a platform for the way I direct my clients to deal with food aggression, this was a very particular incident and we already had excellent ground work in place for Marley to have a positive relationship with humans around food. This behaviour problem can be extremely complex and each dog needs to be considered on an individual basis before advice can be given.

The Wild Side

It became pretty clear that there was our gorgeous Goldendoodle – Marley – willing to learn, eager to please, smart and affectionate.

And then there was this…

A chemical response, 'red mist', hyperactive, unbalanced or whatever you want to call it. Frankly this side of Marley was unsafe and tested my behaviour knowledge to its limit.

From 4 to 12 months I dealt with the following puppy behaviour problems.

Eating his Own Poo

Again the canine behaviourist in me pretty much failed with this unhealthy, socially unacceptable habit taking over my life!

After using every obvious treatment plan, I resorted to standing poised in my kitchen with two saucepans. Ensuring he was midway committed to tucking into his neatly delivered package, I took the opportunity to totally freak out the neighbours and ran outside banging my saucepans while watching Marley flee for his life up the garden. I then stood over said poo while he walked around me back to the house, calmly picked it up and disposed of it and carried on like it hadn't happened. Seriously, was this really what I was resorting too? It hardly put to good use all the finance I had applied to my academic career.

Marley spent the next few weeks running away from his poo but eventually that stopped and he has never even considered eating it again. Not a technique I have ever had to resort to telling my clients to do I might add. It was becoming increasingly clear that the subtle controls for dog behaviour I was so used to using, just weren't clear enough for Marley. His extreme behaviour only seemed to respond to my extreme behaviour but it had to be delivered in a very calm, clear and no nonsense way!

Bullying Other Dogs

Big, small, fluffy or scary… Marley wasn't fussy about who he flattened, launched himself at or hassled. Quite simply he lost his head with anything remotely four-legged and furry. This is an issue that will still haunt us if I don't manage him daily, although he tends to focus on chasing the odd squirrel now rather than just other people's much loved pets!

Barging

Spatial awareness has never been Marley's strong point and I lost count how many times I could be seen grabbing for the nearest tree when he came thundering past, nor do I wish to recall my attempts to stay on my feet when he chose to run through me as if I didn't exist. I regularly found myself on my backside, leaving my pride and business reputation in the mud! This has got better over time and my tree hugging days, thankfully are now over.

Car travel was one thing Marley never had a problem with; to this day he loves a new adventure and will happily sit in the car and wait for the next phase of excitement.

Pulling on the Lead

Marley likes to lead, so four years on his lead work is still something that we practise every day. In the early days I tackled this by taking him running. An iPod, trainers, disinterested attitude and lots of changes of direction and finally the pooch learned to follow not lead!

Low Tolerance

His high energy and reactivity equates to a lack of tolerance. This means I have to manage and correct any low level aggressive responses, whether this be with other dogs or during grooming in the early days. My dedication paid off and apart from telling off the odd boisterous dog, Marley doesn't show any aggressive behaviour at all and that's the way it will stay.

Hyperactivity

An excitable Marley is not one you can encourage. This means high level play at home, lots of high energy or anticipation results in him taking on the persona of something resembling the Tasmanian Devil. A character I have been likened too myself on many occasions. However, I don't use my teeth to bite in these situations or scream my head off (usually anyway!). Sadly, Marley did and so I tell my guests to ignore him and I control any reactive behaviour as it could be potentially dangerous.

Prey Drive

This has been by far the hardest behaviour to manage and to date I still struggle with his hunting instinct. This was opened up at a very young age with the reward of chasing pheasants and as he successfully caught a couple of rabbits it's unlikely my leadership or perfect recall can ever truly be 100% effective. That said it gives me something to work on for the future, otherwise perfection would be dull!

I was to spend many nights with my head in my hands, questioning how could I help so many other dogs but still have issues with my own.

I rang everyone I knew about him to see if I was missing something. Ultimately my turning point came when I stopped trying to fix the problem and took emotional time out. He was a dog after all and reliant on my direction, not the weeping and wailing of a broken woman. It was to mark the start of the fantastic understanding we have today.

Our Relationship

I am tough on Marley, he works to boundaries and I set him up to succeed in every social environment. I protect him from excitable social environments and I ensure my children act respectfully around him. He is fed a balanced diet and is worked mentally and physically every day. We have a fantastic balance of work, play and affection which are all on my terms and 99% of the time it works. He is a dog and I respect his needs and values. The same goes for any dog, whether adverse behaviour is displayed or not.

However, the flip side of this level of control is a constant request from friends and family to let him do what he likes, people asking why I have put him on a lead when I want to stop and talk. Why do I send him to his bed when they visit, why am I so careful about who I ask to look after him when we are away and why they can't give him lots of fuss and cuddles. I manage him this way for a reason; the Marley with the 'lid off' is not pleasant or safe and we haven't seen that side of him for a long time.

We love him, he is loyal and protective, smart and willing and has retained the eager to please attitude he displayed as a puppy. He learns fast and has been an amazing work buddy teaching me a new understanding of the dog's ability to cope. He is also the face of Gencon Head Collars and can be seen on all their packaging and advertising.

My master's degree project was motivated by my experience with Marley and ultimately this has shaped the basis for my learning and developed my skills as a practitioner. I can now truly sympathise with the plight of my clients as I really do practise what I preach. I have always said I have learnt far more from being with dogs themselves over all the text book reading I have done. This large, clumsy, handsome Goldendoodle has contributed a huge part of this learning.

Coping with Another Dog

You may find yourself in the position of bringing home your puppy and having to introduce him or her to your current family dog. Whether this is a 'Marley' or a chilled out family pooch, it is essential that you consider the best course of action for this and understand the needs of your current dog and how they will work with a new puppy in the house.

Marley has been a huge consideration during this process. He is used to other dogs visiting and works well with dogs socially outside but he does take up a lot of my time. A new puppy will be all consuming for the first year and he will need to be able to cope with my potential lack of attention.

Here is Marley on a canine assault course weekend, showing his braver side and jumping through a ring of fire – one of my prouder moments!

I planned ahead and began investing more training time and ensuring he was exposed to a variety of social environments again. It is easy to fall in to the trap of doing the same walks every day. We also started a new dog discipline in the form of working trials (discussed later).

He really loved this but we now take part at a much lower level. Unfortunately, in order to get Marley excited enough to want to work with me, I had to have my leg humped after each exercise, not pretty when you are with a group of other professional dog handlers. In contrast Marley's opposing character trait is to 'shut down'. This is my 'calm' Marley and calm Marley looks at me like I'm nuts if I ask him to run out after a plastic dumbbell. The whole issue of keeping him in a position to be excited enough to work but calm enough to absorb instruction was almost impossible!

Marley is now 6 years old (at the time of writing) and I feel he has reached an optimum stage of maturity where he can show a new puppy the ropes without being threatened by its presence. Whether he would excel at a dog sport or not is irrelevant, I just wanted to make sure he was happy with a new arrival in his little world. My whole experience with Marley has allowed me to show you exercises and provide you with advice, based on my own professional and emotional life experiences, and more importantly, I know what works!

Sadly, in many cases a confused or unbalanced dog inevitably results in poor behaviour such as aggression and serious obsessive behaviours. Many are extremely advanced by the time I visit. It goes without saying that the younger the dog is, the more malleable they are and more willing to conform and adapt.

Set your puppy up to succeed by observing its limitations and remember, every dog is different.

Hogan showing off his eye contact and waiting for a reward.

Task

Recall and document all of the experience you have had around dogs, even if it is just observation at a distance.

Make notes on how you perceive situations where dogs have tried to communicate to you or with each other and consider whether you feel you were correct.

Refer back to what you have written once you reach the end of the book, to see if and how your perception has changed.

CHAPTER 3

Preparing for the Puppy

To begin, we should focus on making sure you are ready for your new arrival in every way and prepared for what you should expect on collection of your puppy.

Your ground work in finding a breeder or choosing where you will have bought your puppy from will have been done by now, but it is worth making sure you have asked all the right questions and have avoided any unnecessary heartache down the line.

Hogan's breeder Derrie giving him a little cuddle when he was ready to leave for his new life with us.

I recommend buying from a reputable breeder but you may also be collecting your puppy from a rescue centre or previous home. Either way, just make sure you gather as much information as possible on the puppy and its background.

The early life of a dog is hugely important in their development, but sometimes we aren't able to have a puppy who has had a perfect start; fortunately dogs live 'in the moment,' so they will adapt well and try hard to fit in with human social order.

To facilitate this, you can be prepared and as clear as possible with your expectations, but always be realistic. Puppies are hard work. It will be the most rewarding but also the most frustrating job you have ever done. Don't put too much pressure on yourself, focus on taking every step a stage at a time and most importantly, work within your puppy's capability.

Physical Preparation/Responsibilities

Prior to picking your puppy up you should ensure you have completed your shopping list of goodies so that you have all your training equipment in hand and ready to use.

It is very easy to get carried away buying inappropriate products and lots of things you don't really need so keep it simple.

Here is a basic list of essential items:

- Crate/small 'down time' area
- Newspaper/Vet-bed (or suitable absorbent bedding)
- Grooming brush
- Food/water bowls
- Toys & treats
- Recall line & Recall whistle
- Kong (Classic) toy
- Collar/Lead/Id tag

Once you have purchased your chosen items you can then be in a position to begin to put them all to good use, this will encourage you to set time aside for socialising and bonding with your puppy, putting structure together for toilet training and building routines and positive habits.

Hogan with his Kong toy.

Hogan's first collar
and lead.

It will also ensure you avoid making early mistakes in the management of your puppy's behaviour, before you are in possession of the physical tools.

In addition to the physical equipment, you also need to familiarise yourself with your legal responsibilities as a dog owner. Aside from just ensuring you clean up after your puppy has defecated (of which fines are now applicable), you also need to abide by the laws of where your puppy is allowed to go and also what level of behaviour and etiquette is considered safe and sociable.

The Law

There has been a significant rise in the level of dog attacks to other dogs and also humans in recent years. This has prompted a review of the law imposing restrictions and guidelines on the management of dogs in all domestic environments, whether this be on public or private land. As a result, dog ownership carries a huge responsibility not only for the safety of you as an owner, but also the public and other dogs. An out of control dog is a danger and you may be liable for an offence, punishable by fines, removal of the dog, or more seriously imprisonment and destruction of the dog.

In the UK this is governed by the Dangerous Dogs Act 1991 (UK).

Dog attacks on children in particular are a serious concern. A recent study concluded most attacks occur between the hours of 5-7 pm, on children aged 3-5 years. These times are in line with what I would consider to be the high 'flash point' periods in most domestic environments.

Hungry, tired and young children combined with distracted parents in the presence of an excitable dog potentially creates a volatile situation. These statistics should be considered as high motivator's for ensuring early training is embedded correctly, while your puppy is young.

Make sure you research the legal responsibilities of dog ownership in your area as these will vary hugely. Fundamentally, wherever you are you will be expected to manage your puppy or adult dog safely and with good control, while also ensuring you clean up any mess and report any damage they may be responsible for.

Financial Considerations

Having worked in a variety of residential areas both affluent and not so, I have experienced a diverse level of care from pet owners. Some have been able to provide a high level of medical care, while others struggle to afford the most basic of corrective procedures. It is also relevant in the social activities that owners are able to engage in. These maybe gun dog clubs and one to one training to basic obedience classes or maybe even none at all.

Finally, the cost of accessories can make even a standard flat collar overly expensive for some owners.

It doesn't mean any dog owner loves their dog more or less but their financial status can greatly affect their ability to provide a dog with some of its essential needs.

As a result, I have put together a check list of considerations to factor in when deciding how best to manage a new puppy alongside your current lifestyle.

Holiday Cover

Planning your yearly holiday will always involve planning for the care of your dog from now on. This is something that often gets overlooked when owners are focused on the excitement of choosing and bringing home their new bundle of fluff.

Hogan and Marley accompany us on most holidays,
minimising boarding costs.

You should remember that a single week is a long time in a dog's life and I have heard and dealt with the fall out of many horror stories from bad experiences in kennels or home stays, including when dogs are left with friends and family.

I would always advise that you seek the help of a professional to care for your dog while you are away, this ensures you are covered for any 3rd party accidents and your dog will receive a daily standard of care as contracted and paid for by you. It also ensures friendships stay intact! There are many dog boarding, kennel or home establishments now and all require a local authority license to function. They will vary hugely in their standard and level of care and so my advice here would always be to ensure your dog is cared for consistently for a 24 hour period (not kenneled in an empty premises over night).

Make sure you can visit the premises and look round whenever you like and ask questions regarding exercising, feeding and physical care regimes. Ask what local vet they use and what is their emergency procedure and training. Are any of the staff qualified in any level of animal care and would they spot if your dog was in trouble. I have seen some really nice kennels and for some dogs it is safer and a more realistic option for them to be housed individually while you are away, for others it may cause unnecessary stress and anxiety and they may be better suited to a home environment.

Be aware that if your dog has behaviour issues such as chewing, vocalisation or toileting then they won't be welcome in somebody's home so a kennel may be a better option.

Your chosen boarding place should not be expected to train your dog unless they offer this as a service, so make sure you give them clear instructions on your dogs' routine, level of obedience and in particular whether they can be trusted off lead. You may be asked to sign a form to take responsibility for off lead time.

Be prepared to travel for the right place, it may not be on your doorstep but if it suits your dog it will be worth the trip. Most importantly look for individuals or establishments who have been recommended to you and have a proven track record. Speak to other dog owners while you are out walking. Often, the best dog care businesses don't need to advertise as they are so busy, so word of mouth is everything.

Finally, plan ahead. In the early days of my behaviour career I ran a boarding service, I was booked up sometimes a year in advance for client's summer holidays as everyone wanted to make sure they had their spot for the school holiday term!

Vet Fees and Healthcare

Having worked in veterinary practice for a good period of my life, I can safely say that veterinary medicine is expensive, it is not an option to ignore this financial consideration.

Wisp sporting an ear bandage by fellow Veterinary Nurse and friend Rachel Bean RVN who runs first aid for dog's courses.

Standard and necessary veterinary care will involve the following:

- Vaccinations – yearly
- Worming and flea treatments – monthly
- Neutering

Veterinary medication is costly for a reason! It's expensive to get drugs licensed for use, this cost is ultimately passed on to the consumer. This means that something as simple as a torn nail could mean the consultation fee, plus expensive antibiotics and pain relief.

You should also keep in mind, the larger your chosen breed is, the more expensive your vet fees will be!

Grooming

For short-haired dogs this may be something you can just do yourself but the majority of long or curly coated dogs need an experienced pair of hands

Marley after one of my attempts at bathing and drying him.
This is 2 weeks after a professional groom. I just do an
interim bath to keep on top of the smell.

to keep things under control. This should definitely be a cost consideration and it may vary greatly.

This is something that won't be a problem for Hogan but Marley visits the groomers every 4-6 weeks. His coat takes way too much time to manage and he sports an interesting smell if he gets wet too often. A good groom is an essential part of his welfare.

Cost of Food

Good dog food can be costly, work out what your puppy will need, what diet you will be feeding and prepare yourself for the monthly cost. Remember what you put in, you will get out, so it is worth making sure the money you do spend is being used for growth, repair and energy for your dog not just excreted as waste!

Hogan putting his 'slow feeder' bowl to the test.
A brilliant invention to slow down your greedy puppy.

Also consider, if you have a puppy who bolts his food like Hogan, you may also need to invest in a slow feeder bowl!

Pet Insurance

Pet insurance is important, not just to cover unexpected veterinary fees but also to ensure you have 3rd party liability cover in the event your puppy is the cause of injury or accident.

There are many companies offering pet cover and you should always research to ensure you get the best possible deal, suited to your financial ability. Ensure you seek 'lifetime' cover, this will give you the peace of mind that your puppy will be financially protected if they develop a lifetime medical problem, such as hip dysplasia or other degenerative illness. Changes can be made once your puppy has reached adulthood and you are more aware of their medical status.

I am aware that not all countries offer pet insurance and also some owners are just unable to factor the monthly cost into their budget. If this is the case, then I always advise owners to open a bank account for their puppy. Even just tucking away a small amount of money each month will provide a financial safety net for emergencies and if you don't need it then the money is still yours!

Provisions for Leaving the Dog Alone

Your dog should never be left more than 3-4 hours maximum for any period of time. If you work, then you should seek the help of a dog walker or dog daycare centre to assist you here.

Welfare Considerations

Meeting the Dog's Basic Needs

The dog is very simple and should be respected for its basic needs and values, you should make sure you have the time and energy for the following:

- Mental stimulation: through training and self-control exercises
- Physical exercise: this will be little and often to begin with
- Boundaries and discipline: the dog needs to have an individual to guide them
- Provide a balanced diet twice daily

Hogan doing his bit for Puppy Coach and interacting with the children.

Space to Accommodate a Dog

Puppies arrive small and in cute little bundles, so you must plan ahead for the size of crate and final size of your adult dog, do you have the room in your house to accommodate a large breed dog if this is your choice? Owning breeds such as German Shepherds and Golden Retrievers can feel like you have another person living in your home so please consider this, they are not small for long!

You should allocate an 'area' for long term use for your dog. This should allow them to view your social space but not be directly in the middle of it. A balanced dog is one that is able to observe and learn human behaviour from a distance, not one that has to try and meet the expectations of human social interaction.

Integrating a Puppy into your Personal Life

Puppy ownership is a commitment that not everyone is equipped to cope with. Family, work and social commitments need to be considered to ensure you are able to provide this intelligent, attentive animal with enough care to sustain its welfare positively. Put time aside to carefully integrate your puppy into your personal life.

It is not acceptable to give your dog a short walk around the block in the morning and then leave them for an 8 hour day while you're at work. They will not cope and destructive, anxious or shut down behaviour is a likely consequence and who could blame them!

Dogs are great company during exercise and mine never miss a run, rain or shine.

Ensuring you have addressed all of the areas discussed will elevate some of the pressure of adjustment when your puppy arrives.

Task

Your task for this section is to produce a final plan of managing your dog and an understanding of the monthly financial outlay.

CHAPTER 4

Collecting your Puppy

It may seem like a straightforward task, after all you just need to pick up your new arrival and bring them home – don't you? However, this may be the last opportunity you have to really understand the level of early learning and social exposure your puppy has had.

Hogan at 4 weeks. This was when I began collecting information and building a relationship with Derrie (Hogan's breeder) so I could understand what his early life with her would entail.

Can you imagine leaving a newborn baby with a stranger to bring up for the first 8 weeks of their life and then you are expected just to take over when you pick them up? It would be a difficult task so it's important that you recognise the areas of importance and knowledge you need so you can be prepared for all eventualities when collecting your puppy!

We will take a look at all the areas you need to focus on. Firstly, paperwork! If you are buying from a reputable breeder there should be a variety of paper work handed over to you. Everything to do with your puppy is yours so you should be in possession of the following:

- Receipt for payment
- Puppy sales contract: confirming private sale and ownership
- Breeder details: this should have their identification, business name and contact details
- Test results for hip, elbow, and eye scores and any others
- Breed lines (family tree)
- Identichip paperwork, if your puppy has been chipped prior to collection
- Details of the vet your puppy was initially registered with
- Guidance on breeding restrictions
- Transfer of ownership for Kennel Club registered puppies
- Vaccination protocol if already started

I started my relationship with Derrie, Hogan's breeder, from the very first phone call. I wanted to gain an understanding of how Hogan would develop in his most impressionable early weeks. You can never repeat this critical period and it is essential that the puppy is positively exposed to the life they will lead in a human domestic environment.

I was in no doubt with Derrie that Hogan would receive the best possible start any puppy could have. He was even sharing his bed with an orphaned lamb who Derrie was hand rearing at the time. I don't think I'll ever have to be concerned that Hogan will be a sheep worrier!

Gaining an understanding of your puppy's early learning is an absolute must if you are to cover all of the key socialisation areas. You should also ask if your puppy has received any parasitic treatments in the first few weeks of their life. If so, don't be afraid to ask lots of questions, you will need to know what they were, what dosage was administered, whether a vet prescribed them and when they are due again.

Finally, you should ask questions about your puppy's routine for feeding, toilet training, social exposure and when they were removed from their mother and/or litter mates. It is useful to ask the breeder before the collection day what their fee includes and what will be provided. Some breeders send their puppies away with a pack containing everything they need for the first week or so. It's worth trying to work out what's included so you can avoid a barrage of questions. Most good breeders will have everything in order anyway.

Choosing an Appropriate Time to Bring your Puppy Home

Before picking up your puppy, ensure you have chosen a time for his or her arrival that will be quiet and relaxed, visitors will need to wait for at least a week or so until your puppy has settled in its new environment.

This may be tricky to implement as a puppy will attract lots of attention but this first week is special time for you to get to know your puppy and begin the bonding process. You don't want this complicated with lots of people bringing excitement and high energy into your home, picking your puppy up and potentially embedding poor behaviours.

Humans can be quite challenging to young puppies, especially if they haven't been exposed to this environment previously. I see many cases where a fear response has been ignored at a young age and the puppy has started to become defensive to avoid being picked up and hugged! Barking and retreating would be early signs of this and are particularly prevalent in small breeds.

Many of my clients have chosen to collect their puppy in the school holidays to ensure their children are involved from the beginning. In my opinion school holidays probably aren't a great choice as children will be out of routine and excitable, you should really introduce children slowly and set a routine for them to interact at key times of the day.

This is easier to facilitate if they are going about their normal activities. Integrating children will probably be one of the hardest situations you face and getting this right is essential if you are to have a happy puppy who is respectful of your child and vice versa.

My children were too young for school when Hogan arrived but being around dogs is totally normal for them so I didn't foresee a problem. Gauge how your children will react. Your goal is to avoid excitability and noise which will be a distraction for you and unsettle your puppy, potentially creating an initial negative first experience. Your children should be taught to respect the puppy's personal space.

Simple things such as leaving the puppy alone while in its crate/down time area, never picking the puppy up and never engaging in running around and screaming to insight a chase response. All this is very much 'easier said than done' so I will guide you through the methods to achieve a calm household in more detail in Chapter 22.

If you have young children under 5 years old, then you may find some breeders wouldn't sell a puppy to you. This is one of Derrie's guidelines and I was very lucky that she considered my profession to be relevant in her decision making process! Don't be alarmed if you have faced this, it will help you really consider the impact on your family of bringing a young puppy into your home.

Our son building his early relationship with Hogan.

Obviously if children are not a consideration for you then it may be you are taking time off work instead. If this is the case, try to start a routine for your puppy that will match the one you will have in place when you return to work. I am not suggesting you leave your puppy for long periods, but you should teach your puppy how to cope with solitary time by managing your behaviour around them, again this will be dealt with in more depth later.

The Journey Home

Travelling home can be a daunting experience for all. Keeping your puppy on your lap provides them with the comfort of you and provides an opportunity for them to get used to your scent and begin the bonding process.

Hogan spent the majority of the long journey back on my lap in the passenger seat, but I also chose to allow him time in the crate, situated in the boot alongside our other dog Marley. This was a personal decision but I feel it was invaluable in starting their controlled relationship. Plus, it was safer as he had begun to move around a fair bit on the front seat with me as the journey progressed.

It is your decision how you travel your puppy but as long as they are safe and close to you, you shouldn't have too many problems.

There are puppies who may suffer from travel sickness. It's worth asking your breeder whether your puppy has ever travelled in a car before and also plan your journey so your pup's stomach isn't full. Have a towel to hand just in case!

Introduction to Other Animals Including A Family Dog

If you have other animals, it is important to keep them to their normal routine and do not make a fuss about introducing your puppy.

Ideally the initial exposure should involve the puppy being contained within a crate or smaller area, both parties should be able to see each other but your puppy prevented from showing too much interest.

If you have another dog who may be a little boisterous or reactive then ensure you take the initial physical association slowly. Have both parties on a lead and don't be afraid to separate them if you are uncomfortable with how things progress.

Hogan and Marley bonding.

If you are confident and clear with your direction, your puppy should learn manners around approaching individuals whether they are human or other animals. Hogan's first experience with our home was to follow a tasty treat all the way from the car, through the front door and straight through to the kitchen. Not only did that associate him positively by allowing him to follow his nose and arrive under his own steam, but it also provided an opportunity for me to reinforce where he would be staying on arrival!

Marley had already been taken through into our garden where he was waiting patiently to give Hogan a guided tour. A lead was left in place so that control could be gained if necessary. This first association requires understanding and patience, giving your puppy the freedom to explore your home from the beginning already sends the wrong message. Being clear about where the puppy's area is from the start is an important part of your relationship and invaluable for toilet training.

This period was positively marked by setting up some controlled down time in separate areas with the use of a treat associated toy. A calm and controlled initial arrival marked the start of Hogan and Marley's relationship; clear and careful handling was required to ensure things went smoothly.

Don't overlook this period if you have another dog. An older dog can easily feel threatened and this may create a trigger for them to display unusually poor behaviour. It is worth setting them up for success prior to your puppy's arrival by making sure they have their own bed area, reducing the level of attention you freely give and being a bit clearer with your direction.

It won't be such a shock then when you suddenly have to start controlling 2 dogs around your home, you will need all the help you can get.

First Few Nights

Hogan's arrival with us was planned over a weekend, so that I would have the majority of the day to settle him and primarily condition him to the crate environment. I recommend that you focus on the crate or den area from the start. It will be essential in your puppy management going forward. There are many ways of introducing a puppy to coping with time away from its owner and dealing with solitary time. The first few days is not a time to consider rushing this process. I always recommend you are in relatively close contact with your puppy for the first 3-4 nights.

Hogan found his place on the sofa pretty quickly.
Boundaries need to be consistently maintained.

You can either take the crate to your bedroom or set the puppy up in its crate or area and sleep downstairs either on a sofa or camp bed, ultimately close by. You should always ensure your puppy can see and smell you but not touch.

Hogan initially had periods of crying on and off in the crate, this is completely normal. You should remember that forcing time away from your puppy is not natural for them. This is essential learning but will easily cause distress if not handled correctly. While I always advise that you need to be firm and clear with your puppy management, you also need to help them cope. There is no sense in allowing a puppy to become overly stressed in the crate or separate area. All this will achieve is to open up their panic response and leave you with an unbalanced, frightened puppy who learns only to display poor behaviour in a bid to rectify the solitary existence.

My goal was to encourage Hogan to become calm while being kept away from me. If you have a calm puppy, then you have a puppy who has the ability to learn and be guided by you. The 'cold turkey' approach to crate training is commonly recommended and involves just totally ignoring your puppy. It is not one I advise. Lots of puppies will find other less invasive ways of coping but many will be left with fight or flight responses that could affect other areas of their lives.

I have treated many dogs suffering separation anxiety who have endured this approach to solitary time, this will be your first understanding of the true impact your behaviour can have on your puppy. Taking things slowly and helping your puppy adapt to being alone is invaluable for building a trusting relationship! To avoid this miscommunication I dealt with Hogan's anxiety by sleeping downstairs and in close contact.

I ignored low level crying, but if this elevated I stood quietly next to the crate with my arms folded and body turned away, until he calmed. There was no verbal or physical contact.

This delicate process can create such a negative association for your dog's first experience away from the litter and in your home, if handled poorly.

You should ensure your puppy is calm and accepting of time in their 'area' or crate away from you during the day but when you are still home, before expecting them to be able to cope when you leave the house.

Any period of detachment from human owners should be a gradual. This process may feel like a lifetime but should be achievable within the first 2 weeks.

Task

Your task for this section is to liaise with your breeder to agree an acceptable time for collection, ask when the puppy will be feeding and what his or her normal routine is for sleeping.

Ensure you are aware of what the breeder will be providing you with.

Discuss with all involved parties how you will be managing the first few days of care for your puppy, draw up a rota if more than one person is involved and agree a process for providing the puppy with structure and routine.

CHAPTER 5

Building a Relationship: Body Language and Communication

There are many routes to developing a positive relationship with your puppy but fundamentally this begins in the home. Teaching manners, self-control and a healthy awareness for personal space marks the start of any puppy's ability to meet our expectations. This should be started as soon as your puppy arrives.

Many owners are so taken up with how cute their new arrival is that they unintentionally start off on the wrong foot. I have lost count of how many puppies have greeted me in their owner's arms when I arrive at the front door. This simple error loads your puppy with the responsibility of the arriving guest, exposes them to lots of high, unbalanced energy and puts them in prime position to feel threatened by facial contact from them. All in all, it's a recipe for disaster and is the start of all the negative front door behaviours people struggle to get under control.

I am sure you have seen dogs who bark uncontrollably at the front door, attack the letter box when the post arrives, jump up at guests and, in worst case scenarios, show aggression. I recently arrived at a home to assess and treat a case where a little French Bulldog had bitten several arriving guests, she was excitable with those that she knew, but strangers were attacked – including me! It didn't take too long to work out that she had developed such anxieties around guest arrival as people were so unpredictable. Allowing her to be present in such a high energy, inconsistent environment with no possibility of offering guidance was the motivation for a very serious end stage, habitual behaviour.

These owners were particularly diligent and have now rectified the problem before it was too late, but this progressive problem is rarely thought about when the puppy weighs a few kgs and is quiet and calm. Things change in a very short space of time, puppies are not puppies for very long, this could be you if you overlook some simple control.

I make a point of telling all of my owners that hallways and front doors are out of bounds unless you are walking your puppy through on a lead. Never allow your guests to greet your puppy here. This is only setting them up to fail and providing an opportunity for poor behaviours to become learnt and embedded.

"The relationship you share with your puppy defines the level of control you have over his or her behaviour, ensure this is calm, structured and positive."

Choosing a Discipline and Lifestyle for You and Your Puppy

Continued learning via canine disciplines such as working clubs focused on gun-dog and working trials through to agility and fly-ball are just a few of those available and they will provide another facet to your relationship.

Marley learning to jump over the scale at working trials.

These clubs are not essential but you should always keep in mind the type of puppy you have chosen, its instinctive drive, working ability and energy levels. If you have a finely tuned working breed then you will need to adequately, mentally and physically stimulate them, obviously in a controlled and balanced way. The disciplines I have mentioned will help you achieve this.

If you already have a discipline in mind you should look to enrolling your puppy early so that they can gain valuable experience in the environment you will wish them to work in at a later date. This can be as early as 12 weeks providing they are fully vaccinated. Even if they are unable to do some of the exercises because they are too young, they can still observe and get used to the behaviour of dogs around them.

Plan ahead with this, especially as some clubs have waiting lists!

Before you even consider choosing a discipline, you should make sure that you have a positive means of communicating with your puppy.

I make a point of educating all of my clients to communicate with their puppy, which includes the following:

- Understanding body language indicators
- Observing facial expressions
- Responding appropriately to stress signals

Stress Indicators, Body Language and Facial Expressions

Sadly, stress and anxiety is as prevalent in the dog as it is for human beings. The only difference being is that the dog is unable to verbally communicate how they feel. The result is often a complete and catastrophic failure of their coping ability and in many cases aggression or obsessive, repetitive behaviours are observed.

To ensure your puppy doesn't develop anxieties it is important that you are able to recognise the early communicators; here I will give you some direction to help you spot them.

Firstly, we will take a look at body language, observe your puppy's posture and tail position. If your puppy is turning away, avoiding eye contact or backing off while still staring at you then they are feeling threatened. A normal puppy should have a waggy bottom, relaxed tail and body position communicating contentment. A tense or uncomfortable stance whether this is in a standing or laying down position should be recognised and responded to by removing your puppy from the current environment.

Also observe your puppy's tail, this sends many messages and a wagging tail doesn't always mean your puppy is happy. Recognise that there are a variety of different wags and that some can display the onset of a challenge, hyper excitability or fear, all of which will result in a negative response. The perfect wagging tail will have a wiggly bottom or it will be low slung, wagging consistently and slowly.

Please note that puppies with docked tails will have lost a very clear means of communicating with other individuals so keep this in mind if you are socialising your docked tail puppy. Fortunately, this is now an illegal practice in the UK.

You should observe your puppy's facial expressions. This can be tricky but there are some indicators you should be familiar with. Training your puppy to look and make direct eye contact provides a platform for them to connect with you positively and avoids them viewing eye contact as confrontational. This is easily achieved by rewarding your puppy every time they look directly into your eyes.

You should observe a relaxed face, with soft eyes, ears should be relaxed and not pinned back, and the forehead should be relaxed along with the lips.

Finally, we will take a look at the dog's vast array of stress indicators, to make sure you can act appropriately should you observe them in an excessive or sustained format.

The Most Common Stress Signals you will See in your Puppy:

- Yawning
- Lip licking
- Stretching
- Pacing
- Aggression
- Scratching
- Vocalisation
- Shivering
- Blinking
- Hyperactivity
- Stiffness
- Excessive drinking
- Scavenging
- Self-harming
- Avoidance
- Overly subdued
- Intolerant
- Unable to settle
- Rapid breathing
- Toileting problems
- Drooling
- Inability to focus
- Excessive grooming

You must remember that your puppy will display some of the subtler signs of stress as a normal part of their behaviour, for instance yawning may just be a sign of tiredness. You will need to assess your puppy's environment and gauge whether the communication is a relevant concern.

Training and Behaviour

Training is very much about teaching the dog our spoken word via a series of individual commands being attached to a positive reward. I recognise this as a highly successful means of managing a puppy's behaviour. However, an understanding of the puppy's body language and communication signals is essential for a human owner to be effective in guiding them though the unpredictability of human life. Without this positive relationship being present, it is unlikely the dog will defer to human guidance readily, leaving room for a lack of control and ultimately safety concerns.

To achieve this relationship, you should adapt your human emotion and reactions accordingly using an awareness of your body language to deliver a clear message of confidence to your dog. My posture is very upright, I look in the direction I am going and retain a consistent and assertive pace, offering occasional reward and vocal encouragement for Hogan's correct behaviour. My relaxed and more vocal behaviour will encourage and accept a play and physically interactive response, useful for recall training and bonding, while my calm, assertive and progressive body language will encourage a working attitude from Hogan. This provides him with clear direction ensuring he meets expectations positively.

Opening up a clear and positive line of communication will ensure your puppy grows in confidence, remains balanced and is successful in all social situations.

Finally, if you understand this concept you will be able to recognise how you or others have potentially triggered an over zealous response from your puppy that you may struggle to stop.

Puppy Classes

This book will give you the knowledge to ensure you cover all areas of your dog's social exposure and domestic learning, along with basic obedience.

This is a group training session put together for the PuppyCoach.com films. All of the puppies are Hogan's siblings. A great opportunity to educate some intelligent, responsible dog owners.

This will include instruction on how to properly socialise your dog. With this in mind you should be able to manage your puppy from this precious time, up to and including adult-hood but this is in support of your practical experience which you can either implement yourself or attend a class.

This is especially important if you have very little ability to safely socialise your puppy. There are some very good puppy obedience classes around.

A good class will offer the following:

• A safe indoor or well fenced outdoor environment
• Good, experienced, qualified instructors
• Small class sizes (no more than 3-4 dogs per instructor)
• Detail on the methods they use to train
• Supporting advice to implement at home
• New exercises to practise each week
• Advice on socialisation
• Short interactive/controlled play sessions with dogs of a similar size and age

- Good obedience instruction
- Consistency and continuity in lesson plans and Instructor attendance
- Progressive platform working towards certification such as The Kennel Club Good Citizen Scheme

Choose your class carefully, remember what you know about how puppies cope and read your own puppy well. If your puppy is nervous you will need professional help from the instructors. If you don't receive this, then this probably isn't the class for you. If you feel your puppy is behaving in an overly boisterous manner or other dogs are behaving in this way, and it is not being corrected firmly and with verbal advice for you or other owners, then again this isn't a good sign. You should feel comfortable with the environment, it should be safe and relaxed. Any off lead play should be controlled and only between 'like for like' in size and age puppies.

The method of training should be reward based, using a toy, treat or praise, you should be instructed in how to deliver this. However, puppies do need consequences for their negative behaviour, but these should never be physically harsh.

I would always instruct an owner to take a boisterous puppy away (remove from the social space) but allow visual sight of the class and encourage methods to achieve a calm behaviour which can be ultimately rewarded.

I never advocate the use of the following:

- Harsh collars
- Sprays
- Shouting
- Water pistols

Or anything similar – it is just not necessary in the young puppy and often adds more stimulation to the problem, making it worse long term. You may see an initial response to these methods but they are always short lived if the puppy hasn't been properly and professionally conditioned to the method.

Removal should be followed by a gradual reintroduction to the class. Control exercises to practise in the park would be essential for a puppy of this nature. If you cannot calm your puppy it is sometimes advisable to tether them a short distance from you and or the activity if it is safe to do so, just until they settle.

- Decide how you will progress your puppy training discipline
- Observe the body language your puppy delivers in different situations
- Learn to spot stress indicators and help your puppy cope
- Be aware of your own body language
- Recognise the difference between training and behaviour control
- Observe how your puppy reacts to your voice in comparison to body language

Task

Your task for this section is to interact with your puppy at different energy levels, with and without the use of your voice. Observe their response and regain control and calm after each interaction by calming your own behaviour.

CHAPTER 6

Working Trials

Having spent years working professionally and socially in dog obedience I decided to challenge myself with something new. I had spent a couple of days working with the Metropolitan Police Dog Section and absolutely loved the challenge of a multi-disciplined dog sport.

As a result, I enrolled my other dog Marley into a recommended club. This gave me the opportunity to practise with an adult dog who would be more than equipped to take up the challenge before potentially embedding mistakes in my new puppy.

While I have an abundance of experience with dogs in general, I can't say I am an authority on any dog sport particularly. Working trials was a new goal for me and one that I was happy to take a back seat at, in order to learn.

Marley learning the long jump at working trials.

The dog world is one of the most diverse I know. Possessing an open-minded attitude is essential for progression as a dog handler or owner, after all you can always teach an old dog new tricks!

Considering the Breed and Discipline

Hogan's predominant breed line is working, meaning he has been bred to cope with a high level of physical demand, focus and concentration. I chose him for several reasons, I have a busy, outdoor lifestyle and would be able to provide him with his needs during my day to day work, plus I was already enjoying the Working Trials discipline and wanted to continue. Having a dog equipped to keep up made complete sense. Whether I really want to still be teaching him new things at 10pm at night when he is still switched on and ready to go is another story, but I guess I knew what I was in for! Make sure your chosen breed fits with your lifestyle, or make your lifestyle fit around your dog.

Working trials is only one discipline of many but I have been amazed to see dogs of all breeds excelling in this environment on many levels. The dedication and patience of many of the handlers is astounding and it really shows what can be achieved when the dog-owner relationship is balanced and positive.

Fundamentally, this environment provided a unique opportunity to see what our dogs are truly capable of when handled correctly.

It is important to point out that, regardless of the level of training a dog undergoes, they still have their own mind and if they choose not to conform then quite frankly they won't!

This should be reassuring for you as a puppy owner when you look around and think everyone else's puppy is better behaved than yours, they are all challenging for an owner at some stage in their lives so avoid putting unnecessary pressure on yourself.

The breed you have chosen may excel in specific areas and struggle in others so always observe the ability of your chosen breed when setting yourself personal goals.

The Rottweiler for instance is a powerful, strong-willed dog who does well with the scale and jumps and is an absolute power house with the tracking element, however they can be stubborn and boisterous so need lots of support to carry out self-control exercises.

Marley and Hogan practising their 'sit' and 'stay' exercise to perfection.

My little chap loves to retrieve and follow a scent so he will do well with the dumbbell, searching and tracking. He does take constant work to keep him to heel though, and he may find the jumps more challenging. Plus, his love of people and attention means he was susceptible to distraction, this is why I spent day after day embedding a calm, controlled behaviour with him in public places from the day he arrived.

Marley with Hogan and Sheba performing
self-control exercises in the park.

Collies are almost over attentive and focused and are amazing at picking up exercises to perfection but they are flighty and easily unnerved so should be kept calm and steady.

I see many Collies for behaviour problems, their working drive is generally very high and they tend to be sensitive and easy to stimulate. This means they require a working relationship with their owner, heavily loaded with guidance and direction if they are to remain balanced. My opinion is that they don't make easy to manage family pets but if you get the balance of work and down time right then they can be highly rewarding.

While first and foremost the dog is a dog, you should always take into account the breed predispositions so that you have realistic expectations in whatever discipline you choose.

Providing a huge size contrast to the majority of breeds. This is my sister-in-law's Leonberger Zeiss, who sadly passed away due to a heart condition.

Working Trials Explained

Working trials is a competitive sport originating from training developed around police dog work. It is a physically and mentally demanding sport for both dog and handler. Competitors work to succeed in individual tests focused on self-control, agility exercises, tracking and retrieval. The sport is a recognised discipline by the UK Kennel Club and in many other countries, competitions take place throughout the year.

This is my discipline of choice for my dogs because the focus is on encouraging self-control for the dog, patience and understanding in the handler, while harnessing and challenging the dogs natural instinctive drive.

Simple commands such as 'sit', 'wait', 'stay' and 'come' are tested in an outdoor environment and with distractions.

There are many dog sports available, the advice I would give when choosing one is to ensure your dog is physically capable of the requirements and mentally suited to the type of learning.

Hogan in one of his very first timed 'sit stays', at 14 weeks.

Engage with your dog positively in whatever discipline you choose, leadership in your relationship is essential if your dog is to remain focused on you in challenging, high energy environments with distractions. Ensure you have control at all times when entering any new situation.

Age of Your Puppy for Introduction to Dog Sports

Your puppy will not be able to partake in any of the physically demanding disciplines until they have reached physical maturity.

Depending on the breed this could be as late as 18 months to 2 years. Their bones are growing at such a rate that it would be damaging to allow any strenuous exertion or jumping, potentially putting strain on delicate, developing joints.

It is important to keep this in perspective. Damage is done when you over exercise your puppy. Hopping up a couple of steps once or twice a day will not cause hip dysplasia. However, hurdling jumps and running up and down flights of stairs at a rate of knots regularly will most definitely tire muscles and overload the skeletal system putting excess strain on delicate joints and growing bones.

I have also witnessed a variety of early bone fractures for puppies who have misjudged or fallen down steps. I always encourage a sensible approach to this when deciding on how you will train and exercise your puppy with or without a disciplined sport.

Early exposure of your puppy to the required environment is beneficial for their future social awareness. Not only will it help them socialise with other dogs and people in an unfamiliar environment, but it will also help avoid high energy excitement when they come to associate it with exciting work and play.

Hogan spending longer in a timed down stay at 6 months of age.

From the moment he arrived with us I ensured Hogan took part in all the calm, self-control led exercises, coupled with positive reward and play to develop his social ability under my guidance. This was a personal decision as he was not initially fully vaccinated. I made an informed decision on this social exposure being invaluable during his critical learning period and the risk of infection being low. The environment was private farm land, with no water present, all of the dogs he met were fully vaccinated and he was managed throughout. This doesn't eradicate the risk but I was comfortable with my decision. I would recommend that you seek advice on this from a variety of reliable sources as each and every situation will be different.

All I will insist upon is that you find a means of adequately and safely exposing your puppy to 'real life' during the critical learning period up to and including 12 weeks. You will never get this time back and it really is essential that you make the most of it. Social encounters only become more difficult as your puppy approaches adolescence.

Taking part in a dog sport is not for everyone so please don't feel you have to. These avenues are available but you can just as successfully entertain and mentally and physically exercise your dog with the right knowledge and available time.

Task

Consider the breed of your dog, their physical and mental ability and what dog sport, if any, interests you?

List the physical considerations you should have for partaking in the following:

- Working trials
- Agility
- Obedience
- Fly-ball
- Tracking

Research what's available in your area and consider whether you would like to be part of a dog training discipline.

CHAPTER 7

Recognising Leadership Skills Through Puppy Development

In any relationship requiring one individual to give another direction, a level of authority needs to be had by the director. You cannot expect your puppy to follow your direction if you offer no guidance and have no authority over their general lifestyle. There are key areas where you can build a positive relationship based on personal space awareness and recognition of primitive motivators, such as food, attention and territory to name a few.

Leadership is essential for a balanced relationship between dogs and children.

Having control over these simple factors ensures your dog is willing to learn from you in any new situation. It is never necessary to be overly verbal or physically harsh but it is essential that you recognise dog values and needs, especially their desire to please and achieve expectations.

In this chapter we will focus on how to become a leader, giving you the ability to guide your puppy towards success in all domestic environments and social situations.

Leadership Explained

The ancestry of the dog is always a cause for debate among dog professionals. However, we have solid evidence that dogs and wolves share the same genetic material (DNA). While we recognise our pet dogs have undergone a huge amount of domestication during their relationship with human beings, we can also consider that they retain many similarities in their rules and values to those of the wolf. We can therefore utilise the information we know about wolves and wolf behaviour to add some clarity to the relatively primitive behaviours we still see in our domestic dogs.

A key characteristic of a group of dogs or wolves is their ability to set a tight hierarchial system to benefit the group as a whole.

Each member adopts a role, whether this be a high ranking role (Alpha), middle of the road (Beta) or low ranking/subservient role (Omega). Each will have its relevance and importance amongst the pack.

It is acceptable within a species that there will be scuffles and disagreements amongst individuals all communicating on the same platform. If this hierarchy system is to be employed by a human owner, then scuffles are not acceptable.

Solid leadership will help you avoid potential 'flash point' scenarios.

You should view your puppy management as you would any office-type environment. I prefer not to liken your puppy relationship to that of your family as this generally brings in lots of emotion and 'grey' areas. A 'work' mentality is essential to safely and clearly integrate your puppy, providing him or her with guidelines, a role and positive praise. If they under achieve or display negative behaviour this should be recognised as a communication error or expectations that are unrealistic.

Leadership Program

In order to manage the dog successfully and safely it is essential to recognise the fundamental differences between dogs and humans. Setting the dog up to succeed can only be achieved through knowledge and recognition of their ability to cope.

The primary mode of communication for the dog is body language and scent, this is inherent and learnt early on in their development and way before their first contact with humans in their ultimate domestic environment.

Humans, on the other hand communicate verbally and body language cues can be conflicting and confusing for the dog when not used with clear intent. This is where problems can arise as the human owner may become frustrated when their verbal communication is misunderstood and add more intent or volume to their delivery. This only achieves a negative result as the dog may view an increase in stimulation as potential conflict.

This, coupled with the relatively primitive and simple nature of the dogs thinking and instinct, means a high level of guidance is required from human owners when integrating a new puppy into their everyday life.

It should be understood early on that dogs are not born with an understanding of our language, no matter how firm the delivery! Each and every word you speak will develop an associated meaning which may not always be desirable.

In short, reacting to your dog when they behave badly is re-enforcing the problem.

Where possible you should avoid tricky situations or use removal or ignoring as a management tool.

To encourage positive word association your puppy needs to

Offering guidance on leadership to a client to help her understand and manage her Labrador puppy.

be calmly conditioned to the meaning of the sound through positive reward, praise and ultimately a desirable outcome.

Meeting 'Tulip' the lamb again. Tulip was hand reared alongside Hogan and his litter mates. This photo shows their first interaction since coming to live with us. Here Derrie provides the guidance and leadership to keep both animals calm.

The word 'No' should be conditioned via clear training, resulting in the removal of something desirable as a consequence for an inappropriate response, not just used in a challenging manner when the dog does something you dislike. This serves only to attach a response from you to the dogs behaviour and invariably encourage it to continue.

In order to apply some structure to the dog's management I have devised some leadership guidelines which will provide new owners with a clear strategy to teach and control their dog in every social environment.

I refer to my owners as 'Leaders'. The job of the leader is to guide a young puppy through the challenging and alien environment of human life and emotion, not to bully, physically or mentally, or act as an imposing or dominant individual.

We are not dogs and so should respect their values and work within their ability to learn, not use forceful physical tools or loud, harsh verbal cues.

Achieving leadership is a complex process and knowledge is essential to create a smooth path for canine management.

Here is a checklist of the areas of consideration followed by a detailed outline of your Leadership program. Remember that these are general guidelines and designed to help you to consider how you manage your puppy. You should seek further advice from a qualified, professional behaviourist if you have specific concerns about your puppy's behaviour.

LEADERSHIP

- Set up a positively associated safe place
- Feed a balanced diet at least twice daily
- Feed away from the family in a controlled format
- Make the dog work for food and teach self-control
- Avoid delivering free attention, this should be on your terms
- Ignore or walk away from unbalanced high energy
- Set restrictions around your home and avoid free access to stairs, beds and sofas
- Do not allow the dog to run to the front door or be the first to greet your guests
- Use your voice for positive praise only and never to reprimand
- Use a lead to teach the restrictions in your home
- Do not allow your dog to barge past you through doorways
- Remove the dog if they display negative or dangerous behaviour
- Provide at least 2 walks a day
- Teach your dog personal space awareness
- Teach a solid recall command (use a whistle)
- Make outdoor time about you, the dog should work for you
- Playtime should be started and finished by you with clear direction
- Toys are possessions and the dog should see them as yours
- Provide adequate and controlled social time
- Communicate primarily with body language
- Keep control of your energy in all environments

To assist in the application of the above points, I have set out below a more detailed version of effectively creating leadership in your home.

Canine Leadership Plan in Detail

Safe Place

Provide your puppy with their own quiet place to relax and ensure its associated with positivity. This can be a crate/kennel/kitchen or utility area.

This creates a safe place for the dogs to observe human behaviour but not be completely immersed in it!

The safe place also ensures your puppy has time away from your family and they do not learn to follow you around the house. This may encourage separation anxiety issues to develop.

Solitary time is alien for your puppy due to its social mentality, by creating time away gradually while you are in the home and associating it with positivity your puppy will learn to cope when completely left alone.

Feeding

I recommend a good quality balanced diet sourced from a reputable company.

This is to ensure the diet is free from additives and preservatives and is as close to a 'natural' diet as possible.

Feed 2 meals a day. Encourage your puppy to sit and wait to be told to eat, never leave food down if they choose to walk away from it!

This is a great way to apply structure and routine to your puppy's day and it also gives you two opportunities to work on your relationship and obedience, as food is your biggest bargaining tool!

Feed your puppy after the family have eaten, ideally in a separate room.

This will provide your puppy with a clear routine and structure around food, it also allows you to teach calm and steadiness around high prize rewards.

Attention

Be aware of the amount of attention you deliver to your puppy upon their request. You should actively seek your puppy out for fuss but only on your terms. It is important you do put time aside to play, walk and groom, so they know they are accepted within your social environment.

This ensures a good balance to the relationship between you and your puppy.

If attention insights high energy, stop and walk away. Ignoring an undesirable behaviour is the only way to ensure it is not repeated.

High energy when not exhibited through exercise or working drive, nearly always leads to undesirable behaviour.

Boundary Control

Be mindful of when/if you allow your puppy to jump on stairs and sofas, and avoid any overnight stays in the bedroom. This will ensure balance.

Your puppy is an opportunist and will look for various ways of ensuring a close physical bond with you as their owner, this will be detrimental to your ability to manage them, so my advice here is to avoid it or carefully manage it.

If you are facing problems indoors then it can be beneficial to leave a lead attached to your puppy's collar to help you physically manage them.

If you chose to attach a lead, then be calm and confident if you have to use it and leave it in place only when you are supervising or someone is in. Never overnight or when left alone for safety reasons.

This is a safe way of ensuring physical control of the dog around the home without inciting a challenge.

Use the lead to gently move your puppy away from a challenging situation do **not use** your voice, grab the collar or pick your puppy up.

Having physical contact like this will cause the dog to respond in a negative way.

Use your voice only for positive reward, if your puppy displays high energy stop using your voice altogether, there should be no shouting.

Vocal communication invariably creates more stimulation and confusion and will also make the dog more aware of any anxiety from the owner.

Remain consistent with your boundaries. If you think your puppy may struggle with a situation, then set a boundary using a smaller room with baby gate.

The use of a boundary ensures your puppy does not try and take responsibility for a social situation, it also allows them to observe your handling of a social situation.

Do not allow your puppy to run to the front door, set a boundary either visual or physical.

Being allowed to run to the front door sends a message to your puppy that you

Post-walk relaxation! We have a no sofa rule a home but as you can
see by the blanket in place there are times where rules get broken
and allowances are made. Marley has chosen to lay on the tiled floor,
we haven't enforced this. Controlling your puppy's physical boundaries
provides an easy route to retain leadership. If you are going to break rules
you have to be comfortable you still have good calm control overall.

have an expectation of them, when the humans do not respond in a predictable
manner this may become distressing for them. Your leadership will also begin to
fail if this happens frequently.

Set a boundary and enforce it when people enter your home. It is important
to control any roaming/pacing behaviour as well, so if your puppy is in the
living room they should display calm energy not try to demand attention/
jump up, pace around, lie at your feet or behind your legs. Ensure your puppy
shows personal space awareness.

Creating calm energy in your puppy ensures they are much more amenable
and in a good position to react appropriately, using learnt behaviour rather than
falling into a 'fight' or 'flight' response.

If you see any high energy behaviour remove your puppy swiftly with minimal interaction and do not allow them to re-enter until the situation is calmer. Remember, timing is key. If you leave your puppy alone for hours they will never learn which behaviour is desirable.

Never allow your puppy to barge past you through doorways.
This provides you with an opportunity to teach them manners and allows you to take the lead and provide direction in all new social situations.

Exercise (mental and physical stimulation)
Your puppy needs at least 2 walks per day and ideally one of these should be off lead, teaching recall. Ensure you leave the house with a calm puppy, do not let them barge past you either on the way out or in, they should wait to be invited. *The length of time you exercise will vary depending on age and breed of your puppy but it should be clear that they all require at least 2 breaks away from the home to explore normal dog behaviour.*

Hogan learning the early stages of self-control.

Ensure that the first and last part of your walk involves controlled lead work. I advise that you spend time training your puppy to walk to heel on a normal collar and lead.
Spending time at each end of the walk with the dog walking politely on the lead will associate you with good control and reinforce that you are making decisions on what happens during the walk.

Never allow your puppy to walk in front of you when you meet people.
If you allow this it will again send the wrong message, reducing your ability to lead and direct.

Do not allow your puppy to sit on or lie at your feet or behind your legs, ensure they are aware of your personal space.

Guarding breeds will guard their personal space in these situations and this can be potentially dangerous. Needy breeds will over-bond and nervous breeds will use the owner as protection. The dog needs to learn to be comfortable in its own skin and not take unnecessary responsibility.

Ensure a strong recall command is in place so your puppy can enjoy a life of free time.

You need to train your puppy to a solid recall command to ensure safe off lead management.

Delivering exercise at a repetitive level is advantageous. By this I mean teaching your puppy to go running with you if this is something you enjoy. Training them to run alongside a bicycle or even training them to use a running machine for 10 minutes before any off lead time, will help to dispel any initial high energy and keep them in the correct frame of mind to focus on your direction. This may not be possible and if not, you should use other methods to stabilise the dog and allow them to exercise mental ability to prevent giving in to over excitement and obsessive behaviour. Obviously care needs to be taken with exercise during your puppy period, you will not be able to do any of these activities fully until your puppy's bone growth plates have closed at around 18 months – 2 years of age. However, you can begin to teach early association to routines to help them adjust later on.

This is a really good way of achieving balance and calm in your puppy, encouraging the production of endorphins: powerful, positive chemicals produced during exercise, allowing them to perform their instinctive behaviours.

Play

Keep high energy activities to a minimum and don't allow your puppy to play with anything that is not specifically designed for them. Remember, play should be on your terms.

Possessions are considered a 'resource' to your puppy so dog toys should have a purpose and be managed by you. Ensuring play is elicited by you reinforces your importance in your puppy's little world.

Toys and chews can be given but ensure these are given in the kitchen to begin with and ideally have a level of interaction with your puppy to encourage them to work for their rewards.

Controlled play sessions are a regular occurrence at our house. They are always fun and relaxed and provide a great platform for learning and bonding.

This will also associate time away with something pleasant and should be encouraged.

Use playtime as quality interaction with you. This can be achieved with 'seek' and 'find' games, specifically designed dog puzzle toys and obedience work which can be trained in the home with the use of a clicker to modify and encourage desirable behaviour.
Dogs are intelligent animals so this should be explored.

Play with a tug toy can also be good fun but make sure you remain in control and do not allow your puppy to become too hyperactive.
Although this may be a fun game some dogs will see this type of game as a challenge that has to be won, I would always avoid this altogether in Bull type breeds.

Socialisation

Adequate and controlled socialisation is of paramount importance in creating balanced behaviour in your puppy. Expose your puppy to different dogs but only if this can be done safely, the dogs you choose should be calm and balanced themselves.

You as the owner should decide upon a situation, and whether it is safe or not, your puppy will learn successfully from another dog but this will only be positive if the other dog is balanced and well managed.

The relationship you share with your puppy is reliant on a solid understanding of each other. Leadership, patience and communication are all required to ensure your relationship develops positively.

Puppy Developmental Stages

The key to understanding your dog's ability to learn and process information is to have a clear awareness of the life stages your puppy will go through during his or her development. Once you recognise these you will be prepared for behaviour changes as and when they occur. The most predominant behaviours that are likely to occur and may cause concerns are: fear, caution, testosterone-led dominance, reactivity and sensitivity.

Good self-control techniques, social learning and handler knowledge and skill will ensure you avoid any unnecessary negative experiences.

The life stages are as follows:

Neonatal Period (0–12 Days)

Your puppy is able to respond to touch, warmth and smells, but body function regulation, elimination (urination and defaecation) and temperature control are not present.

Transition Period (13–20 Days)

Your puppy's ears and eyes are open but sight and hearing are limited. Awareness over body function control begins to develop and tail wagging is evident.

Hogan with his litter mates at a few days old.

Awareness Period (21–28 Days)

Sight and hearing have developed in efficiency and your puppy is beginning to learn the ropes of becoming a dog, it is essential that a stable environment has been created where the puppy's needs are being met and the predictability of a structured routine is in place.

Here is Hogan testing out his new senses on one of Derrie's chickens! (Puppies will still be with the breeder generally at this stage and so this job is down to them but it will still be a necessity to help the dog transition into life with new owners later on).

Early chicken socialisation!

Canine Socialisation Period (21–49 Days)

Puppies learn the early rules through interaction with the mother and litter mates, canine behaviour cues are being rewarded and recognised and your puppy is developing an understanding of the difference between interacting with litter mates and with humans.

Human Socialisation Period (7–12 Weeks)

During this time the puppy should be beginning to interact with lots of different humans from children and babies to the elderly, they should be exposed to all variations of 'the human' and be recognising huge differences in visual, body language traits and auditory characteristics.

This is the best time for the puppy to be going to its new home and is likely to be when you were advised to collect your puppy. Everything is in place for your dog to learn and begin developing manners and responding to simple word association training commands such as 'sit' 'stay' and 'come'. Toilet training begins and learning is developed through a process of association.

Early learning. Hogan following his mum's guidance.

Filming for the PuppyCoach.com series showing how puppies and children can interact positively.

In addition to this, the permanent new owner bond is established and the puppy has the ability to absorb the difference between acceptable and adverse behaviours through an awareness of right and wrong, developed through clear owner guidance and consistency.

Fear Imprinting Period (8–11 Weeks):
You will need to be mindful of the puppy's reaction to fear or being startled during this period, any traumatic or negative experience during this time can have a lasting effect on the puppy's behaviour and development.

Introduce the puppy to all sorts of people including children but be careful not to allow over zealous behaviour to minimise adverse conditioning. Experiences and learning at this stage are permanent.

Also make efforts to introduce your puppy to other 'balanced' dogs, do not expose the puppy to dogs with high energy or aggressive tendencies.

Hierarchy Classification Period (13–16 Weeks)
This is the period that a puppy would be coming away from its litter/mother in the wild, a critical time when dominant behaviour patterns may be witnessed and leadership skills are being tested.

Meeting Sheba in a controlled format for the first time at 9 weeks.

Mouthing is evident if not already controlled and periods of 'high energy' may become the norm! Praise and shaping positive introductions in social environments is essential learning and helps the puppy learn a means of coping with and interacting with human behaviour.

Flight Instinct Period (4–8 Months)

Puppies may push boundaries during this period, beginning to ignore any vocal commands and developing confidence levels away from the owner, it may last between a few days to several weeks. Your management of rewarding positive behaviours and ignoring/controlling negative behaviours will be highly relevant here. Your puppy may also be struggling with teething issues during this time so providing a consistent object to gnaw on is essential.

Second Fear Imprinting Period (6–14 Months)

This is relevant to social situations. This period may also correspond with growth spurts and may occur at different times depending on the breed of the dog. Small breeds may experience this period earlier than large breeds. This is where the puppy needs to really learn inner confidence and self-control, avoid negative handling and also sympathetic vocalisation during times of fear or stress.

You should be well practised in your efforts of managing negative behaviour now and be competently dealing with your puppy with patience and kindness, allowing the puppy to work through social scenarios and setting them up to succeed during interactions.

Maturity (1–4 Years)

Maturity varies from breed to breed. Some giant breeds continue to change physically after four years of age but the average dog can be considered fully developed between 1–1 ½ years up to 3 years.

Some owners may see an increase in dominance-led behaviours and potentially aggressive responses as dog's test for leadership status. You will need to have little tolerance of this behaviour and engage in active training to ensure rewards are still forthcoming for positive behaviours but likewise keep in place a 'removal' consequence for negative behaviour. It is your home and you command a level of respect and manners.

Staying consistent with your boundaries and ensuring you keep things

'Jake' the Belgian Shepherd displaying maturity at its very best!

clear and simple will ensure you are received effectively by the dog. It is here you will really start to run into trouble if you have failed to establish a clear difference between the dog's life and your own.

Your puppy is growing and developing at an incredible rate, both physically and mentally.

As a rough guide, your 6-8 month old puppy is at the equivalent life stage of a 3-4 year old child.

You cannot afford to take your eye off the ball during these precious early few months. What your puppy is learning now will be setting them up for the rest of their lives. A year of focused, tough work now will ensure you have many years of a balanced well-mannered family pet.

Task

Implement the structure and routine that will work in your home to ensure you have the ability to clearly and safely 'lead' your puppy.

Observe your puppy's life stage and note the behaviours you are observing to assess how well your puppy is progressing.

CHAPTER 8

Crate/Down Time Area Training

A properly used crate is an absolute must for all new puppy owners. It facilitates toilet training, provides a safe haven for your new arrival away from a busy family environment, prevents the destruction of prized possessions and all in all makes most owners lives a whole lot more bearable.

However, as with any human invention designed to make our lives easier, it is also easily abused, potentially creates socialisation issues and encourages a puppy to reach a 'shut down' anxiety led state if not introduced and used correctly.

In this section I will talk you through the best way of associating this invaluable piece of training equipment positively and ensuring your puppy bounces into it and settles down happily.

Hogan curled up in his bed next to his crate. He has learnt an association to a bed area away from the crate. This allows control in different environment's when it may not be viable to take the crate along.

Choosing your Crate or Down Time Area

If you have a small room or safe, undisturbed, sectioned off area such as a utility room or similar then this with also suffice as an area to manage your puppy from.

Please, never use closed doors when your puppy is removed into their space (a closed crate door is fine as they can hear and see through it).

If you are using a room, or your crate within a separate room then please purchase a stair gate (baby or dog gate) to put across the width of the door. Hogan's crate is situated in a busy social space in our house.

Early positive crate association with constant reward in the form of food.

Closing a solid door on your puppy isolates them and impacts on their social learning, it also means you won't develop the positive relationship you are striving for. Likewise glass doors are not safe and should be considered a hazard as puppies do jump up to begin with!

It is invaluable to have a means of containing your puppy in a positively associated area. I consider this essential to help the puppy adjust to a busy domesticated environment and provide an avenue of teaching the puppy self-control and solitary time, whilst also ensuring the puppy's safety when not supervised.

The area should be used for feeding, sleeping and down time. The puppy should not be totally isolated from family life but likewise should not be placed in the thick of social activity. A happy balance is necessary for a positive experience.

Size of Area

Please make sure you have chosen an area or crate of adequate size for the breed of dog you have chosen. Your puppy will grow quickly and you will probably still want to be using an area up until they are fully grown. Your puppy should be able to stand up, turn around and lie down flat and outstretched throughout.

Purpose of Area

The introduction of the crate into a domestic environment has provided a means of physically managing the puppy, keeping it safe when not attended and providing valuable 'down time' away from the hectic lives of many family environments. However, incorrect or poor training may mean the crate could have a negative effect on the puppy's welfare.

It is essential that your puppy is correctly and positively conditioned to its crate to avoid distress. I have seen many crate trained puppies who are unhappy but appear to be calm and relaxed. A stoic behaviour does not mean the puppy has accepted the crate, it may be they have run out of ways of communicating their upset.

Setting your Puppy up to Learn from a 'Trigger Word'

Your puppy can learn that the crate is positive much faster if you use a 'trigger' (or clicker) word. This is one word you will use to positively associate your puppy's good behaviour. It is reinforced with a treat. You can simply associate it by using it when your puppy does something you like.

There are many different approaches to this but if you can understand the concept you can find what works for you.

I like to teach my dogs using eye contact as this associates the trigger word alongside a behaviour that you will really want to embed throughout their training.

This is achieved as follows:

- Sit down on a sofa/couch
- Hold a piece of food in the palm of your hand and make a fist
- Call the puppy to you
- Stay quiet
- Place the closed fist on your knee and wait
- Ignore the puppy's attempts to free the food and wait
- Once your puppy makes eye contact release the food and say your word, for me this is 'Good'
- It is important that your timing is spot on, say the word and deliver the food immediately
- You may only have a split second to spot this before your dog looks away
- Repeat

Your puppy will start to associate the trigger word with a positive reward plus seek out eye contact from you, giving you more control over their behaviour.

NB: You will also build on this method to introduce the word 'No' later on.

Perfect eye contact in training from Hogan.

How to Condition your Puppy Positively to its Area

To ensure your puppy is happy to enter the crate you should follow these steps:

- Set the crate up in a quiet area with a bed at one end and newspaper at the other
- Ideally have a toy or something familiar for the puppy in the crate before you start

- Sit on the floor by the open crate door
- Invite your puppy over and deliver attention
- Encourage the puppy to show an interest in food in your hand (you can always use something else your puppy likes, such as a ball)
- Once you have the pups interest, throw the treat into the crate
- As soon as the pup enters the crate to take the treat, deliver your trigger word 'Good'
- Throw another piece of food on to the floor outside the crate so your pup feels the freedom of being able to walk out and collect a second reward
- Repeat this process until your puppy is entering the crate to wait for the food

Closing the Crate Door

You must ensure that your puppy is happy to take itself in and out of the crate before closing the door, also look for key times to practise doing this, such as when the puppy is sleepy. Give your puppy something nice to keep it busy and distracted when you close the door for the first time. A Kong toy stuffed with tasty treats works really well.

Once your puppy is distracted, follow these steps:

- Walk towards the crate
- If your puppy looks at you, make no eye contact just calmly show them the flat palm of your hand, this is the start of your early body language communication signals
- Quietly close the crate door
- Repeat the hand signal and step away
- If your puppy cries you should wait for a quiet moment, walk back to the crate, stand sideways to the door, fold your arms and say nothing
- Your goal is to help your puppy cope at this stage not bully them to stay where you put them
- Once your puppy stops trying to get your attention, show them the hand signal again and slowly open the crate door
- If your puppy attempts to charge out, just gently close the door and repeat

- Once your puppy is waiting, you can then invite your puppy out with an 'OK' and use your trigger word 'Good' as they approach you

Periods in the crate should initially be short, it is advisable to place your puppy in the crate whenever they fall asleep in your home. This is so that they get used to sleeping in one 'safe place'. Do not rush this process, you will be using your crate successfully for months to come if you ensure the association is delivered correctly.

Make sure you are not attempting this with a really busy house, lots of stimulation outside of the crate will just encourage the puppy to want to join in, a calm patient handler is the most important factor if this is to be successful. Build the solitary time up gradually and make sure you never leave your puppy in the crate for longer than a 3–4 hour period, even if they are positively accepting of the crate.

Teaching your Puppy to Transition from their Space to Yours

Puppies incorrectly conditioned may be quiet when the door is closed but explode from their crate when the door is open, displaying unbalanced, high energy and excitable behaviour. This behaviour can only usually be tolerated by most owners for a short time before the puppy is returned to its crate again. So, teaching the dog how to transition from its crate to human social space is essential for balanced behaviour.

In order to do this, you should really focus on the level of energy your puppy displays when you open the crate door. It is not acceptable to allow them to charge out and jump all over anyone stood in their way, even if you have missed them and want to lavish them with attention!

To avoid this situation developing you should add in behaviour controls around changes in your household dynamics.

People entering or leaving your home should not engage with your puppy in any way, they should wait until any excitable behaviour has passed and the puppy has settled down again before engaging with them, this includes eye contact. There is no exact period of time for this, it will depend on the perseverance and character of your particular puppy. This is the start of you recognising your puppy's responses to high energy social situations and what common body language signals they use.

Hogan relaxing in his bed.

Stay calm and never try and physically or verbally stop your dog reacting, they learn best when they work things out for themselves. Once your puppy has responded you should then work through your controls around the crate door, as you have already practised and invite your puppy out into the social space but with guidance.

I advise that you use a lead and direct your puppy to a bed within your social space, this gives you the ability to manage your puppy calmly and without having to chase them around. It also desensitises them to the attachment of the lead, aiding the development and understanding of lead control.

Ultimately you are looking to teach your puppy all the tools they need to develop their self-control, and also preventing all the early unwanted behaviours such as mouthing and jumping up being rewarded by you or visiting guests.

Common advice is never to use your crate or down time area as a punishment and I do agree with this in principle. However, I advise all my new puppy owners to regularly use this area as a means of controlling your puppy, teaching them how to behave in new social situations and helping them to cope! For me this comes down to the effective handling of a puppy in every social situation.

I recommend that you NEVER use aggressive, vocal, or physically invasive body language to direct your dog into their place of comfort. This will definitely make sure they never want to go there willingly.

Here the lead is in place to show how I initially trained Hogan to stay in his bed.

However, I do highly recommend that you place your puppy in their area prior to any change in dynamics in your home, such as a guest arriving or children coming home from school. By managing the first 15 minutes of a change in energy in a social space and allowing your puppy to watch the activity in your home on a boundary line, you are helping them cope and adjust. This is also the reason I have stated that you should never shut your puppy behind a closed door. A good baby gate or crate door allows the puppy exposure to social activity but prevents loss of control or the rewarding of poor behaviour patterns by family or a third party.

If you consider that your crate provides a 'safe zone' for your puppy to defer to or be deferred to when they are struggling to elicit self-control, then you will use it appropriately. I always set my puppies up for success, this means they are invited to join social time and given direction. This direction is likely to be focused around staying in a particular area or on a bed, the direction is reinforced twice and if the puppy is still struggling to be calm I would then remove them to their down time area and repeat once calmness is achieved.

At no point should this process be erratic, seen as a means of reprimanding the dog or attached to anything negative. Use a very calm and matter of fact attitude with gentle clear handling. I also use the 'flat palm of hand signal' to communicate this calmness and offer control to the puppy.

I have used this method with all my dogs to teach them what level of energy is expected when socialising with humans and it creates an invaluable platform for them to learn as a puppy. Marley spent the first 5 months of his life choosing to lay in his down time area in the evenings rather than to sit with us. He found our busy social environment far too intense. Allowing him to take this at his pace through his adolescent months now means we have a very balanced adult dog around the house.

Task

Your task for this section is to ensure you:

- Successfully condition your puppy to its crate
- Spend time making this experience calm and positive

CHAPTER 9

Toilet Training

Toilet training is exactly what it says, you are building a habit for your puppy to toilet in a specific place outdoors. In the early days this really is only habit forming, puppies do not get full control of their bladder or colon until between 14-16 weeks of age.

That said, effective training may mean your puppy appears clean long before this time as you have built a solid routine, leaving little room for mistakes. I employed the same habitual training with my own babies, building a habit of visiting the potty after food, as soon as they woke up and after any play or entertainment. They were both dry day and night by 22 months of age. Proof that children and dogs do learn similarly when they are young!

**Hogan doing his first wee on command.
You have to document these things!**

Timescale

If you have a small breed dog, you may find toilet training takes a little longer; just remain clear and consistent you will get there in the end.

If you are still having soiling problems from 5 months onwards, and have stuck to a solid training plan, this is likely to be due to other medical or behavioural factors. As a result, you should seek further professional advice. I have many clients call me with adolescent dogs who are soiling the house, commonly this would be in specific areas, such as upstairs, by exit doors or in the centre of prime living space rooms. This is indicative of a more complex issue; it is likely that they know very well where they should go to the toilet but they are choosing to use the act as a means of communicating an issue!

Method

Effective toilet training begins as soon as you bring your puppy home. I do not advocate the use of 'puppy pads,' in my opinion this just teaches the puppy to soil on a substrate similar to your carpet and in your home! Get them outside as soon as possible.

For accidents in the crate or 'down time area' use good old fashioned newspaper!

The most successful toilet training comes from early outdoor exposure, so take your puppy out regularly and at key times.

Always go with your puppy to make sure you are there to deliver the reward immediately. Don't interrupt them or talk to them while they are wondering around

Build good habits around toilet training from the start. Hogan was already used to toileting outside before he arrived with us.

and definitely do NOT engage in play or attention-giving as this will act as too much of a distraction.

Ideally it is beneficial if you allow your puppy to follow you out into the garden rather than picking them up, this allows them to build a clearer association of leaving the house to go outside.

You should be patient and reward with your 'trigger' word (mine is 'good' and I've associated it with a food reward), back this up with a treat. Remember this is early habit forming and not something that your puppy will pick up immediately so be patient, calm and consistent. Never reprimand your puppy for accidents in the home, send them away while you clean up and act like it hasn't happened. Avoid using bleach-based cleaning products. When beach is mixed with the ammonia in urine the result is a toxic substance. Also avoid any cleaning products containing ammonia as these will just encourage your puppy to soil in the same place again.

You will get used to your puppy's toileting behaviour signals, recognise these and make sure you step in early with guidance. Attach a verbal command such as 'busy', or 'toilet'. You can then begin to instruct your puppy to go before you have to leave them alone.

I have always used the word 'wee-wee's' for all my dog's and I start to say it when I step out of the house, while gesturing for the puppy to go to the grass with my hand signal. With my first Labrador I also used to say 'do a poo' and he knew the difference. It doesn't sound very pretty but it did the job and was easy for me to remember for consistency. Use whatever words you like but make sure everyone is using the same! It is important that this is delivered calmly and repetitively, don't deliver attention directly to your puppy until they finish. Don't interact at all and more importantly don't get frustrated, it may take a while for it to click, if this is the sound they hear every time they go to the toilet they will soon make the link.

If you wish to use a specific 'toilet' area you will need to take your puppy to it and be clear with this, make sure you clear up the mess or it will put them off.

Checklist for Effective Toilet Training

- Newspaper (for accidents in crate)
- Take out every 2 hours or more

- Immediately after food
- As soon as the puppy wakes up
- After any high energy play or interaction
- Always go with your puppy to deliver the reward immediately
- Don't interrupt them
- Reward with your trigger word and treat
- Never reprimand your puppy after an accident
- Avoid using bleach to clean
- Observe your puppy's body language
- Attach a command such as 'busy'
- Decide if you are using a specific 'toilet' area and take them there
- Keep the toilet area clean

Toilet training will be the focus of the early weeks with your puppy. It will motivate you to keep control of the puppy's environment, to avoid soiling in your home. As with all your training keep it positive, end on a good note and allow the puppy to work out what you want themselves.

Task

Your tasks for this section are to:

- Set up your toilet area
- Set yourself a routine
- Start to build in your associated word to encourage them to toilet outside

CHAPTER 10

Feeding and Nutrition

Food will be your most effective tool to teach your puppy, so ensure you have maximum control around its delivery. Remember dogs are hunters and are used to working for their food, so focus on this primitive drive by encouraging them to deliver respectable behaviour with manners.

Just a simple period of calm is enough to begin with, and if your puppy charges for the bowl as you present it then just pick it up and repeat. Never take your puppy's bowl away from him or her while they are eating. This is often well documented advice, it is poor advice and will potentially cause aggression problems in your dog later on.

Just apply common sense to this and imagine if somebody did this to you when you were about to tuck in to your favourite meal. They might get away with it once, but the next time you would be ready for their approach! Instead your puppy should recognise that your hands bring food, not take it away. Spend time stroking and grooming your dog while they eat, and periodically drop something tasty into the bowl as you do so.

As with anything, don't overdo it, just once a day and for a short period. If this makes your puppy rush his food take it even slower. Be guided by your puppy as this is all about you communicating a positive message, some puppy's need a very clear and slow approach to all new associations.

Puppies who Bolt their Food

This problem is particularly common in the Labrador and as a result I sought other means of feeding Hogan instead of just from a bowl. If your puppy is eating too fast this can cause gastric upset, as much of the early digestion begins in the mouth during chewing.

You can see the prongs in the slow feeder bowl standing up which encourages Hogan to eat around them, therefore making the process much more difficult and slower.

I would advise you use the following options as alternative methods of feeding to slow this process down:

- Use a slow feeder bowl
- Hand feed some of the puppy's quota through the day as rewards for training
- Deliver the food inside a Kong toy or similar

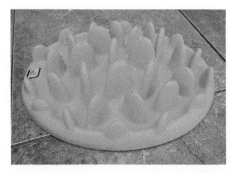

There are a variety of different slow feeders.
They all do a similar job; this is the one I used for Hogan.

Choosing a Type of Food

The dog food market is flooded. I know that for many owners choosing a brand of food can be challenging. I try to take a simple and realistic approach to this process and consider all affecting factors.

To begin to understand where to start you should familiarise yourself with all available methods of feeding, understand the positives and negatives and ensure the diet you choose will work for the breed and energy level of puppy you have.

These are the various different types of food available:

- Dry food
- Wet food
- Raw feeding barf diet
- Commercial dog foods
- Complimentary dog foods
- Tripe
- Semi-moist
- Frozen
- Freeze dried
- Complete dog foods

During my veterinary nursing career, I was privy to the scientific research and educated on the nutritional values of a variety of different dog foods, in particular, dry food. While in principle dry food seemed to tick lots of boxes, especially the convenience of storage and ease of feeding, it wasn't until I began my career in behaviour that I began to look seriously at the effects of food on the behaviour cases I treated.

I am not in a position to scientifically underpin the thoughts and opinions I have on the subject, nor can I say that they are exclusive across the board. I have had the opportunity to trial a variety of foods but certainly not all, and I am aware that some companies invest hugely in achieving a quality product. I can only speak from my experience and advice here should be seen as personal to the dogs I have treated.

Dry food provides an easy and relatively 'clean' way of feeding the dog, but bowls are often left down all day if the dog chooses not to finish a meal. The dog is a natural predator and will scavenge and eat whatever it comes across, you should question why a dog is leaving food, hiding it or picking at it during key times through the day. Food acts as a powerful avenue for the dog to communicate its role within a social group. Any grazing behaviour is not normal and an owner's leadership will definitely be in question if this is occurring.

With this in mind, if you are choosing to feed a dry food product then ensure you set a clear routine and make control obvious. This is simply achieved by making the dog sit and wait for you to place down the bowl and then release them to eat. As soon as they move away from the bowl you should remove it. Never leave food down for 5-10 minutes or any other period of time, it reduces the importance of their food to them generally, and encourages fussy poor feeding behaviours.

If you observe the ingredients on the bag of many dry foods, you may also find they contain the following:

- Corn germ meal
- Corn gluten meal
- By products
- Grains
- Cereals
- Meat
- Animal derivatives

None of these ingredients are beneficial for your dog and some may be harmful long term. Understanding the ingredients label of a bag of dry food is confusing for the majority of pet owners including me at times!

Ultimately I try to bring a common sense approach to any problem. I recommend that you do sufficient research to ensure the chosen food has been safely prepared and sourced by a reputable company. It should be balanced with a mix of protein and vegetables. If raw feeding is your choice I suggest you do not prepare your own food, due to the risk of meat related bacteria when handling and storing it.

There are many positive reasons for choosing raw food, the dogs thrive on it, are calm and balanced, have healthy coats and a significant reduction in the amount of faeces they produce. However, there are also some considerations to ensure you are aware of.

As a veterinary nurse I assisted with many abdominal procedures whereby dogs were suffering blockages as a result of poorly chewed and digested bones, so I highly recommend that you use a recommended supplier. Unless, of course you are experienced in this mode of feeding.

Many dogs are fed dry foods with no apparent issues, and I do not wish to prolong the debate of raw versus dry feeding. I feed raw food and this is just my choice. I do so using a company I trust and with knowledge of all potential concerns. That said I am also aware that raw feeding may not be viable for all. It can be costly, time consuming and you do have to be organised with defrosting and storage. It may not suit all dogs so you should speak to your veterinary surgeon for guidance on this matter. There are many dry and cooked foods available with good nutritional value so just ensure you find what works best for you as well as your puppy.

Finally, I always suggest you don't feed human food to your puppy. Aside from the behaviour management aspect of this, there are also many foods that may be harmful to dogs. The following list will help you identify what you should avoid.

Toxic Subtances

- Chocolate
- Yeast
- Cherries
- Apricots
- Pear pips
- Peaches
- Almonds
- Apple core pips (contain cyanogenic glycosides = cyanide poisoning)
- Macadamia nuts
- Potato peelings
- Foods that have gone mouldy
- Rhubarb leaves
- Grapes – all vine fruits
- Coffee
- Tea
- Tomatoes

- Hops (beer)
- Raisins
- Plums (kernel)
- Broccoli
- Avocado
- Onions
- Citrus
- Coconut and coconut oil
- Garlic
- Chives
- Cooked bones
- Raw eggs
- Baking soda and powder
- Nutmeg
- Mushrooms
- Salt
- Xylitol (found in peanut butter and chewing gum) HIGHLY TOXIC

Amount of Food

As a rough guide your puppy will require 4 meals per day until he or she is 11-12 weeks old, this can then be reduced to 3 meals a day until around 4-5 months and finally down to 2 meals daily from 5-6 months. This is highly dependent on your particular puppy, their energy levels, amount of physical exercise and calorie requirement. You may find your puppy guides you with this and begins to drop meals accordingly if they are not hungry.

Using Food as a Training Tool

Feeding your puppy provides a fantastic opportunity to build your leadership relationship and also encourage them to work a little harder for their final reward of a meal. Asking for a simple wait before delivering the food can be built on by adding in the 'sit' and increasing the period of time you expect your puppy to wait.

Hogan doing his best not to drool all over my leg and trifle! Reinforcing the importance of creating a boundary between your dog and your food.

You can then move on again by removing yourself from the area and still requesting the dog wait, this is achieved by the introduction of a solid release command such as 'OK' with a hand gesture.

Your puppy should not move until you deliver the release command. You can ask for more control via the sit and wait as your puppy develops.

You can also embed positive behaviours with the use of food and in particular it is really useful for training a solid recall. I also like to use food to build positive relationships with family members, especially children. Allowing children to have an involvement in their puppy's development in a controlled and calm manner is invaluable. It also teaches the puppy an awareness of children as important individuals in the household.

Finally, you can use food as a positive avenue for training your new puppy to be accepted by an established family dog. I never recommend that you interfere in the dynamics of this relationship, however it is important that you involve your other dog in the feeding regime your puppy has.

Educating children in a feeding regime for their puppy Rottweiler
(refer to Chapter 25).

Your puppy will be fed 4 times daily to begin with so at each meal it is useful to establish control by feeding both dogs, a distance from each other but at the same time. Even if your older dog just has a treat in the bowl. This will ensure your puppy is not delivered special privileges above your older dog which may create tension.

Task

Your task for this section is to research a chosen brand of food, consider where your nearest supplier is and whether you are able to store in bulk.

If you have already sourced your food, observe the ingredients and check how many waste products are included.

CHAPTER 11

Obedience Training

It is essential that your puppy eventually recognises the vocal commands associated with individual behaviours, in order for them to have a solid platform for communication to develop. This takes time and care, your puppy is not programmed to understand the human spoken word, so each word you use should be singular and clearly associated with a desirable behaviour. You should recognise that the dog is primarily responding to and following your body language and scent.

For them to understand and learn 'words' they must be calm and focused and have a solid relationship with the handler.

Training and socialising Hogan in a group walk.

Successful obedience work requires a confident and clear approach. As a new owner you will have to ensure your puppy wants to be with you and work for you, so your leadership skills are essential. There are many areas where having good obedience in place makes life a whole lot easier.

Health Checks and Veterinary Visits

Good obedience and awareness of commands allows you to communicate in a clear fashion to your dog when they may be unnerved or concerned such as during a visit to the vets or when they meet something for the first time such as trains, prams or bikes.

To prepare for this you should actively put time aside to condition your puppy to general handling in a controlled and serious manner.

Begin by spending time stroking and touching your puppy, picking up their feet and tail and looking in their mouths, all the time associating the activity with something pleasant like food or play.

You can build on this and make it more structured once you have more control with a sit and wait command.

I always put my puppies on a table to do this so it mimics the association they may have with the vet.

I chose to go one step further with Hogan and taught him to lay flat.
I used treats to guide him into position and then showed him the flat
palm of my hand to ask for the wait before using 'OK' as the release. We
practised this to increase the amount of time he is content to lay flat.

Always keep this interaction short, positive and focused and do it as early as possible, lots of puppies learn to dislike their paws being touched at an early age so it is worth spending time drying paws positively. Don't wait until you are back from a walk and in a rush as it's chucking it down with rain. Rushing will definitely give your puppy cause for concern. Some puppies can be uncomfortable being picked up as well so it is important that you recognise what your puppy tolerates and what they don't.

Always remember dogs in general have a very 'black and white' attitude. This means if you hesitate or are not clear with your handling you are liable to create a negative reaction. You should scoop them up with confidence, one hand supporting their bottom and the other controlling their head

Make sure your puppy is wearing a lead and collar so you have full control and take a structured approach to examining your puppy's general physical health.

Mouth

Observation of the dog's mouth should involve a thorough look at the following:

- **Teeth:** Is there any plaque/tartar build up? Are they intact? Note any chips or breaks. Puppies have 28 (deciduous) baby teeth and these will start to erupt from 2-3 weeks old and all should be present by the time the puppy is 8 weeks old. Almost as soon as all the baby teeth are through the roots begin to resorb to make way for the adult teeth, they will eventually have 42 adult teeth.

- **Gums:** Are they a healthy pale pink or is there inflammation, any lumps, or any sign of bleeding? Sometimes you will see black pigment on the gums, this may be normal for your puppy but observe for any changes.

- **Tongue:** Is it a healthy pale pink in colour? Can you see any yellow or white residue?

If your puppy is drooling or pawing at their mouth, then you should also seek veterinary attention.

Make sure you know what the 'normal look' of your puppy's mouth is, some will have pigment in their mouths and you will see black areas as a result, the 'chowchow' also has a black tongue and this is normal for the breed.

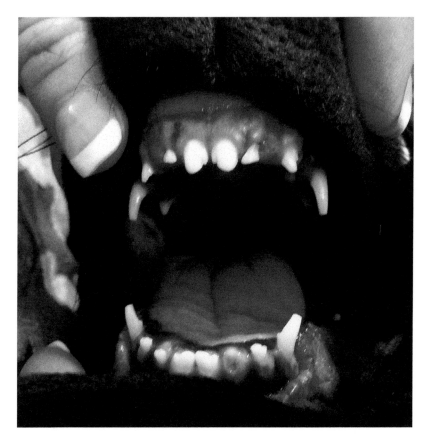

This is Hogan's mouth at 5 months of age providing insight as to why puppies chew continuously all the way through their puppy and adolescent period.

Ears

Lift up the ear flap and observe the skin on the inside. Ensure it is free from inflammation and dirt, can you see wax at the opening of the ear canal and if so is it a normal light brown/yellow colour or is it thick and black?

Is there a smell and is your puppy tolerating you doing this? The dog has two ear canals the horizontal and vertical, with the ear drum (tympanic membrane) being situated at the base of the vertical ear canal.

Although all dogs can and do get ear infections, certain breeds of dog are more susceptible. These would be your long eared breeds such as Spaniels and those with thick heavy coats such as the Newfoundland and Bernese Mountain dogs.

Perfect poser – "Show me your ears Hogan!"

The Labrador along with other pedigrees are prone to developing an allergy condition known as Atopy and the ears can be a real focal point for this. My first Labrador, Merlin, suffered excessively with atopy and food allergies. Despite this predisposition I was able to keep him managed and free from infection with medication, general hygiene and ensuring I dealt with little problems before they became big ones. There has been so much research into food allergy and atopic conditions now and there are many veterinary products available to treat the underlying immune system problem, so always involve your vet in your puppy's care if you feel their ears or skin in general are problematic.

You should also keep in mind that there are parasites that can cause ear infections and these can be easily treated. Never try to treat an ear infection yourself, if your puppy has a perforated ear drum you could cause serious damage.

Eyes

Your eye observation is limited as this is really a specialist area and I would not advise you do any poking around here. It is just useful again to observe what is normal for your puppy. What colour are their eyes? Is there any redness or discharge? Obviously this along with any irritation is a matter for your vet to investigate.

There are obvious conditions affecting the eye that are easily treated with the right medication (such as conjunctivitis), infections can cause eye ulcers and you will not necessarily realise the extent of the problem. Eyes are definitely an area where you reach for the phone and visit your vet.

Nose

Using the 'wetness' of your dog's nose to decide on their general health is not advisable and generally isn't taken seriously by any veterinary professional. A very healthy dog may have a warm dry nose while a sick dog can still have a wet cold nose. Do NOT use this to make important health decisions on your dog.

The nose, however, does act as a means of temperature regulation and this along with the pads on the paws allows for the secretion of sweat. Dogs don't have normal sweat glands in their skin and so this temperature regulation is confined to these small areas along with panting from the mouth.

You can see how a dog can very quickly become over heated, so be mindful of this when the weather warms up!

Mucous Membrane

The mucous membrane is a particular type of epithelial tissue and you will see it as the gums in the mouth and conjunctiva of the eye. It should be a healthy pale pink in colour and there should be no sign of any blood in the form of pin prick hemorrhages.

This area is often observed and tested to check on your dog's circulation, this allows you to consider their general health. It is also a good barometer for the presence of oxygen in your dog's blood. Make sure there is no bleeding and that the area is free from lesions and damage.

Genitals

The genital area may be difficult to check as many dogs will dislike you looking, however as with all areas of the health check it is worth ensuring you know what is normal for your puppy.

You will find the female genitalia under the tail below the anus and in the male it will be underneath and between the legs.

It's useful to know what your female puppy's vulva/genital area looks like as this area will swell as an indicator of a season. This is important when you are on the lookout for their first one!

A common problem in developing male puppies is 'paraphimosis'. This is where the penis gets trapped in the prepuce (foreskin) and swells. Don't panic, you can try and ease it back in using some lube or if you're a bit squeamish then a vet visit is needed.

Don't leave it to rectify itself though. You shouldn't panic but the penis will dry out and become vulnerable if not treated.

Contact your vet if you are unsure of anything in these areas.

Observing the genital area in your male puppy is easy as they generally sit backwards on their pelvis showing off all they have. You should be able to get a good look to tell what's normal.

Anus

This area is not one owners like to observe but you should ensure it is kept clean, is free from hair and look for any skin damage (particularly in very hairy dogs).

I have seen may dogs with thick fur suffering from a condition known as 'flystrike'. This occurs when flies have laid their eggs in the warm, damp fur around the anus resulting in the hatching of maggots. Maggots do extensive and life threatening damage to soft tissue in a VERY short space of time. It is essential that you keep this area clean, particularly if your dog spends lots of time outside in warm conditions. Flystrike will also occur in ears and anywhere where there may be skin damage.

The anal area also houses the 'anal glands'. Situated on the inside of the anus they are positioned at 10 to the hour and 10 past the hour if you imagine a clock face. It is a common area for trouble especially in dogs suffering from allergies. The scent produced by these glands is designed to coat the faeces and deliver many messages of communication to other approaching dogs. As a result of the feeding of different diets the faeces from some dogs is too soft to ensure the glands are regularly evacuated. In some cases, they can become blocked causing pain and irritation.

Ensuring adequate fibre content should assist with this, but if it does occur you will see your puppy 'scooting' their bottom something often associated with worms.

If you are confident your worming program is up to date, then it is worth getting a vet check to rule out an anal gland problem.

It is possible for you to learn how to empty these glands yourself but if there isn't a problem then leave them alone.

Hogan tucking into a bone.

Be aware if you take your puppy for a pamper session, some groomers will empty the anal glands as part of the grooming procedure. I advise that you ask them not to as they may cause unnecessary irritation, creating a problem that wasn't there to begin with.

Paws and Nails

Allowing easy observation of your dog's paws and nails can be facilitated by teaching the paw command, as follows:

Sit in front of your puppy quietly and follow these steps:

- Place your puppy into the sit
- Pick up one paw and deliver a treat
- Repeat until your puppy is giving you their paw to receive the treat
- Once they are naturally doing it you can attach the word 'Paw'

This will build confidence in your puppy giving you their paw to examine, you can lengthen the time you hold on to the treat to extend the examination time.

The nails should look healthy with no cracks or breaks, the nail bed (where the nail attaches to the skin) should be free from discharge and damage. Broken nails can be a source of infection so make sure you get a veterinary opinion. The pads will be soft and shiny to begin with but will soon become hard and cracked once they are used. Small cracks are normal but any that are causing pain or discomfort should be checked properly. The skin on the paws should be free from inflammation and shouldn't smell.

Skin and Fur

Puppies will have a variety of different coats and also skin colour depending on their breed, so again make sure you get used to what's normal for your own puppy. It is normal to observe dandruff and lots of scratching when they are in their early puppy period.

Your puppy's skin and immune systems will always be a little over reactive while it adjusts to new environments but it shouldn't result in physical harm. It should also get less as they grow.

If your puppy is fed a good balanced diet and is well cared for, their coat should shine and feel soft to the touch, unless you have a wire-haired or fluffy coated breed and these may appear a little rougher/coarse. It should also be free from excessive dandruff and grease and the skin should be clear and healthy with no smell.

A normal 'doggy' smell may occur if they get wet but make sure you dry them thoroughly to avoid infections.

Bright eyes and a shiny coat.

Canine Communication

To begin with you should concentrate on communicating in a format your puppy will understand. They are body language and scent communicators so your focus should be on quiet body language signals. If you view the PuppyCoach.com films, you will see me use the 'flat palm of my hand' throughout.

This is the clearest means of requesting calm and balance in your dog, as shown below.

My signature hand signal delivered at various heights and intensity provides a different level of communication.

Self-control is everything and should be your primary focus in all social events and during training sessions.

Keep in mind your puppy's concentration span, for the first few months of their life you should be looking to do very short (max 10 minutes) periods of focused work.

Finally, remember that your puppy will have a more solid understanding and learn quicker if you allow them the opportunity to work things out for themselves. You may get frustrated and want to push their bottom into the 'sit' position for instance. All you will achieve is a puppy who doesn't understand why you are invading their personal space so firmly and you will build negativity into your relationship. To encourage your puppy you should guide them with food or wait for them to try out different things, rewarding the desired behaviour immediately.

Recall

Recall is dealt with as an independent subject in Chapter 17, but I have included it here also as it is very much linked to your obedience training.

Teaching Harley the early stages of recall, sending him out for a ball and guiding him in with the long line. This is making me the focus for his enjoyment so it is always fun to return to the handler. Having the ability to prevent your puppy ignoring you is essential for consistent recall training.

To be successful with your recall commands you should embed your puppy's return to you early and with a clear, consistent sound. I always recommend the use of a gun dog whistle. This gives a consistent tone and it will allow you to develop a variety of different whistle patterns alongside different meanings, such as to direct your dog left or right or to go 'down' or stop.

I use two short beeps to recall Hogan right back to me and one long and loud sound to direct the STOP command. This means he must stop what he is doing and stand still until I either recall him or catch up with him.

You should have a deep understanding of how relevant your relationship is in recall training. A solid leadership based relationship coupled with basic obedience training and social learning will facilitate a positive response.

The Fight, Flight, Freeze or Avoid Response

The fight or flight response manifests itself in many ways. In most cases this is through unbalanced high energy, stress relieving behaviours and vocalisation, particularly when scenarios of high stimulation occur. It should be viewed as an undesirable chemical response, occurring as a puppy's coping mechanism fails. In this scenario your puppy will always resort to an instinctive response, which almost mimic's a human panic attack! We have all experienced the effects of stress at some point in our lives, your puppy will be susceptible to similar physical and mental feelings as they produce the same survival chemicals as we do in intense situations.

To challenge this response with direct physical or vocal reactions will only serve to heighten and encourage a negative response and should be avoided at all costs. Managing high energy and unbalanced behaviours from the start provide an excellent platform to avoid this ever being a problem.

It is essential to understand that a puppy who is experiencing the chemicals involved in the fight or flight response does not have the ability to access or retain learnt information. This is important when you wish to focus on teaching obedience commands. If you become frustrated, the situation will only get worse so stay calm and consistent.

Flight animals such as sheep will be natural triggers for the dog's prey or chase drive. This is Hogan reaffirming his relationship with the young sheep who was born and reared at the same time as he and his siblings. Positive calm socialisation provides a platform for self-control and reduced reactive responses.

Obedience Commands

Obedience commands are developed as a result of a positive, leadership based relationship between a dog and owner. A dog has the mental ability to associate vocal sounds with particular behaviours and repeat these as instructed if they are taught properly.

I see many dogs who have had poor early learning or do not view their owner as their leader. These puppies or adult dogs display poor behaviour even though they have been through puppy school and in some cases still attend obedience type training classes! Just because your dog or puppy has been taught the behaviour attached to a particular word, it doesn't mean they will want to do it for you. An understanding of this is essential from an owner's perspective as it highlights where work needs to be done.

"Focus on embedding a series of common behaviours attached to individual spoken words"

Follow these Do's and Don'ts to achieve this successfully:

- Find some quiet time
- Sit down with your puppy and a pot of treats or a toy
- Use the treat (or toy) to guide your puppy into the desired position
- Reward with your trigger word (good) and release a treat
- Stay calm do not get over excited
- Repeat until they are performing the exercise with less direction
- Attach the single word command (such as 'sit' or 'down' etc.)
- Repeat
- Keep training sessions short
- End on a good note
- Signal that the session is finished by removing the pot of treats and sending the puppy away
- You can apply this method to all self-control commands

Self-Control Commands

REMEMBER:
"Your puppy is not born to understand human vocal communication! They will not understand the meaning of the word 'NO', unless you have taken the time to teach them properly".

This level of control provides a great platform to integrate children around your puppy.

1. Sit

This is probably one of the first commands you will teach your puppy as they will naturally sit for you if you stay calm and quiet. It is generally the first behaviour they will offer you if you are armed with a reward and some patience.

Remember to wait and be sure your puppy's bottom is firmly on the floor before introducing the command. Say it only once and immediately reward with your treat/toy or praise. Keep the reward low key, you don't want to excite them so their bottom comes up and you reward the wrong thing!

Repeat the process until you are confident your puppy knows what the word means. Never attach any other words to the behaviour as this will cause confusion and make it more difficult for your puppy to focus. If your puppy is reluctant to sit you can guide them by placing the treat in your hand towards the end of their nose and guide the nose backwards and down into the sit, releasing the treat as you do so.

2. Down

To encourage your puppy into the down you should sit on the floor. Place the treat on the end of their nose and push gently towards them and down. As they follow the treat, take it between their front legs and guide it forwards so they creep down. Deliver the treat immediately, but again, don't attach the word until you are confident your puppy has worked out what they did to receive the reward.

Make sure you don't link the 'sit' and 'down' behaviour together here as this is an easy mistake to make. Your puppy will probably naturally sit first but don't reward that or ask for the sit, just encourage them to go straight into the down.

3. Stay

Your 'stay' command is different to 'wait'. Stay means your puppy should freeze in the position they are in and not move until you return to their side physically and deliver them the release command.

Stay is a command that develops over time as you ask for longer periods of calm. It is brilliant for creating control in busy environments as the dog will only ever receive the reward from you once the exercise is totally finished. This requires a huge amount of self-control and young puppies will only manage short periods to begin with. Don't ask for too much too soon.

**Here Hogan is practising his sit and stay in a pub on holiday.
There is always an opportunity to train your dog.**

I develop this by beginning with the 'sit/stay'. This involves placing your puppy into a sit on a lead, asking for the 'stay' with the flat palm of your hand raised, taking 2 steps away, re-enforcing the command returning and delivering the reward followed by a calm release such as the word 'ok'.

As your puppy begins to understand how to receive the reward you can put more distance between you and them and increase the time.

You can also practise the same command while your puppy is in the 'down' position. This training should be delivered with calm and quiet, it is not useful to get too over excited with your puppy's success as it will attach high energy to the command and that will raise the puppy's anticipation of the type of reward.

Finally, always release your dog and send or call them in the opposite direction to the way they were facing, this reduces their desire to come towards you while they are in the stay position.

4. Wait

Practising this command around feeding time is a really good way of developing your control positively.

You would use a similar format to the way you have taught stay, the difference is your puppy just needs to learn to wait for a release command, they don't need to wait until you return to them physically. You would place them in a calm state, this can be in 'sit', 'stay' or 'stand'.

Teaching self-control in every environment provides a good opportunity to develop your puppy's social ability.

Live Consult: Feeding Protocol

A screenshot from the PuppyCoach.com films showing Kerry and her puppy Willis working through a feeding regime.

Teaching this command around meal times provides an easy opportunity to teach the behaviour several times a day.

Use the flat palm of your hand to instruct the body language communication and step away, place the food bowl on the floor and reinforce the command with the hand signal. If your puppy moves, pick the bowl up and repeat. It is useful to have someone to help you if you struggle to manage the food and the puppy at the same time.

This is also a great way of involving children but a lead should be attached and the puppy controlled physically to avoid any problems arising.

5. Heel Work

Of all the obedience exercises, I feel that manners on the lead is the most difficult to manage, and focused heel work is almost impossible for many dog owners who just want to physically exercise their dog. I want to give you a different perspective on how to address this task. Firstly, we should separate 'loose lead' walking and 'heel work'. I feel the two are very different and to be successful you need to be able to do both.

Your knowledge on how the dog views the lead is important and will be your motivation to stay patient and consistent. The dog is designed to pull into a force, a human would apply rationale as to why they may feel tension or resistance and most of us would stop and try and work out what the problem was. Dogs are not able to do this. Their instinctive response is just to pull harder in an attempt to get away from whatever is creating the force!

When your puppy grows this problem will make the process of lead walking miserable at best, but at worst potentially dangerous and physically hard work.

I began this process by allowing Hogan to drag a soft, light puppy lead around my house with little interference. They should get used to the weight of something round their neck first without the force attached. Once he was accepting this I then did the same thing outside.

I then started to pick the lead up and encourage Hogan to follow me with a toy and verbal praise, once he reached my side I gave a treat reward and dropped the lead. All the time encouraging positively until he was happily bouncing along next to me on a loose lead waiting for his treat.

If he chose to go in another direction I just stood still, stopped the energy for a moment, waited and then as soon as he re-focused on me I repeated the encouragement.

Hogan showing off his heel work during socialisation training with my horse.

This is essential groundwork. I also believe that working on eye contact and a balanced relationship in general puts you in a better position to be successful here. This is not an exercise that is only achievable with training, a solid relationship is a huge factor.

To make Hogan engage and work with me with eye contact, loose lead and walking to heel waiting for instruction, I used treats, but any positive reward will achieve the same result.

I found that treats gave me the opportunity to 'fine tune' his body position from the minute he arrived at my home. I also began the process of conditioning in my garden away from distractions.

It was not realistic to expect Hogan to do his street walk or socialise with his head constantly looking up at me, I taught him just to walk on a loose lead but made it clear when he needed to work with me and when he could relax and just trot along taking in his surroundings. This control was achieved by stopping the walk every time he went out in front of me. He effectively self-corrected by walking into the lead and then stepping back. At this point I would advise that you make a few changes of direction and even walk a figure of eight to encourage your puppy to follow you.

In order for this to be successful it is important that you retain full control over the lead, never let your puppy drag you, swap sides, weave in front of you or greet other people or dogs before you! The lead is your only means of physical control and your puppy should learn to defer to you when attached to it. Also remember, once you attach the lead you have removed 3 of a dogs 4 means of coping if they feel threatened, so make sure you are guiding them.

Using the opportunity to socialise Hogan and build his confidence in new surroundings.

A concerned dog will choose to flight, freeze, avoid or fight. Your puppy's only viable defence is to fight once the lead is attached if an owner isn't controlling a situation, most dogs will do everything in their power to avoid confrontation especially when they are young so this is a really damaging position to put your puppy in. If your puppy is avoiding something, then move on and put some distance between you and whatever the problem was.

This is the reason why I see so many dogs who are aggressive on the lead. A simple fear behaviour is ignored when the puppy is young and this develops quickly through adolescence into full blown aggression if it is not recognised, and dealt with appropriately.

I spent every walk with Hogan in his early weeks totally focused on protecting him, I didn't allow anyone to stroke him until he was in the sit position and calm and even then I instructed them on how to approach to avoid him jumping up. I avoided most other dogs on leads and only allowed him to engage with them where the owner was happy to just walk with me for a little while so they could get to know each other while the walk progressed.

I chose where I was comfortable allowing him to socialise but this was never out in front of me with a lead attached. This only serves to make you irrelevant and the other dog becomes a rewarding factor encouraging your puppy that pulling on the lead reaches a desirable and fun outcome.

Creating a static environment for your puppy to meet another dog is potentially challenging for them and you will have no idea how another dog will react once you and another owner begin to engage in conversation. So avoid this at all costs.

While this may make you feel uncomfortable when engaging with the happy dog owners you meet, you can deliver this in a friendly way, after all it will be you who is battling poor behaviour from your puppy if they learn the wrong thing at this impressionable age.

You will have a small window of opportunity to embed your puppy's behaviour on the lead before they begin to grow in confidence and really challenge you to take the lead literally on your walks. Puppies dragging their owners along the street is an all too common sight. Put the work in when they are young and you will avoid the embarrassment of your dog taking you out for a walk for years to come!

Practising canine communication skills with Sheba.

Most importantly, never give up – use every walk as a training opportunity. Socialising your dog effectively requires good self-control and you will need to start this process by teaching your puppy to follow your lead. If they trust you then you really are half way there.

Always keep in mind that your dog learns everything by association so as soon as they see your walking boots heading for your feet they are already in the park running around like a lunatic. The anticipation will be too much to bear by the time you attach the lead and actively hit the street.

Take this into account and use every opportunity you have to calm your dog down, re-engage their brain and build a distance between each stage of the walk and the actual off lead time. You can use doorways, gates, openings to fields, hedges, fences or anything that allows you to create a boundary. When you reach the area for free time make sure you keep your puppy on their lead for a few 100 yards so as not to let loose a little mad ball of excitement. CALM, CALM, CALM is the key to effective lead training.

I can honestly say that while Hogan has excellent lead manners, to this day I still work on this on every walk. The walks are a pleasure because I have worked tirelessly on this aspect of his learning but it isn't easy.

Having a well behaved dog on the lead is an asset on every level.

Positive Association to a Mat

Training your puppy to respond to a command to go to a visual point of contact is a really useful means of teaching your puppy self-control. It is a command that I taught Hogan early on so that I could have an area associated with calm while I introduced new objects or social situations.

There are a couple of ways to teach this but I chose the most difficult. This involved lots of patience…

I used a square carpet tile as his point of contact and began by placing it on the floor within a room.

I stared down at the carpet tile while Hogan walked around the room. Initially I stayed in close contact with it until Hogan delivered me the behaviour I wanted.

This began with him just standing on the tile, where upon I delivered his trigger word 'good' and followed with a treat.

Mat control outdoors. First attempt at working trials – perfect.

The next time I waited a little longer until he sat on the mat, and I repeated the reward.

To make sure Hogan didn't just leave the mat as soon as I acknowledged him, I used the flat palm of my hand to indicate the wait, put a treat down a metre or so away from him and then gave the release command 'OK'. If he moved before I said OK, then he was not given the treat.

It now means I can place the mat anywhere, give the command 'mat' and he will go to it and lay down and not move until I tell him 'OK'.

This requires practise to lengthen the time and expect him to stay when I am out of sight but the early learning was embedded by the time he was 4 months old!

The dog will always learn better when they work a problem out for themselves rather than relying on you to physically direct them. As with all my instruction you should stay calm and patient, use your body language, eye contact and energy to help your dog out rather than vocal or direct physical control!

Task

I would like you to ensure you develop structure to your lead association and walking.

Build in 10 minutes at the beginning and end of your walk whereby you work to get your puppy focused on you. If treats don't work, then take a favourite toy or throw a ball to mark good behaviour.

Your walk should involve control, 'free time' should be something that occurs immediately after performing good behaviour.

CHAPTER 12

Teaching Self-Control and Establishing a Routine

In order to encourage self-control your puppy should have a lifestyle that is managed with structure and routine.

While you shouldn't be letting your puppy boss you around, it is advantageous to create a form of expectation through consistent daily routines. This helps your puppy understand what is expected of him or her, improves your ability to communicate and goes some way to helping you achieve a calm puppy.

We practise 'down stays' on most walks so Hogan learns
to be calm and balanced in all environments.

If you have created this situation you have every opportunity to build on your puppy's self-control, something that is often overlooked until problems arise.

I have seen so many over socialised and over stimulated puppies. There is a social awareness of the importance of puppy socialisation but unfortunately little clarity is given as to how to successfully achieve this process and ensure your puppy is balanced and well mannered.

Often the puppy learns early on that people and other dogs are great fun. By allowing them to bounce around and jump all over members of the public and visiting guests you are embedding behaviours that will take a lifetime to correct. Your guests will not be so willing to receive your puppy in the same way when they are a fully grown adult dog and this behaviour around children and the elderly is dangerous.

Establishing a Routine

Hogan's routine began as soon as he arrived with us, in fact my busy life of family and work commitments meant that I put together an itinerary so that I could factor in realistic and necessary puppy time.

**Involving our children with Hogan early in his life reduced the
excitement factor when he finally arrived.**

The routine was led by realistic expectations; you may have a plan in your head but actually your puppy has other ideas. Like peeing on your floor seconds after you have just let them out, a very common problem as your puppy finds its way around and gains the confidence to toilet outside.

I can remember trying to set my routine for my daughter when she was born, 2 hours into my first morning I was an hour and a half behind the regimental detail of my itinerary!

By the time I had my second child my expectations had significantly reduced, and although I was never a 'PJ's at 11am' type of mum I still found that my routine had to be a lot more flexible if I was to avoid feelings of failure! This thought is easily translated to how you manage your puppy.

The life changing experience of a puppy's arrival takes time to adjust to, so expect your planned routine to evolve and go with it, in the grand scheme of things it won't take long to get some sort of control back and the time flies, so just enjoy it! Begin by establishing a checklist of all the things you need to achieve to successfully lead your puppy through human life ensuring positive experiences and correct learning.

If there are a few people in your household, it is always worth having a rota set up so everyone gets to be involved in the puppy's development.

Your routine should look something like this in your first few weeks:

- **5-6 am** release from crate/area for toilet
  Some focused attention but remaining calm
- **6-8 am** Deliver food in controlled way
  Toilet break
  Replace in crate/area (your time to get ready)
  Free time respecting house boundaries
- **8-10 am** Social time/walk
  Down time away from owner
- **Noon** Deliver food as above
  Toilet break
- **12-2 pm** Controlled attention/training for 10-20 min
  Down time
  Social time/walk
- **2-4 pm** Down time
  Toilet break/training

- **4-6 pm** deliver food as above
  Toilet break
  Down time
- **6-7 pm** Toilet break/free time
  Social time/walk
- **7-9pm** Down time
- **9 pm** Bed in crate/area (ignore your puppy during this period)
- **11 pm** Last toilet break – no attention

Prepare to be kept very busy!

Now that Hogan is settled, the routine is less intense but he recognises the time that is for him and time away. All in all, this helps him cope with the high energy and chaotic activities that occur in our family home, particularly when the children are present!

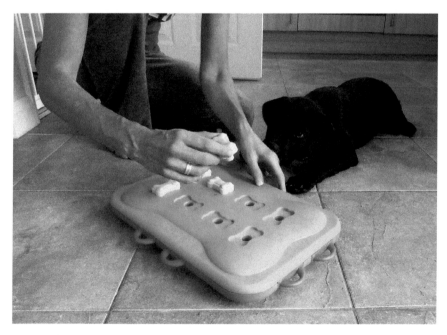

Some interactive play time focused on working Hogan's mind but
keeping him calm.

Building your Puppy's Confidence

How your puppy greets you sets the bench mark for how he or she will approach your family, friends and strangers and creates their expectation of what response behaviour they may get in return. If the response they receive is inconsistent, which is highly likely, this will chip away at your puppy's understanding of human life and ultimately their confidence.

Whenever you play with your puppy or allow someone else to interact with them, you must always consider whether their behaviour and energy level would be safe and acceptable around an elderly person or child.

Your puppy needs to be managed correctly and have an awareness of human personal space boundaries. Simple errors and a lack of control could find you and your puppy in really negative scenarios. It is advisable to make sure you teach and guide your puppy into performing the correct behaviour around other dogs and humans at all times and from their very first interaction.

I regularly witness owners allowing their new puppy to take the lead in social situations while people deliver attention. When the puppy is a cute ball of fluff this interaction is encouraged, and any behaviour good or bad that the puppy does receives a reward in the form of a response from the interacting individual.

The next time you see your puppy jump up onto your legs and scratch for attention or nip the hand of your children while they are playing, ask yourself if this is the behaviour you would still want to encourage when your puppy is a fully grown adult dog.

The chances are this will be a 'definitely not' response! So don't make this mistake.

Walk away from your puppy when and if you see this behaviour, if the behaviour persists then remove the puppy calmly from the room, wait until the puppy calms and then invite them back into your space but this time make sure you encourage calm.

Giving the puppy something to do while they are in your social space is advantageous, I used Hogan's bed area as a base and gave him a Kong toy lined with a small amount of soft cheese and then frozen. This kept him busy while I got a few jobs done. It also had the added advantage of associating the children's high energy play with something positive and reinforced that he didn't need to be involved in what they were doing!

Putting Self-Control Exercises into Practise

Whenever I socialise a puppy with a new situation inside or outside the home, my goal is to focus on providing them with as many opportunities as possible to correctly read and learn from their visual observation. They are only able to do this if they are in a calm and stable frame of mind.

This means I spend time on every walk, making them practise on and off lead heel work and particularly down stays at a distance. They are also encouraged to look to me for high level rewards throughout, for this reason I am always worth coming back to!

Never back off on your training, free time is obviously highly rewarding but your walks should always have an element of 'training'.

You should be beginning to build a picture around your puppy's development, it is complex and there are many areas to address to ensure you get the process right. It is imperative that you acquire and develop knowledge on all aspects of the dog, from their behaviour, how they learn, their ability to cope and the importance of their relationship with you as an owner.

Obedience and physical training are areas of our relationship that have previously been the focus for a well behaved dog. The close physical relationship we now share with our dogs in current society means we have to address their learning in all social environments.

Task

Set yourself up to address lots of different social environments with your dog and practise your down stay in each area.

I took Hogan to the local supermarket and put him in a down stay while people walked past. I occasionally let the odd person drop him a treat but I didn't allow any physical contact. You should do the same.

Repeat this at the park and other social situations you may visit. Tell members of the public that your puppy is in training!

CHAPTER 13

Human-Led Play

Puppies are not born with the ability understand how a human plays. If given no direction they will either play as they would with another puppy or become over excited or anxious if the human doesn't conform to their expectation. Either way, a puppy's idea of play is very different to yours and it could end with injury and the embedding of poor behaviours if not dealt with correctly.

The correct application of play provides many avenues of positive learning for your puppy.

We can identify them one by one:

I. Bonding with an Owner

We should focus on building a 'play' and fun relationship with our puppy based around an object so the stimulation is gained from interacting around something rather than risking mouth and human skin contact. A puppy will naturally bite hands and clothing, or anything that's waved around in front of them.

Keeping them focused on something also allows you to signal when you want play to start and finish. This shows the puppy that you are in charge and so prevents demanding or over excitable behaviour in the future.

I have also set families up with a means of building a way to integrate children with the new puppy using play.

Taking the child to the local pet shop to choose 'their' toy is a great way of giving them a connection to the puppy. You can also teach them to only engage in play when they have their toy. This means a parent can be alerted to puppy-child contact time as the child runs round looking for their toy. It also signifies consistent approach of play to the dog and reinforces the importance of the child within the family hierarchy.

Hogan showing self-control around play interaction with me.

I see far too many dogs bringing me their entire toy box when I arrive to conduct an assessment in order to get some sort of recognition from me. They are not impressed when I ignore all their attempts!

This in itself isn't a problem as such but it certainly can become one if the dog starts to view the toys as significant possessions. A toy box should belong to an owner and contain a variety of balls, toys and training tools such as a whistle, recall line, plus grooming equipment. Keep it out of the way and it will become a focus for fun and learning when you use it to engage with your puppy.

A simple bubble blower create's a lovely
interaction with Hogan and the children.

2. Providing a means of Mental and Physical Stimulation

Hurling any toy at lightning speed across an open space will always instigate a high level reaction in all puppies – even the most docile. Doing this consistently can be damaging both mentally and physically for your puppy and even adult dog.

I will explain why…

From a physical perspective this exercise creates the potential for injury to any dog, in particular when they are still young and developing. The speed and force created during this blast of energy then has to come to a stop. The force of a sudden stop results in a transfer of force and energy through your puppy's delicate and growing skeletal system and should be avoided. Some dogs perfect the grinding halt while others partake in the odd somersault. Your uncoordinated puppy is likely to end up in one big heap left wondering what just happened!

From a behaviour perspective, the reason they may appear a little bewildered is because you have just opened up their chase or prey drive response, otherwise known as the hunting instinct. While this is inherent in dogs, it will be a behaviour that is much nearer the surface for some breeds and personalities. Any fast moving object triggers a compulsion to chase which will overtake any other behaviour that you may prefer them to have.

Hogan entertaining himself with a ball full of treats.

I personally always advise this high response reaction is avoided unless you are incorporating training. It generally only spills over into all other areas of the dog's life and before you know it your cute puppy is now causing carnage at the heels of joggers, cyclists, children playing football and not to mention chasing anything that's small and fluffy.

Teaching self-control in highly stimulating environments by building on your sit and wait commands is essential learning during your puppy's early socialisation.

You may feel this advice is a little bit on the overkill side as I am aware many puppies will happily chase a ball or toy with no adverse effects. If this is your puppy, then that's fine, but if your puppy appears to be taking on the 'over-charged' behaviour of most then add some clear control to how you associate them to toys.

I do throw balls and toys for Hogan but as with everything this is focused on teaching him how to behave while having fun at the same time. The excitement comes from me when he returns with the toy in his mouth. Retrieval behaviour is instinctive in Hogan but for those puppies who choose to run with an object, you can attach a longline (extra-long material lead) to intercept this and build a new positive behaviour focused around you.

Engaging in ball play with Harley. It is possible to work with most breeds with toys even if they aren't natural born retrievers.

Your puppy should be developing a positive relationship with you which means there will be no greater pleasure for them than pleasing you. Utilise this thought and make the toy interesting to you and even more interesting for the dog if they return to you with it.

Ensuring toys maintain your dog's interest is easy – if you love it then so will your dog. That's one of the reasons why they will always seek out your most favourite shoes to have a nibble on. Set the play situation up by bringing the toy into the social space, let your dog 'win it' a few times, reward for their recall by offering treats and then throwing the toy away for them to chase. Using the 'chase' behaviour in a controlled way is a great way of achieving positive reinforcement of good behaviours.

Having this avenue of bonding in your relationship is invaluable and provides you with an excellent platform for shaping their behaviour and teaching them new vocal commands, and all while they just think they are having a great time.

3. Providing an Opportunity to Learn Self-Control
I always use toy motivation to help teach puppies self-control. This is something I am really keen for puppies to learn early on. Human beings tend to be very over excitable with high energy around a puppy and this energy transfers into negativity really quickly if you do not teach your puppy how to deal with it.

Controlling the energy around play helps a puppy learn self-control.

I use a toy to instigate contact time, I will also expose a puppy to excitement from me, this is important as they will meet excitement from humans for various reasons in their lives. You need to teach them how to deal with it.

As soon as I feel the puppy is reaching a high level of excitement themselves, in which you may see more mouthing, jumping or even growling – the play is stopped immediately.

This is achieved by the removal of the toy, a change in my body position to the normal standing position followed by calm, quiet and aloof energy until the puppy mimics the same behaviour or loses interest.

This is a behaviour that a more mature dog may use when interacting with a youngster to teach them when enough is enough without having to instigate a challenge by showing aggression. You may have seen this take place in the park as a confident dog will stop movement, stand very still and give very passive but assertive body language as a strong indicator that things are going too far.

I have found this provides a good opportunity to teach your puppy about human play, when and how it is initiated and stopped. It also teaches the puppy how to get their high energy under control.

4. *Providing an Avenue for the Puppy to Express its Innate Behaviour*

In Hogan's case his innate or instinctive behaviour is to retrieve. A dog is never happier than when it is performing what comes naturally to them. Having the ability to perfect this and shape the natural behaviour into one that works around your household really builds your communication platform with your puppy.

I tapped into this by teaching Hogan that everything he picked up he should bring to me as I would reward him highly for doing so. This meant whenever he took some of my children's toys, stole a sock or anything else he would come charging to me to see what exciting thing he could trade it for. Perfect for avoiding a distraught child and a trip to the vets!

There is a big difference in the trading of an object in this way and waving food in front of a puppy's nose to get them to drop something. Especially if you have spent the last half an hour chasing them around the garden. All you are doing is teaching the puppy that whatever they have must be very highly prized and they should hang on to it.

In the very worst case you may also be teaching your dog to swallow the object so that you can't grab it from them. I have treated several 'stone swallowers' who have all undergone surgery before I met them for exactly this reason.

The first thing I do is teach an owner to ignore it and NEVER CHASE. Don't fall into this trap, remember if you want it they will want it more. So take no notice and just call them over to you, pop on their lead, stick some tasty food in your hand and wonder off up the street. You will soon find they have forgotten what's in their mouth, have dropped it and are looking at you longingly for whatever interesting thing it is that you have.

When considering your puppy make sure you understand what their instinctive drive is – what have they been bred to do. It may be that you never want to open this up as it could cause more problems than if you avoided it.

To give you some examples, Collies will want to naturally herd, Shepherds will naturally guard, Husky and sled dogs will naturally pull, and Terriers will want to flush out every rabbit hole while fluffing out their chests and displaying the best territorial behaviour they can!

I also advise that anyone owning any type of Bull breed should avoid playing high level tug games with them as this may open up their reactive side. These dogs make fantastic family pets and I have had the pleasure of working with some amazing Bull breed owners, but I also regularly see them being exercised (so called!) hanging from tree branches by their mouths or being swung round off the floor to make them physically strong. This is not acceptable (not something I have ever seen from one of my clients), nor is it advisable if you expect that dog to integrate successfully with human beings. Quite frankly this is a classic example of human abuse of man's best friend!

Research your breed, its origin and what line of work it was bred to do. You can then decide whether you may be able to utilise natural instinct to facilitate learning. If you can't then it's still possible to teach them something totally new.

Hogan's natural behaviour is to retrieve, harnessing this helps him grow in confidence.

**Proof that the world's best guard dog breed can be soft at heart.
They just need some patience and understanding.**

I first met the 14 week old Rottweiler above when he was 10 weeks old. He was already causing some concern with his behaviour, growling and early signs of aggression were reported. After just a few sessions we channelled this challenging behaviour into something positive.

With the help of this awesome little retrieval toy we focused his busy little brain on a positive interaction with lots of self-control. Keeping this process calm and positive avoided any flash points and created an excellent means of communication with his human owners.

5. *Facilitating a Platform for Interacting Two Dogs Together in the Same Household*

I found toys to be a great way of bonding for both Hogan and Marley when Hogan was very young. It can become a flash point so you should always observe interaction with possessions, toys or otherwise. For my two it was the turning point in their relationship. Marley really began to view Hogan as a play mate rather than something to avoid or remove!

They still have great fun pulling at each end of a soft toy even now.

That said I have my limitations for play around my home. This is only ever allowed in the garden and has to be focused on the toy. I monitor it and never allow it to escalate to an unbalanced level.

Many clients ask me if they should interfere in their dog's relationship in multi dog households. From a leadership perspective you have to be in charge and to easily create this platform you must treat the dogs equally.

They will sort out their own hierarchy, it will evolve naturally. More problems are created when an owner tries to decide who may be the lead dog, so leave well alone.

Marley and Hogan in their favourite pose!

Regarding play, I suggest you view the behaviour objectively. If your dogs are behaving in a way that would be unacceptable if they were interacting with a small dog or child, then stop it! Allowing it to become their most prevalent form of interaction will only result in difficulties when they meet other dogs.

You should also spend time interacting with them both. To achieve this, I make Marley wait while I throw a ball or toy for Hogan and then switch them over. This requires massive self-control so keep your expectations low. Once you crack it – it's hugely rewarding.

6. *Building Solid Foundations for Owner Control Through Positivity*

Finally, building your relationship through play provides a fantastic avenue to develop all sorts of social learning. I have taught Hogan patience, self-control, recall, heel work and most importantly, when and how to have fun with a human.

It is a really important part of your puppy's social learning. I have rehabilitated several rescue dogs who have never had this early learning and as a result many new owners struggle to engage with the dog because of it.

Put time aside for this as part of your training. Keep control of the toys – the toy box should be out of sight. You should always take away those toys that you are using as high prize indicators and only leave down the ones you aren't interested in.

Motivation for Play

The focus of play should not just be on physically wearing your puppy out. This may be detrimental to their joints and bones, plus you may create high energy and excitement that quickly becomes unbalanced, leading to poor behaviours such as mouthing and jumping up which you should be discouraging as early as possible.

Play should involve short periods of focus on an object or on you, particularly if you are teaching a new command.

In order to control this, I ensure there are regular periods where the movement is stopped or the toy is removed and Hogan needs to focus to give me another behaviour (such as Sit or Stop) in order to resume play. This has the added positive effect of teaching Hogan self-control.

Also, finding a variety of objects to entertain your puppy on a controlled level will expand his or her concentration and keep training varied and fun for all.

Using Play in Training

Play is most successfully developed when it is focused around teaching manners and positively associating behaviours with individual words. Such as 'sit', 'heel', 'come'.

Some puppies would rather engage with an owner through play than receive a food reward, but also food can sometimes send puppies into a frenzy making them difficult to work with – so work with what best suits your puppy.

This is Hogan's brother 'Harley' demonstrating perfectly how important human praise is to him during recall training.

As an example, in order to reinforce Hogan's heel work I was consistently using food. However, the desire for a food reward in a Labrador is great so I found myself with a puppy displaying lots of high energy, jumping up and whining.

To combat this, I introduced a toy, popped it under my arm and progressed with the walk. Each time Hogan checked into to my heel I dropped the toy for him to receive. This had the added advantage that he didn't know when I would drop it and so consistently delivered the positive behaviour in anticipation of his reward. It was also received with a lower energy enabling him to focus on the direction I was delivering.

I performed the same training technique with little Harley, but before we started I spent 10 minutes making the ball the most important object in his life.

Teaching Harley the fun that can be had with a ball game and using this to positively associate good behaviour.

Types of Toys

There are thousands of different puppy and adult dog toys on the market and this can be overwhelming. They generally fall into brackets of use such as:

- Distraction
- Comfort
- Interactive

Ideally you should provide your puppy with one from each range, keep them back and rotate them. My dogs have a few toys to pick up, chew or throw around and then I separate ones that are considered 'high prize' and used for training and relationship purposes.

My advice is always to consider the breed of dog you have and their size and energy level. Choose toys that meet safety standards and are highly recommended and don't assume that any toy is indestructible. Trust me, some dogs will destroy any toy you give them regardless of durability.

Play should always be delivered on your terms and the end of play should be clearly stated by the removal yourself and or the toy. This really is essential if your puppy is to learn when it is acceptable to engage with you and when it isn't!

Task

Assess the situation you currently have with your puppy toys, ensure you have chosen correctly and monitor which ones evoke a response from your puppy and whether this is in line with their breed predisposition.

CHAPTER 14

Puppy Play – The Good, the Bad and the Ugly

One of the things you will observe when your puppy plays is the constant flood of body language communication they are using. It is important that you have some understanding of this so you are able to decipher good play, unbalanced play and when to pull your puppy out because they are not coping.

What is Normal Behaviour for Puppy Play (Play Indicators)

You may witness many behaviours in play that mimic those observed during a fight such as:

- Mouthing
- Biting legs and paws
- Scruffing and pinning to the floor
- Chasing and tackling
- Growling, barking, whining
- Baring of teeth
- Placing their chin over shoulders of the other puppy
- Rolling on their backs

Before you panic that you have invited a mini-monster into your home, I can assure you that these behaviours are very normal in the young puppy. The level to which these behaviours develop is likely to be related to the level of energy involved in the game and you will notice that the higher this gets, the more intense the responses become.

Play between siblings is generally much more volatile than with other dogs, so teaching self-control and monitoring play is important for their learning.

Biting or mouthing will be particularly prevalent. I can remember watching Hogan with his first small raw bone. While I sat there wondering what on earth he was going to do with it, I was impressed see how he was totally fixated on the objective of demolishing it as fast as he could!

Bite Inhibition

While these bones made my life so much easier as they would keep him busy for hours, it did highlight for me the strength of his jaw and how he had to learn to measure the impact of his bite when playing with other dogs in order not to do damage.

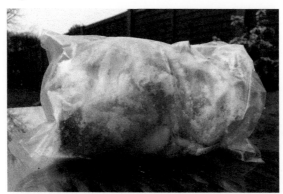

Hogan has now progressed on to the larger bones as the small ones are no longer appropriate for his size. You need to be aware of this to avoid a choking incident.

From a survival perspective it makes sense that the puppy is able to deal with chewing and digesting live prey, although they have evolved in many ways this primitive behaviour is still retained and chewing should be a natural part of a puppy's daily routine.

You may have played with your puppy and noticed the force they use when mouthing your hand is hugely reduced to that displayed during the chewing process. This is important learning and is referred to as 'bite inhibition'.

When to Intervene

To understand whether interaction is play or fighting you will see two fundamental differences.

In play there will be lots of give and take from both parties. Puppies will also inhibit the force of their bite to avoid injury, something that definitely doesn't happen in a fight. You will also be able to intervene in play to stop it, if you intervene in a dog fight there is a huge possibility the dog may redirect on to you.

Use your knowledge and common sense in all scenarios. If you are not comfortable then stop the play, take hold of the more forceful puppy and see if the other one tries to continue play. If they don't, then leave them alone and continue on your walk, if they do, then separate them and calm the situation down by taking back control before allowing play to resume.

Why is it Important?

Puppy play is an important developmental stage for your puppy, it will be where they begin to develop their communication skills, learn right from wrong, burn off excess energy and establish themselves within a social environment.

Many primitive behaviours can be witnessed and if you observe puppy play, you will also view signs of immaturity and clumsiness as well.

Between 2-4 weeks of age a puppy will begin to develop their play skills in the litter with their mother and litter mates. This is when the early learning around bite inhibition begins. Puppies naturally use their mouths to communicate a variety of messages, they will learn to measure the intensity of their bite in order to ensure a balanced relationship with the individual they are playing with during these precious learning stages.

This is Hogan playing with this sister Flossie. The play was extremely high energy and not something I wanted to reinforce. It was observed for just a few minutes before they were split up and managed calmly for the rest of the afternoon. Flossie's owner was horrified that her little female pup was involved in such high energy interaction!

Bite Inhibition Explained

A puppy who bites too hard will receive a squeal from the receiving puppy and play will cease, they quickly learn that the fun of playing will end if they do not take more care. For this reason, it is important that a puppy is not removed from its litter mates or mother until at least 7 weeks. It is difficult to replicate this early learning otherwise.

Once your puppy is with you the temptation to engage in excitable play is high, especially if you have children present. This is where accidents happen, you should understand how a puppy would play with a litter mate is not the way you would like them to interact with your children or visitors.

To begin to teach your puppy that mouth communication is reserved for other canine's only, I advise that you do not allow any mouth to skin contact at all. This is particularly important in the early weeks. It should be enough to just remove yourself or your puppy from the play moment immediately, should this occur.

I never advise you adopt the squeal of another puppy to signal harm, I find

Clear handler guidance was required to keep the dogs calm and balanced.

in most cases by the time this occurs, the puppy has reached a heightened state and your vocal response only serves to reinforce the behaviour.

If you find your puppy is engaging in play that you are concerned about, you should consider the energy level being used.

Mild to moderate play even if it looks challenging is usually fine, however the same behaviour patterns can be dangerous when delivered at a high energy level. I find most of my clients are able to tell the difference pretty quickly.

I also advise that you try and allow your puppy to interact with another puppy of a similar size and age. This will be different to when they interact with an adult dog. The temperament of the puppy is relevant, rather than the breeding so use your judgement to manage the situation.

Puppies really are learning at such a fast rate and it doesn't take much to embed the wrong behaviours. A boisterous 14 week old Mastiff could terrify a Yorkshire Terrier of the same age, even if there is only minimal interaction. Always be realistic about what your puppy will cope with. Instead of having to pick your puppy up out of a situation and create a problem, don't put them in it in the first place.

Finding safe places to effectively socialise your puppy with others can be tricky. This is precious time for the puppy's early learning about other dogs and so you need to get this right.

A well run veterinary puppy social class or introductory puppy obedience classes can be great. Just do your research and ask to go along and have a look at the class before you take your puppy. You can find more advice on this in Chapter 5.

Also trust your instincts. If you are not comfortable with the way your puppy is interacting with another then you are probably right, there is no harm in stepping in to calm things down whether you were right to be concerned or not!

Task

To underpin your learning for this section, observe your puppy in lots of different situations, their behaviour around humans, adult dogs, dogs they know and dogs they don't.

This will help you gauge how this differs when they interact with a puppy more on their level. It will also help you see how your puppy's character may develop, how confident they are and how tolerant.

CHAPTER 15

Lead Association and What to do if your Puppy Won't Walk on the Lead

It comes as a surprise to many puppy owners if their playful puppy shuts down and refuses to walk when they attempt to leave the house. I have had several situations where owners have had to resort to picking their puppy up in order to get them to and from the car.

Flossie and her owner were facing a daily battle of wills on their walks. Flossie regularly sat down when she felt overwhelmed. This is frustrating for her owner and could have affected the balance of their long term relationship if not addressed.

This is actually a common problem and is led by several factors:

- Owner – puppy relationship problem
- Poor collar and lead association
- Rushing the process of lead association
- Too much constant pressure on the lead
- Fear
- Sensory overload

Fundamentally, if you have conditioned your puppy to the collar and lead well at home and established a solid leadership relationship with your puppy whereby they are used to following you around, then this problem should be straightforward to solve.

This shows what NOT to do when your puppy sits down. Stopping and interacting in this way reinforces the concern and embeds the behaviour. You should stay upright facing the direction you are going, offering encouragement as a leader.

Follow these steps to introduce your primary physical control: lead and collar

- Use a soft puppy or flat collar
- Apply the collar and distract the puppy, ideally during a play or feeding

session, ignore and distract your puppy if they pay too much attention to the collar

- The collar should be tight enough so that it doesn't pull over your puppy's head but you should be able to get two fingers comfortably between the puppy's neck and collar
- Don't attach a lead straight away, wait until your puppy is comfortable with the collar
- Attach the lead at home and do NOT put any pressure on it at all, just let the puppy get used to dragging the lead around
- Distract as before if the puppy shows any interest in the lead
- You must see the lead as yours, do not allow your puppy to play with it or chew it, use distraction to achieve this
- Get your puppy used to following you around and make yourself interesting. Your puppy should naturally be observing you so this should be straightforward.
- If they are ignoring you, add energy to the training and incite a chase by running in another direction and calling them
- Once your puppy is happy with the lead at home, you can then begin to pick the lead up and encourage your puppy to follow you using praise, treats or a favourite toy

If you have completed the above and tried to encourage with food but your puppy still refuses to walk, you should ensure you remain facing forwards in the direction you are going. Never look back or apply human sympathy to the situation. Your puppy is relying on you to convey a message of confidence so you have to show them there is nothing to worry about!

Ensure the whole experience is positive so as not to scare your puppy as you follow these steps to encourage your puppy to walk forward and trust you:

- Walk in a confident upbeat manner
- Always look forwards in the direction you are going
- Never get distracted, especially by mobile phones
- Gently handle your lead, you should have a relaxed loose lead with no tension
- When your puppy stops, take one step forwards and gently move your

arm in the direction you are going (it should be very relaxed, gentle, enough to move the collar only), offer a treat for encouragement

- Stay facing forwards while you move the lead in the direction you are going
- As your puppy tilts forwards, immediately relax, encourage and repeat, offer a reward when the puppy begins to trot next to you
- Try to avoid engaging too much with your puppy while they are learning this, the reward can be a treat or a simple 'good'

IMPORTANT: Before using this method you need to be confident you have put your ground work in. This should not be physically distressing for your puppy, just a polite reminder to keep moving forwards. The reward for them moving is an immediate removal of any pressure felt and subsequent positive praise, food or toy! If you have associated the lead correctly, you should find that there is very little pressure on the lead at all.

Rules for Heel Work and Loose Lead Walking

Lead training mistakes are usually made very early on in the puppy's life. I have met lots of owners who are inclined to allow the walk to be all about their cute puppy and as a result the puppy is allowed to do what it wants and go where it wants. This sets an owner up to fail at the task of having any control over the lead and the puppy very quickly becomes the leader in the relationship.

The bulk of your lead and collar association should be done in one room of your home with minimal distractions. Don't expect your puppy to cope with the lead, collar and their first experience outside all in one go.

You must recognise the importance of taking control of the lead and ensuring your puppy sees this time as 'work'.

- Keep your puppy in place on only one side of you
- Make sure you stop each time your puppy walks out in front of you
- Change direction and keep your puppy focused on you

These are the basics for managing a puppy on a lead. Follow these tips from the very first walk and you will already be sending your puppy a strong message of guidance.

Derrie (Hogan's breeder) working on Hogan's heel work off lead.

The DO's

- Start your walk with calm control around a boundary line
- Leave the house with a calm puppy
- Walk proactively, with your head up and shoulders forward
- Make your puppy work with you and stop at all roads, practising the 'sit'
- Take a positive approach and make the walk enjoyable but on your terms
- Use the opportunity to bond with your puppy, keeping them focused during distractions
- Use a long line to allow freedom rather than letting your short lead go slack

The DONT's

- Allow your puppy to weave in front of you
- Let your puppy stop and sniff every blade of grass
- Encourage pulling
- Keep tension on the lead
- Stop and chat to every passer by
- Allow passers by to reward your puppy
- Move at a slow pace if it can be avoided

Practising lead control with Harley (Hogan's brother) using the long line to facilitate free running providing a contrast to the short lead training.

Types of Lead/Collar

There are a variety of collars and leads on the market, most of which would be unsuitable for a young puppy. If you have conditioned your puppy to a basic flat collar and lead appropriately there should be no need for any other training equipment in your puppy's early few months.

However, should you run into problems with pulling on the lead or poor lead behaviour as your puppy approaches adolescence, I suggest you enlist the help of an appropriately qualified trainer/behaviourist to guide you.

I have treated many dogs who have been exposed to some of the harshest methods of physical control by the time I am called in to make an assessment. A problem that focused around simple lead manners very quickly escalates if negativity, pain or anxiety is attached to a particular response.

Every dog is different and should be professionally assessed prior to advice being given. Don't make the mistake of reaching for the first recommended product you see on the internet. Some are highly effective, but some can cause serious mental and sometimes physical damage. All will need expert direction in how to use them in the most efficient way. Even a simple flat collar will harm your puppy if you are too harsh on the end of the lead.

Most importantly there is no quick fix so addressing lead and collar association and manners when your puppy is young is invaluable.

Best practise is always ideal, but I am realistic and aware of the level of commitment lead work requires. This isn't always easy for people to focus on but really is an area that quickly becomes problematic if not approached in the correct way.

Remember everything your puppy learns in the early weeks will be embedded for the rest of their life. Taking 10 minutes to pay attention to how your puppy reacts when they see the lead in the house and how they enter and leave your home can make a huge difference between educating a calm well-mannered puppy, or unleashing the Tasmanian Devil on an unsuspecting public!

Task

Your task for this section is to focus on maintaining calm in your puppy before attaching the lead. Perfecting your sit and stay really helps with this but remember not to fall into the trap of repeating commands or shouting. The calmer and quieter you are, the better your puppy will respond.

Practise leaving the house, taking a minute or so to stand calmly at your front door with the door open before inviting your puppy outside.

Pay attention to how your puppy walks and make sure they are more focused on you and the progression of the walk, rather than stopping to sniff every lamppost.

CHAPTER 16

Keeping your Puppy Focused on You and Avoiding Problem Behaviours

One of the most challenging tasks you will have as a new puppy owner is to keep your puppy focused on you in all environments. While this may be fine in the comfort of your home when you're armed with a treat and minimal distractions, it is significantly more difficult when the distraction level increases and you introduce traffic, livestock, wildlife and the general public with their dogs.

Direct eye contact is often seen as a confrontational communication by a puppy to begin with, introducing it should be done carefully and slowly. One of the worst mistakes owners make is to carry their new puppy to the front door to meet guests. Placing your puppy at face height to an arriving stranger is a recipe for disaster and something I strongly advise against. This will almost certainly frighten your puppy and make them avoid eye contact for the foreseeable future.

To avoid this becoming a problem, place your puppy in their 'down time' area while your guest greets you and enters your home. This then gives you a great platform to make the first meeting at their level and associate the guest arrival with a positive reward. It will also allow the energy and excitement around the front door to become a distant memory and not a potential flashpoint for the future.

Teaching 'Look'

If you have attended dog training classes before you may have noticed, one of the first commands taught will be the 'look' or 'watch me'.

The reason for this is that your puppy needs to know how to engage with you if they are to learn, they also need to be encouraged to read your facial expressions and they should learn not to find this threatening or confrontational.

It will become the basis for helping your puppy cope in challenging environments giving them direction in social environments and generally providing you with an effective means of communicating.

To establish this positively you will need to begin the process in the home with minimal distractions before you expose yourself and your puppy to external situations.

Eye contact can be established within your normal day to day activities as well, your preparation should begin immediately. It will initially focus on you developing a positive, leadership relationship with your puppy. You will be the one to decide on the direction of the walks, you provide the daily food on your terms, you manage social time calmly and quietly. This is the basis for whether your puppy chooses to listen to you or not. Having these elements in place encourages your puppy to follow a routine and this includes the person setting it!

You can then build on this by teaching the simple command 'look'. Once you start teaching this command you are dealing with the 'learnt' centre of the brain. This part of the brain stores information picked up during social learning and is therefore not instinctive. It will also be easily overridden by emotion and so avoiding excitement or high energy is essential for positive learning.

Hogan demonstrating perfect eye contact. Practising this at home first will enable you to be more effective when faced with distractions.

In order for you to embed a vocal command and link it to a particular behaviour you need to put time aside to teach your puppy systematically. Developing and shaping their natural behaviour into something you require and repeating it until it becomes learnt.

If your puppy is happy to connect with you through eye contact it will add depth and understanding to your relationship. To teach the 'look' you should follow these simple instructions:

- Sit on a sofa or chair and call over your puppy
- Arm yourself with some tasty treats or a toy
- Be calm and patient and wait
- As soon as your puppy makes eye contact with you, reward immediately
- Use 'GOOD' and release the treat

Once you have repeated this exercise a handful of times your puppy will be making eye contact with you almost immediately. You will need to repeatedly reinforce this process until the vocal sound 'look' is automatically linked to the behaviour when you say it. Ultimately you are looking for a habit to form each time you say the word.

I will often use 'look' to get Hogan's attention when we are out and he naturally offers eye contact to check in with me. It provides a valuable window of opportunity to intercept danger, allow time for me to assess the presence of risk, or control him before he reaches another dog.

Attaching Energy to your Control

In order to maintain this contact and keep your puppy entertained, it is important to change the tone of your voice and have a toy to hand. Throwing a toy behind you for your puppy to chase while you continue to walk forwards is a great way of adding energy to your communication, making you interesting and fun.

Never chase your puppy to get the toy back, instead run in the opposite direction calling their name so that you maintain the fun and exciting element of your interaction.

If you need to attach a lead, then you should also make your puppy work for you first. Remember your puppy will enjoy the mental stimulation that work provides and this shouldn't be seen as a chore, so walking them to heel, asking for a sit-wait or down stay should all be seen as interesting and stimulating activities. Your puppy doesn't need to be running around in a highly charged state in order to exercise, often this will result in them becoming even more excitable.

Providing Guidance and Leadership

To maintain a good relationship with your puppy and ultimately adult dog, it is essential that you focus on the key areas that allow you to create authority and provide guidance. Having authority should be seen as a positive element of your relationship, not a negative. Dogs need guidance and consequences. Not everything can be fixed by waving food but likewise it is not necessary to lose your temper, or be physically or verbally harsh with your puppy.

There are many situations I have encountered where owners are frustrated and have physically reprimanded their puppy because they don't know what else to do. I always advise that you should avoid responding negatively "in the moment". Instead, learn to recognise your puppy's motivator and set them up to succeed.

To achieve this, you should be sure you have addressed all of the puppy's basic daily needs as follows:

- Is your puppy in good health?
- Do they have structure and boundaries?
- Have you provided a clear 'down time' area that the puppy is happy with?
- Have you addressed boredom issues?
- Is your puppy teething?
- Have you provided adequate mental and physical stimulation?
- Have you reduced your puppy's access to high level environmental stimulation?
- Consider whether your puppy is having a negative response to food?

Make sure you keep your puppy calm before entering social situations. Never allow another person to excite your puppy and if play has occurred then take the time to calm your puppy down again.

Perfecting the 'down', and 'sit', 'stay' in social environments has been much of the focus for Hogan's training. I had no need to add energy, he came with that in abundance but my responsibility was to teach him self-control so this really was a huge focus.

Finally, you should always recognise the importance of solid leadership in every area of your relationship. Focusing your control around primitive motivators is a great way of establishing this easily:

- **Control over delivery of possessions** – make possessions fun but add a working association
- **Awareness of personal space boundaries** – teach your puppy not to invade personal space
- **Control around guest arrival and general greetings** – never allow greetings freely
- **Management of space within the home** – restrict your puppy's access to key areas (hallway/living and bedrooms)
- **Manners around food** – make your puppy work for their food
- **Basic obedience** – spend time teaching the human spoken word
- **Control on the lead** – never allow your puppy to direct you on the walk

Protecting your Puppy from Risk

I have treated many aggressive dogs who are totally ball focused. A ball can appear to be a positive distraction for an owner but in actual fact it may empower the dog and trigger possessive behaviour or make them overly excited.

If you are able to develop a balance in your relationship, then you will find that you naturally provide an element of security to help your puppy cope in situations they may find challenging.

It also allows you to manage your puppy safely while you assess potential risks from other approaching dogs or dangers within the environment.

Whilst your role as a dog owner is comprehensive and full of responsibility you should keep a realistic perspective. It is not possible to read every situation your puppy faces and often they will be fully equipped to deal with dog interaction better than you, so try and relax.

My advice would be to be choosy over where you walk. Make your walks productive and don't linger or just walk the same field every day. Assess your areas and what sort of dogs and owners frequent these areas. Do they have generally good control and respect for other dog walkers or not?

Hogan and I paid a visit to Hogan's mum. It was lovely to see that I still had good control despite having some competition!

Remember it is always 'deed' not 'breed' so try not to stereotype the dogs you meet. I focus on an approaching dog's energy, where the owner is and whether they appear to have control.

Avoid large groups of owners meandering along chatting while their dogs run amok and make sure you are respectful of others. It is etiquette to put your dog on their lead if you see another dog walking towards you on a lead. This will take the pressure off the other owner and ensure your puppy doesn't get themselves into trouble by trotting over to say hello!

You will also be sending a clear message of control to your puppy, teaching them that not every approaching dog wants to interact with them. If you keep them focused on you and deliver your treat as you pass you will also create a positive training opportunity.

Building Trust

Trust between you and your puppy is invaluable. If you build it correctly your puppy will grow in confidence, look to you for guidance and pay attention to your control signals. It also provides the basis for you to be able to effectively socialise them with a variety of different animals, situations, children, vehicles e.t.c. If you are calm and confident then your puppy will take that as their cue to ignore the situation or lean on you.

To build your trust you need to be clear with your puppy from the start in directing them and giving them rules and boundaries. Keeping a positive approach to all of their interactions with you but ensuring you are not associated with unbalanced high energy.

An easy way to create calm is to stop vocally communicating with your puppy, particularly if you are resorting to shouting. This makes you appear unbalanced, will raise your puppy's energy levels causing confusion and in some cases make your puppy fearful of you.

Use a common sense approach to their management. If you don't want a full grown adult dog diving for your dish washer to lick the plates every time you open the door, then don't allow it when they are a puppy. It may be cute but you are setting your puppy up to fail and ultimately creating a flash point.

I stayed very quiet in all Hogan's early association with animals, objects, people and children but in all cases he was told to 'sit' and 'stay' via a series of hand signals prior to the meeting. It was successful and enabled Hogan to learn to take life challenges in his stride.

Hogan and Marley. Hogan's first meeting with a cow. The moment lasted just a few minutes but has set him up to respond calmly around livestock and take my lead.

What is a Problem Behaviour?

As your puppy develops and interacts with you, you will notice some behaviours he or she does that may be undesirable during human contact.

It is normal for all puppies to display a series of common behaviours that could easily become problematic if not addressed. The intensity of the situation of the high street has triggered Hogan to jump up at me for re-assurance during this training exercise.

Some examples of these are:

- Mouthing
- Travel (car) fear
- Fears in general
- Hyperactivity
- Jumping up
- Digging
- Chasing
- Aggression

Humans have played a huge role in the evolution of the dog, but the domestic dog still retains and lives by primitive dog rules and values. In addition, we have also bred individual behaviours to be prevalent in certain breeds in order for them to fulfil specific roles in our lives.

We therefore need to recognise that these behaviours may need to be performed or redirected to ensure there is a manageable outlet if they are not required to perform them for working purposes.

Why do they Occur?

As an example, Border Collies are bred to 'herd' and this behaviour is essential for their working role with sheep. As a result, the Collie is well known to display the behaviour when not always ask for, trained for or wanted! If prevented from expressing this natural drive and their energy is not focused elsewhere, stress behaviours may prevail. If this occurs, owners may find themselves in a volatile situation and the puppy may be difficult to manage. I have treated many Border Collies who obsessively chased their own shadow. It is difficult to manage and distressing for the owners, requiring a vigilant behaviour modification program to achieve a successful result.

You may also find that problems arise if instinctive puppy communicators (mouthing, jumping up) are not stopped as early as possible or have been inadvertently encouraged.

You should also take note of where other people reinforce poor behaviour for you. If an arriving guest greets your puppy when they are jumping all over them, poor behaviour will be rewarded. Protect your puppy by removing them to begin with.

Finally, negative or physical handling will certainly result in your puppy responding poorly. Be aware of how you are treating your puppy in all scenarios. Your relationship is based around clear communication so it is important you get this right.

How do we Control or Stop Poor Behaviour?

In all cases, you should first and foremost recognise the simple and clear direction required for dog ownership, set the dog up to succeed by guiding them through human life with boundaries and direction and ensure you are aware of the instinctive drives for your chosen breed.

If it is not possible to allow the dog to perform the breed associated behaviours, you should ensure you are keeping their 'busy brain, busy' with regular learning and controlled social exposure.

Your dog will be crying out for guidance and this is the key to a positive relationship. Just imagine how concerned and confused you would be if you had to suddenly live with a pack of dogs who all communicate and act in a way that is totally alien to you! Only then can you truly appreciate how adaptive the dog really is, but this also makes it easier to understand how things can go very wrong.

Allowing an overly physical and emotional relationship with little guidance for your dog does not provide a positive platform for you to set your dog up for success. Setting early boundaries around interaction and attention, approach into your personal space, areas of your home that are out of bounds, and control around the entry and exit to your home all provide positive communicators to your dog that you are the 'risk assessor' and he or she does not need to take a lead role.

If you set these simple rules as soon as you bring your puppy home it becomes normal life for them very quickly.

Discipline and Control
(This subject is addressed in more detail in Chapter 19)

Whether to discipline a dog or not provides the canine profession with an area of conflict, with many trainers choosing to only use treats and toys to positively reinforce good behaviours while others use overly physical or harsh methods to create fear and submission.

While I appreciate that my experience is not exclusive, I feel there is value in considering the communication and interactive behaviour of the dog as an independent species. I prefer to adopt a more open minded approach and work with whatever situation is presented to me at the time.

Every individual needs to test boundaries and be reminded that they exist. This is what provides we humans with some level of respect and self-control in today's society and enables us to develop respect and social awareness in the relationships we create, whether these be with people or animals.

I fail to see how drip feeding my children chocolate and sweets to keep them quiet on the supermarket run would ever teach them how to behave in every social scenario. Nor Is it acceptable, necessary or beneficial to physically punish a child to correct poor behaviour? I much prefer to advise them on how to behave and provide a reward for their self-control at the end of the event, using the removal of the reward as a consequence for a lack of self-control.

This can translate to the management of the dog. I do not agree with negative or harsh physical handling or high level vocal reprimands when the dog doesn't conform to expectations. I much prefer to give them the direction to succeed, remind them and remove them if they cannot display manners. After all, if you spend any time observing the dog or wolf naturally you will see that this behaviour is one of many they use to set a boundary and create manners and respect in younger individuals.

Your method for implementing this clear direction should be as follows:

- Make sure you are calm and confident (you will fail if you are aggressive or anxious)
- Attach a lead to your puppy (only if they are used to one)
- Do not use your voice. Use direction with body language
- Invite your puppy into the social space and place them on a bed (use the lead)
- Go about your activity
- If your puppy moves, then replace them
- If they move a second time towards the activity, then remove them calmly and with no fuss
- Repeat the process
- Your puppy should be encouraged to stay in their bed but may get bored easily so provide something to chew

This should provide you with a clear consequence, a platform to teach the puppy and an avenue to avoid stress and anxiety. If your puppy remains in a calm state, they will learn. This may require work, particularly if you have a very high energy puppy with no self-control. You can build on this gradually.

Your goal is to teach your puppy to cope in a social environment but ignore the activity unless invited into it.

Hogan learning time out around meal times. He is trained to stay on his bed. If your puppy chooses to leave the bed area more than twice then you should remove them completely from the social area to help them settle.

Task

Your task for this section is to perfect your discipline, observe your leadership skills, consider whether you feel your puppy has manners around your personal space.

You should also cease to use your voice to communicate with your puppy for a period of 48 hours, this will allow you to view your puppy from their perspective and encourage you to communicate with them via their primary communication mode – body language.

CHAPTER 17

Recall

Basis for Positive Recall Training

Before considering your recall methods, you must take into consideration the status of your relationship. Your puppy will initially see you as the focus for their attention during their first few weeks (7-14 weeks). This provides a fantastic opportunity for you to start to embed positivity around them coming to you when they are called and generally being attentive to your direction.

Nurturing this behaviour in the early days will make the progression to successful recall so much easier. Do NOT miss this valuable opportunity. Let your puppy off the lead as soon as possible as you will never have a more productive period to build a solid recall response. After this time your puppy will begin to become more confident and curious of the world around them. They will be easily distracted by the behaviour of other dogs and people and will also be more susceptible to fears and phobias.

If your puppy persistently runs towards people and other dogs at this impressionable age you will be guaranteed to have an ineffective recall and your puppy will be learning all the wrong behaviours, receiving high level responses to their attention giving!

Your goal should be to make sure your puppy considers you their primary means of survival and routinely looks to you for guidance. If they are regularly used to checking in with you on a positive level but also respect that the walk is on your terms, then this gives you a great start point to build on the behaviour required for teaching recall.

There are important things you need to do to ensure you maintain a confident approach to the management of your puppy off lead, but also facilitate their socialisation and make the walk enjoyable for all.

Where and How to Walk

Choosing where and how you do your walk can make a difference to how receptive your puppy is. If you are too predictable, walking in the same place, following the same route and out for the same period of time, daily, then there really isn't anything interesting about this for your puppy. The walk then becomes less stimulating and your puppy will begin to find other more exciting ways of entertaining themselves which may not be so desirable.

This approach also makes the environment intense as it is likely other dog walkers will be doing the same. They may find one particular field quite challenging if it is frequented by lots of other more confident, older dogs. Don't put your puppy in a potentially intimidating situation where they are likely to feel threatened.

Additionally, walking with no particular purpose sends the wrong message to your puppy so make sure you are aware of your body language, take a positive stance and walk with confidence. Encouraging periods of 'work' for your puppy, either to retrieve a toy, perform a short 'sit-stay' or check in and walk to heel, will all make the walk focused around you and provide interest for your puppy, potentially distracting them positively from other environmental scenarios.

All of this advice is to ensure your puppy recognises that you are a positive focus for their enjoyment and direction. If you have this in place, then you are well on your way to being able to teach a solid recall.

Use these following points as a checklist for success:
- Leadership
- Positive direction
- Good communication
- Solid boundaries
- Owner awareness and respect
- Progressive means of learning human spoken words
- Positive, enjoyable dog-owner relationship

Equipment

You will require the following to develop a recall command:

- Flat collar and name tag

- Long line (approx. 20ft)
- Recall whistle (ACME Gundog whistle)
- High prize treats: liver/meat and or toy/ball
- Treat pouch
- Praise and patience in abundance!

Recall Equipment: Treat bag, whistle, ball, treats, longline, and standard lead.

Method for Training

I find that its useful to give my owners a simple program to follow when embedding recall. While the behaviour is organic to begin with, it doesn't stay that way. Having an owner focused on moving forward with clear direction and goals to achieve is far more beneficial than giving some basic advice and leaving things to chance.

Let's look at each phase individually.

Phase 1

This is the amazing period of human bonding during your puppy's early arrival (7-14 weeks) that is handed to you, as an owner for free so grab it with both hands and find every opportunity to encourage your puppy to come to you for rewards. This should be several rewards at once: praise, treat and release.

Hogan now at 10 months is well practised in the behaviour required for treat training.

Avoid using a command at this stage just focus on getting your puppy to chase you or create an interest in a toy and interact. When your puppy comes over, periodically run away and repeat the praise and contact as your puppy follows. Make sure you make a huge fuss of your puppy as they return, this is not the time for a simple 'good'. You need to be interesting and really exciting.

Attaching this behaviour to some clear body language signals such as opening your arms wide and crouching down can be great markers to begin an early recall communication.

Creating energy around your body language by running backwards as they approach is also a really useful trigger to keep your puppy's interest.

Never chase your puppy or allow them to move away from you, you should be the one to cease contact in every situation. If your puppy appears disinterested it is up to you to regain their contact; hide, run away, squeak a toy do whatever you need to do to get things back on your terms before finishing on a positive note. This is a common problem when practising in safe social environments such as homes or back gardens so be aware.

Phase 2

This phase begins once your puppy has settled into their routine with you at home, around week 2. This is where you will be looking to introduce a clear signal attached to recall.

While many people just use the dog's name or a particular word, I strongly advise against this. Your recall command needs to be consistent if it is to be strong enough to infiltrate a puppy focused on something highly stimulating. I find the human voice is hugely inconsistent and lacks clarity, plus the voice will highlight any human anxieties providing a clear reason why a puppy may choose not to return to its owner.

With this in mind, my advice is to source a recall whistle early in your puppy's training. I find a positively associated whistle can work in much the same way as a doorbell. The doorbell signals a guest arrival and the usual high level reward that follows via human contact. I have had many occasions where a dog will respond to the doorbell without a guest even being present, just because they are conditioned to do so. My first Labrador was totally food driven but would still always stop eating to check who was arriving if the doorbell went during a mealtime.

We can take this learning and apply it to our recall training. Your puppy should now be interested in your movements and used to following you around, not just because they are insecure and require reassurance but because they want to. You are now interesting, fun and the individual that guides them. Attaching a noise to this behaviour should be straightforward.

Structure your training so you have clear 10 minute periods in your day focused on productive learning.

I use an ACME 210 1/2 Gundog whistle. I trust this is good quality and will deliver a consistent and clear sound.

Set up the moment when your puppy is running towards you as practised in phase 1 and as they enter your space give 2 short beeps on the whistle. Finish by delivering the high level reward as before. Repetition is how you build on this association so make sure you regularly practise this at home.

Attaching this response to a meal time and/or play will give it even more impact.

If you have chosen just to use a word or wish to use a word such as 'come' then you should deliver the word just before the whistle. However, I would advise that you focus on one or the other to begin with until your puppy is responding willingly.

Don't be tempted in the early days to test your command while your puppy is distracted, you are likely to fail and will need to be in a position to interrupt their behaviour so that they don't ignore you. As with all your training, set yourself and your puppy up for success not failure.

Phase 3

Phase 3 can start within a few days of you beginning phase 2. This final leg of your recall journey involves associating your command and or signal outside away from home.

Adding in distractions can bring a whole new level of stress for both you and your puppy if you are not adequately prepared. It would be very easy to destroy all your positive ground work by just letting your puppy off, expecting the recall training to be strong enough.

Hogan in Phase 3 of his recall journey. Wearing his longline and sporting his own gundog whistle, placed for the purpose of the photo only of course!

To ensure your puppy doesn't ignore you I would advise that you attach a long line. I prefer not to use flexi leads for a variety of reasons but most importantly you will want to leave the line attached and drop it at some stage and you would be unable to do this with a flexi lead.

This allows you to begin to trust your training but also gives you the opportunity to pull your puppy out of a situation safely and without chasing should they ignore you.

This final phase should be taken in 2 week periods:

- Spend 2 weeks holding on to your long line, testing your recall
- The following 2 weeks you should be periodically dropping the line, running away and building confidence
- Your final 2 weeks involves mentally 'letting your dog off' but the line stays in place and is just there for emergencies, your puppy should be totally focused on you by this point if you have built your training well

I kept a long line on Hogan until I felt it became dangerous (he was around 8 months old when I removed it) I hardly touched it throughout but my experience suggests that it only takes one episode to set you back, so I wanted to be sure he could never ignore me. Now, I rarely call his name and just direct him with body language commands, his whistle and the occasional 'come'.

Avoiding a Poor Response

If you have followed the direction above, then it is unlikely problems will be persistent. Most can be spotted early and in all cases you should just take one step back and drop down a phase for a week or so. However, I am realistic and problems can occur even if you are doing everything right. Walking your puppy in public places leaves you vulnerable to the behaviour of other individuals and their dogs.

Taking note of these simple points will give you the best chance of enjoying every walk with your puppy safely:

- Maintain physical control of your puppy at the beginning of your walk
- Use your long line

- Don't over use your recall command
- Don't allow your puppy to ignore you
- Actively use praise, food and toys to reward
- Don't always associate recall with the lead being re-attached
- Carry your lead across your body not in your hand
- Don't be afraid to call out to people if you need them to ignore your approaching puppy
- Don't expect other dogs to teach your puppy manners
- Keep the walk progressive
- Vary the locations of your walk and the routes you take

What to Do if Things Go Wrong

Should your puppy ignore your recall and charge over to someone, then you should expect them to react in some way. Whether this is negatively or positively it still leaves you with a poor behaviour that has been rewarded. This is why your long line is invaluable.

If you really can't get your puppy to come back you should walk over to the situation without speaking to your puppy, give the long line a gentle tug and holding the line walk away. As soon as your puppy is trotting along with you again you can then engage and reward. You should never scold the puppy for ignoring you as this will reinforce the poor behaviour and chip away at the trust in your relationship.

Having a solid recall command in place will give you a basis to keep your puppy out of trouble and safe. It will also portray you as a responsible dog owner and make you feel proud to have such good control of your young puppy. It will also set you up to have a respectful and well-mannered adult dog.

Recall runs much deeper than just your dog returning to you when they are called. It is a barometer for your relationship as a whole and speaks volumes about how balanced your dog is overall.

Allowing our dogs to run free in public places is a privilege and one which we don't want to lose. Respect for other members of the public and their dogs can only be achieved with good off lead control, reinforcing the importance of this early learning.

Task

Your task for this section is to recognise the level of attachment you have with your puppy. Does your puppy willingly run to you or are you finding you are chasing your puppy around?

To test your control, pop your puppy in the garden or outside space, close the door and leave them for 2 minutes, go back and call them in, do they come straight away? If not, close the door, walk away and repeat. Don't keep calling with the door open. Once your puppy is waiting patiently at the door, open the door and make them wait before inviting them in.

CHAPTER 18

Understanding Poor Behaviour

What is Poor Dog Behaviour?

The behaviour of the dog and whether it is good or bad is very much down to the perception of the individual observing. There are many scenarios where I would view a dog as being out of control or unbalanced and potentially dangerous but because there appears to be no sign of aggression the owner and other members of the public would possibly disagree. This failure to observe the dog's communication signals prior to an altercation or negative response is one of many reasons why our dogs are being set up to fail.

Hogan showing how connected dogs are to our instruction when we get the relationship right.

It is also common for an owner to interpret a dog's behaviour from their perspective and this is totally normal. The words 'guilt' and 'jealousy' are common descriptive words used to explain why their beloved pet has growled at them or destroyed furniture. My explanation that these behaviours are a result of a failure in the dogs coping ability and an indicator for distress and anxiety, often comes as a shock.

In society today, dogs are physically and mentally entwined in the lives of the human owner, they are exposed to emotional responses and expected to cope with the sometimes erratic, highly stimulated and fast pace of life. It is seen as acceptable to have them up on sofas, in beds and meeting guests at the front door, creating a position of authority for the dog and providing them with an expectation of 'leading' rather than being 'led'.

This innocent face made several attempts to make himself comfortable on one of our sofas. Although he wasn't necessarily causing a problem I continued to enforce the 'no sofa' rule to ensure my leadership was as strong as possible. This is so important for other areas of your relationship such as recall, so never overlook the simple communicators.

Given that dogs ultimately learn through experiences; this lack of clear direction can have a negative effect long term. The majority of poorly behaved dogs are not born 'bad', their behaviour deteriorates as a result of this social learning. While the dogs brain has all the same structures as ours they are limited in their ability to process complex information and can be prone to anxiety if effective communication is absent.

The dog is totally receptive to our emotional energy, regardless of any thoughtless handling, therefore it comes as no surprise that spending time in our dog's physical space exposes them to any negative energy we possess, usually this energy is created through stress.

Ensuring an opportunity exists where the dog is simply allowed to co-exist with the human is not only acceptable, it is recommended for your dog's welfare.

The Dog's Brain

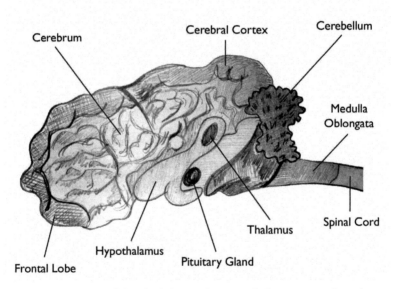

A simple sketch of the dog's brain showing all the major and similar structures to the human brain.

While I am aware my next point could be seen as controversial, and it certainly isn't true of the entire population of dog owners, I feel it is valid and if it goes some way to make a new puppy owner consider how they are behaving around their puppy then I shall take the risk of upsetting a few.

We have all seen the current approach to canine management adopted by some, I would like to think this is a lack of education rather than an inherent need to put one's emotional self before the needs and welfare of the dog.

I am referring to the dogs who are carried around in handbags, pampered and dressed up and dogs who have had their fur chemically coloured. This would include dog's seen on social media being forced to interact with an out of control child or positioned overly close to a newborn baby just to grab a few 'likes and shares' for the cute factor.

In these instances, the dog's perceived role bounces from one of entertainment and fun for the human, to acting as a supportive emotional crutch for day to day stresses. When not needed for one of the above, confusion and anxiety prevails, resulting in needy attention seeking, destructive and boisterous poor behaviour in an attempt to rekindle the closeness with the owner.

In these instances, the dog is quickly deemed a nuisance, dangerous and can become a commodity the owner could live without. Rescue centres bursting at the seams and new breed specific rescue charities appearing are testament to this being a serious concern.

I realise it might be unfair of me to label all dog owners in this way, and to the contrary, the people I have the pleasure to meet are dedicated and enthusiastic, wanting to learn and do the very best for their new family member. Sadly though, I do see enough evidence of cases to warrant a raised awareness of how detrimental this human behaviour is to our canine species.

We are truly blessed to be able to share our lives with such an amazingly adaptive, loyal and intelligent animal. They deserve every respect and as much understanding of their communication and values as we are able to give them.

Evidence exists to suggest human stress is on the increase. The dog is totally receptive to our emotional energy, regardless of any thoughtless handling, therefore it comes as no surprise that spending time in our dog's physical space exposes them to any negative energy we possess. Usually this energy is created through stress.

Evidence of this has been around for years. It is well known that working dogs work better if they are housed predominantly away from the human owners home and only enter when invited. Once this threshold is breached the dog develops a very different relationship with its owner. While this was thought just to be solely due to hierarchal and leadership factors, we can now also add our observations of the dog's behaviour around human energy to clarify the relevance of human emotion on the dog's responses.

Having worked with dogs for most of my life I tend to use the energy of the dog to gauge how balanced or unbalanced they are. An unbalanced dog will nearly always display behaviours of concern but often they are reported when they are seriously embedded and then it becomes difficult to correct them.

So now that we can begin to understand how we may be partly responsible for poor dog behaviour, we should determine what is recognised as 'poor'.

Behaviours Deemed as 'Poor'

Many behaviours are actually extreme versions of what would be normal survival behaviours in the wild. This table depicts the motivation for these behaviours both in the wild and within a domestic environment.

Table displaying behaviours and their instinctive and domestic motivators

Behaviour	Instinctive reason (wild)	Domestication reason
Jumping up	Establishing status play Feed from the mother	Frustration/challenge Seeking attention Anxiety release
Mouthing	Communication Teething	Boredom/teething Attention Frustration
Boisterous	Play Adolescence	Stress Lack of leadership Adolescence Play
Digging	Hunting Create a cool place to lay Nesting Play	Stress/frustration Boredom Hunting

Chewing	Play/teething Entertainment Pain relief	Anxiety/boredom Play Teething Pain relief
Chasing	Uncertainty Play Hunting	Play Hunting Stress relief
Pacing	Scavenging	Poor diet Stress relief Boredom
Destruction	Play/frustration Teething/pain	Anxiety Teething pain Boredom
Vocalisation	Warning system	Warning system
Aggression	Reproduction Hierarchy Pack protection Food related (hunting) Resource guarding Protective Territorial Predatory Survival/self-protection	Negative experience Fear/anxiety Challenged/threatened Lack of leadership Self-protection Resource guarding Protective Territorial Predatory

In my experience a puppy who has been managed with routine, boundaries and discipline alongside positive mental and physical stimulation performs these 'so called' negative behaviours far less, if at all.

When a puppy struggles to find an effective means of communicating, frustration and anxiety are likely outcomes. A deterioration in the puppy's overall behaviour would be expected in these cases.

Aggression has to be at the top of my list when considering poor behaviour. This adaptive behaviour is just one of many means of communication that the dog has and it may be delivered at various levels of intensity depending on the original desire or motivation.

The media on TV and on the internet have created a huge awareness of isolated dog attacks over the last few years, but let's get this in perspective. You are far more likely to trip over a loose slab on a pavement or fall down a flight of stairs than you are ever going to be injured by a dog. Most dog attacks are invited, not necessarily always by the victim but by a succession of events and poor management, leaving the dog with no alternative. If you are able to get yourself into an educated position around dogs you will be able to respect and observe their communication, therefore avoiding conflict.

There has been a notable rise in dog attacks in society both in public and private places. This is becoming increasingly worrying and we should all question the reasons for 'man's best friend' becoming so volatile.

I regularly visit the homes of dogs with human and dog aggression problems. Entering the territory of these dogs can be challenging as this is where they are at their most confident. Additionally, owners are always intent that I see the nature of the problem to its full extent which means I am often unnecessarily offered up as bait!

I generally find my relationship and understanding of the dog develops within the first 10 minutes, as we display respect and control of our boundaries.

Anybody who ever questions the use of boundary control that I implement with my dogs should come and observe the behaviour of a confident dog on their own territory. Dogs will also draw an imaginary line on the floor of a particular living space and potentially block and stand their ground if I choose to cross it. My reaction to this is not to bulldoze my way through but instead to show respect, distract, get control by attaching a lead and pacify the confrontation before tipping the bar in my favour, setting my own boundary and making the dog work to enter my social space.

This is never about physical ability or a power to weight ratio. If it were I am sure I would be ejected soon after my arrival. I use my knowledge, experience and physical height, always choosing the moral high ground to rein in control and avoid a negative reaction from the dog. My goal is to build the dog's trust through confidence and authority, I don't attach any hesitation or create grey areas. I arrive, direct, build trust, create calm and leave, hopefully with owners who are successfully implementing all my techniques.

Nevertheless, aggression occurs for many reasons and often appears unpredictable to most people. Just because a dog displays aggression it doesn't necessarily mean the dog is inherently aggressive, but it does mean an owner needs to recognise the severity of the problem and address it, not just expect it to go away or hope that it was a momentary blip.

It is rare that any dog will use aggression naturally as a means of first line communication. Most will do everything in their power to avoid it or remove themselves. Often the aggression cases I am called out to see have been problematic for some time, owners may have made allowances for behaviours but not really understood the reason for them. This allows the behaviour to become embedded and the dog develops a confidence in their delivery as they know it will work.

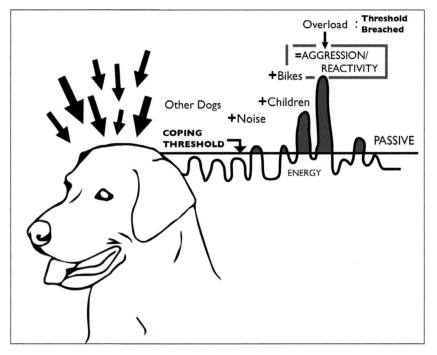

Diagram: Depicting the coping threshold and daily triggers. When your puppy faces high level stimulation this is when they will be most likely to react. Teach huge amounts of self-control to avoid poor behaviour.

Ultimately aggression in any form should be viewed as 'end stage' behaviour, it is deemed the most severe of all the negative dog behaviours I treat. The majority of aggressive outbursts are delivered for effect, meaning injury is unlikely, but the behaviour has the desired result due to the psychological impact on another individual. Ultimately it has not been necessary for the dog to deliver a damaging bite, the noise and energy with which an attack is delivered is enough to receive a result.

This is the reason I always teach my clients to only ever take their behaviour to the level required. There is no need to drag your dog to its bed if they are happy to go with just a finger click and a point. This is how you develop a trusting relationship and the dog understands, after all this is how they would conduct themselves generally. Problems arise when early behaviours are ignored, the dog is prevented from communicating, sustains an attack themselves or goes beyond the point of reasonable self-control.

The best way to understand the process is to liken the dog's behaviour to a boiling kettle. Keeping the electricity pumping will ultimately result in the necessity for an outlet, imagine the lid popping off as the heat and pressure gets too much. This is ultimately what is happening with the dog during a reactive moment.

Why does it Occur?

It may be that the dog had a negative experience at some point in its life, this doesn't have to be catastrophic, just something whereby the dog felt overly threatened. The next time the dog meets this situation they will have a learnt association and will therefore be more anxious than normal. If the situation disperses quickly then the dog will recognise that it may not need to feel so threatened next time. If the dog is challenged in the moment, then they will try their best to communicate their discomfort. If this is ignored and the moment doesn't pass, then the anxiety heightens and the dog begins to display similar symptoms to those seen in a human panic attack.

To understand this process, you should recognise that the dog's ability to cope is managed by the 'fight or flight' response (as discussed in Chapter 11). Once this chemical response is triggered a series of behaviours are displayed in order to protect the dog and preserve its life. This is ultimately seen once the lid to your kettle has come off!

If you recognise that the negative behaviour from the majority of dogs occurs in challenging, intense or high energy moments you will realise quite quickly the need for creating and maintaining a calm confident attitude when walking your puppy.

Keeping the energy low when passing other dogs and not allowing your puppy to run up to other dogs uninvited will go some way to avoiding confrontation.

The key reasons for aggression to become problematic are:

- Negative experience

- Genetics
- Feelings of being threatened
- Learnt association
- Their negative behaviour has reached the desired outcome: reward

This is one of my client's dogs practising calm self-control in a local busy park. Creating a confident and calm puppy will help them avoid confrontation.

How do I Protect my Puppy?

I am regularly asked by clients how they should manage a negative situation if their puppy is challenged when out walking. Unfortunately, there is no certain means of protecting your puppy. My advice would be to reduce the potential risks rather than avoiding them altogether.

Never pick up your puppy – Firstly one of the worst things you can do if another dog is approaching in a challenging way is to pick up your puppy. You immediately instigate interest and potential conflict by doing this and more importantly you put yourself at risk. Dogs will communicate with each other much more efficiently than humans and dogs, so it is always better to try and stay out of the communication as much as you can.

Drop the lead where possible — It is always advisable that you try and drop the lead as well. Your puppy will feel more threatened if they are unable to get away or avoid a situation and a lead will prevent them being able to do this.

Obviously, if there is a chance your puppy will bolt away from you completely then you won't be able to take this risk.

A balanced adult dog won't see a puppy as a threat and for the most part they will just want to try and instigate play. Whether your puppy welcomes this or not it is always better for them to learn how to communicate rather than you enforcing fear or anxiety.

Shout out to the other dog's owner — If you are really uncomfortable with another dog's approach then don't be afraid to shout out to the dog's owner, while it is always possible they will have poor control it is worth asking them to recall their dog if you feel your puppy is being put under pressure, they may just not have noticed your concern.

Carry a pop up umbrella — There are other simple methods that you can try if an owner is unable to recall their dog. A pop up umbrella can work wonders as a deterrent and it also shields your puppy from the approaching dogs direct eye contact. I also advise you carry a rape alarm or something similar. The shrill sound these give off is often enough to send most dogs in the opposite direction, I have often used mine in an emergency to separate 2 dogs. It is much safer than attempting to physically pull two dogs apart.

Try not to panic — While all of this can be really unnerving, especially if you are new to dog ownership, I can assure you that the majority of negative incidents are just noise and drama or 'handbags at dawn' as I often describe it. Dogs can sound like they are tearing each other to pieces but often there is no damage to be seen. The less the humans react the quicker things will calm down.

What to do if Your Puppy Sustains a Negative Experience

If you are unlucky and your puppy sustains some damage, then you must get the details of the owner and consider whether they should be reported. A dog off lead and out of control is deemed dangerous and the dog should be under some form of restriction. This is likely to mean the dog wears a muzzle and lead in future, but ignoring it and thinking it may be a one off is not acceptable.

There are dog laws and they exist for a reason, if you don't feel another owner is responsible enough then you should report the incident.

If your puppy is injured, even if it only appears to be minor, you should always visit the vet. This is important as a dog bite does not just cause skin damage but it is also a crushing injury and damage may have occurred beneath the skin that isn't always evident. Additionally, your puppy is likely to have a degree of shock which in itself needs monitoring and potential treatment.

For the benefit of your dog, it will be important that you carry on as if the incident has never happened. Adopt the same confident and assertive attitude you should be used to by now. An incident will have unnerved you but you have to continue to provide guidance and positivity for your puppy. If you hold on to the negative association so will your puppy.

Puppies are resilient and often carry on as if nothing has happened. Follow their lead, but if possible try to find avenues to build your puppy's confidence. Walking with an older, calm and balanced dog or 'buddy dog' is brilliant for this.

Confidence comes from positive associations so try walking somewhere different to begin with and using lots of positive reinforcement before re-visiting the place of attack. You should be in a confident frame of mind before you do this.

It is not uncommon to find your puppy may be more vocal or nervous and if this is the case then you and your puppy may benefit from a one to one session with a qualified behaviourist. Each case is different and it is beyond the scope of this text to provide guidance in every possible scenario.

Always remember a dog will generally do everything it can to avoid a serious negative scenario.

Go back to basics: some treat training on the outskirts of the place of
attack can begin the rehabilitation process.

If you are educated, sensible and have an awareness of canine behaviour
then there is no reason why your walks need to be fraught with worry.
Incidents do happen but just assess your risks, reduce them where you can
and be prepared.

Task

Your task for this section is to note the variety of behaviours you
have seen from approaching dogs, consider whether the behaviour
could have been, or was, problematic.

Recognise behaviour in your puppy that could become a
problem as they grow and focus on how best to intercept it or
correct it.

CHAPTER 19

Discipline and Control

Discipline Explained

The word 'discipline' is certainly one that creates conflict within the dog behaviour and training profession. The dictionary definition describes discipline as the *'enforcing of rules and application of correction for poor behaviour through punishment',* so it makes sense why it wouldn't necessarily be well received.

It is my opinion that every individual will have their own perception of discipline, dependent upon their life experiences and social learning. My use of the word is not so literal. I prefer to consider discipline as a means of providing a basis for guidance and learning, NOT using 'punishments' to correct behaviour but applying clear boundaries and setting a non-intrusive consequence to highlight a distaste for an undesirable behaviour.

I will never be physically harsh or cruel to a dog. Cruelty is something that I believe is created when you set a dog up to fail. Surprisingly, cruelty can be created by mistake when dog owners are encouraged to only use one method to train an undesirable behaviour out of their dog. For instance, treats will not interrupt an instinctive drive, or panic response related problem as the dog will be too charged to think about food. Thus the owner and dog will fail, often with catastrophic consequences.

Dogs should be given clear and consistent instruction on how to behave within human social space, if they are to do so safely. In order to achieve this, it is important to create a practical, fair and safe means of communicating to the dog what behaviour you expect from them. While I am positive and reward all correct behaviour, I do believe every individual needs to recognise their boundaries and limitations and this also applies to the dog.

I would urge all my clients and readers to take a common sense approach to managing their puppy, whatever words are used to describe an action, you need to be comfortable you are guiding your puppy and setting them up correctly.

I will explain the methods I use to achieve control within this chapter.

Using a Consistent Means of Management

The most important advice I can give a new puppy owner is to always be consistent with whatever management technique they choose.

The dog takes an extremely 'black and white' attitude in its perception of experiences. Creating 'grey' areas by being lazy in your approach, acting differently, using lots of different verbal commands and/or using rough handling, will result in a negative experience and your puppy will not learn anything positive. In fact, it is likely this will encourage a higher level of negativity and create frustration and anxiety in both parties.

You should also consider your living environment:

- Where will you put your puppy to keep them safe?
- Are you going to use this area to manage their behaviour?
- How many people live in the house and are they all on board with the training?
- Do you have an open plan home?
- Does your puppy have easy access to your front door?

I will now talk you through a clear means of setting your puppy up for success.

The 3-Stage Control Method

Your puppy should wear a short puppy lead (cloth) in the house.

This will give you the physical control you will need without having to chase your puppy or keep grabbing the collar or picking them up, which will create negativity. The lead keeps you dissociated from the guidance and allows you to manage your puppy without rewarding just by giving a response. Leave the lead on after a walk and make sure you distract your puppy if they show any interest in the lead.

Hogan's first cloth puppy lead that doubled up as his house line.

Stage 1: Set up your area of 'control' within your social space in your home

This will be just a bed or mat in your living room or main social space, it should be something the puppy is used to lying on.

Positive association to the bed facilitates calm control in busy environments.

Stage 2: Calmly walk your puppy through into your living room and place them on their bed or mat

You should stop your puppy briefly at the doorway and show them the *flat palm* of your hand to calm down their energy and reinforce the positive behaviour you would like them to display.

Stage 3: Use your body language to ask for the 'Sit' and again show them the flat palm of your hand to request the 'Stay'

Do NOT use your voice here. Your voice will add to the stimulation in the environment. Do NOT bend down into your puppy's space, use a treat to get them to sit if you need to and don't walk away until you feel they have calmed.

The first time you practise this it would be useful to entertain your puppy. Provide them with a stuffed Kong toy to chew. This will also reinforce that the bed area is a positive place to be.

Hogan and his Kong stuffed with food and some live yoghurt!

You have now given your puppy clear direction in how you expect them to behave around your home.

When and How to Use a Consequence

It is likely that your puppy will move the first few times you do this, so this is where your consequence comes in…

A. When/if your puppy moves you should get up and calmly replace them back on the bed

Be firm in your action but non-confrontational and non-aggressive. Use the lead ONLY, don't grab them or chase them. If you add energy to this your puppy will not learn.

B. Should your puppy move again then you should do one of the following

Either calmly take them back and hook the lead over the end of a radiator, secure it through a sturdy piece of furniture (or something similar), or remove your puppy and its bed to its area (as discussed in Chapter 8).

Hogan in his crate. The crate was used to manage his behaviour as well as provide a safe place to be. This could only be achieved if the behaviour management was delivered calmly, with no high level anxiety or aggression.

The removal is delivered calmly and consistently with no eye contact. If you are clear with your direction and perform the techniques in a confident and no nonsense manner, then your puppy will learn quickly.

Always be aware of the level of energy you are using as this is really relevant and could make the difference between the technique being a success or failure.

Positive Reinforcement

I have found Hogan to be compliant on many levels with the solid leadership that is present in our house and I have utilised a variety of different techniques to improve upon our relationship and his understanding of my expectation.

In my work I will use a combination of techniques to communicate with a dog and further their level of understanding, so the journey with Hogan provided me with the opportunity to experience my professional methods on a very personal platform with great success.

A heavy focus is put on trainers and behaviourists in today's social culture that all dogs should be trained solely in a 'positive' way. The general thought is that this means we should only be delivering food and toys to train our dogs. I agree that whenever possible positive behaviour needs rewarding and encouraging. However, little guidance is given in how to manage dogs with severe behaviour problems such as aggression and high level anxieties, when treats alone don't work.

I can assure you that this is because there is no place for food rehabilitation in such cases. It doesn't work and I have met many demoralised and emotionally stressed owners who have felt they have failed their dog because of this advice. More importantly many dogs are never given the correct treatment to help them through a problem.

There is a physiological reason why food will never be strong enough to intercept these types of behaviours at the time of a reaction. Once the dog is displaying extreme poor behaviour or hyper-excitability they are being led by a chemical response. The response is designed to maintain a heightened state as a means of protection for the dog. We previously touched on this in an earlier chapter where I defined the behaviour as similar to a human panic attack. These chemicals mean it is impossible for the dog to focus on anything other than the trigger and their appetite is absent in this moment.

I do agree food can play a part in early social rehabilitation in an attempt to avoid a potential conflict, but without some form of consequence and control from an owner this is unlikely to be beneficial long term when faced with a sudden trigger.

I remember clearly coming across a lady walking her little terrier while I was out riding my horse. I could hear the dog barking and the sound of a 'clicker' before even turning the corner of the covered bridleway I was on. What I witnessed was a classic example of human error in re-enforcing poor dog behaviour. The clicker is conditioned as a 'positive reinforcer' usually with food. It means that whatever behaviour the dog does when they hear the sound and receive the reward, this is the behaviour that's now positively associated (with the click sound). In short, they will think that's the behaviour you want from them.

One example of a variety of different clicker training aids available on the market.

The owner was clearly trying to get the dog's attention, making the sound and waving chicken under the dog's nose.

The dog was solely focused on the legs of my horse and why wouldn't he be, he was hearing his clicker, seeing his chicken and giving it his all to meet his owner's expectation, or so he thought! Fortunately, the dog was on a lead and I have a very compliant horse. I walked past unscathed but shocked at the level of poor understanding an owner could have of a powerful training technique.

The internet is flooded with opinions on the subject of positive reinforcement and conflict exists between professional's as a result. Ultimately the dog is an individual who has a different means of communication to humans and requires a level of support to be able to successfully live in a human domestic environment.

The management of the dog requires a good understanding of their primitive behaviours, values and needs. Owners should recognise their clear body language communicators, of which there are many and which also vary between breeds and individual dogs.

Food and toys are a great way of developing a relationship with your new puppy but they are not the 'be all and end all' and in some cases can interfere with the development of self-control and authority. Keep an open mind and apply a solid common sense approach for when to use them.

I rarely use treats for Hogan's 'down stay' now, I found treats continued to encourage him to jump up in excitement, before I could return to him, therefore breaking his stay. Lesson learnt, he now waits for a calm stroke and belly rub, just as rewarding providing leadership is present.

How to Achieve a Balance of Control

In general, I use a very successful means of management that covers a broad spectrum of techniques, all of which I consider to be positive. Ultimately I have developed them to help the dog stay balanced, calm and free from conflict. I have used these methods to help integrate new puppies into domestic homes and to successfully rehabilitate troubled dogs.

My Top Tips to Achieve Perfect Control

- Implement a solid and consistent leadership program
- Communicate with body language and energy control
- Teach the dog the human spoken word and simple obedience commands
- Build a fun and interactive relationship through play (on owner's terms)

I use toys and food to reward specific behaviours such as 'leave it,' 'come', and 'stay' and also marking and shaping specific commands such as teaching the 'roll over' on to their side, useful during a veterinary examination.

I choose not to feed my dogs before their first early morning run, preferring to take high prize food and deliver it during recall. This also allows the dog to exercise some primitive behaviour, after all, in the wild they would go out to hunt and then return with their kill to eat.

This motivation allows me to become the food provider when the dog has an empty tummy, a very powerful position to be in. This is about using every opportunity to ensure you remain the dogs focus for survival.

Task

Your task is to write down your thoughts on discipline and consider your own opinions, recognise where you are helping your puppy cope with their new environment and where you are leaving them to their own devices.

Begin to utilise the '3 Stage Control' method and remember not to use your voice for delivering authority, reserve your voice for obedience commands only.

CHAPTER 20

Teaching Skills for Creating an Owner-Led Relationship with your Puppy Outdoors

Leadership was discussed in more detail in Chapter 7 and it definitely begins in the home. However, it is valuable for the development of an owners control away from home and I will make reference to it throughout this chapter.

Controlling the Environment

Walking your dog in a public place comes with many risks, primarily because you are unable to control the actions of others. You will consistently face challenges from the terrain you walk on, weather conditions, wild animals, livestock and everything else you meet. Nothing will be predictable and entering any environment with a brand new puppy can be completely overwhelming for some.

I want you to be prepared and take a sensible approach, so I will provide you with the confidence and knowledge to know how to deal with situations.

Firstly, you should lower your expectations, it is impossible to control your environment and trying to avoid scenarios will just make the walk a stressful experience. Focus on walking, training and educating your puppy rather than what others are doing. These early walks will pave the way for how every walk will be as your puppy grows. So set a solid benchmark and good focus around you.

Never make the mistake of being distracted from your puppy. Being too vocal and constantly interacting will devalue your leadership. Walking and chatting on your phone will do the same. You should adopt an air of quiet confidence, only calling your puppy to give direction or deliver a high prize reward, instead of constantly whistling and shouting!

You should focus solely on what you can control, your puppy! There is no better reward than being a proud dog owner and creating a relationship others will be envious of.

How to Maintain Leadership

Leadership will be in place at your home but transferring this control begins as soon as you attach the lead. Often the control over the puppy's behaviour is lost before an owner steps out of the front door, as the puppy has become over excited and difficult to physically manage.

Here Marley and Hogan wait patiently for me to get prepared to battle the rain!

When faced with this problem you need to be very careful that you take time to stop and calm things down. Your puppy won't be small forever and it is very easy to find yourself physically challenged by your dog as they grow.

Just slow the process down, leave the puppy on their bed until you are ready to leave the house and then call your puppy to you. This not only builds in a level of control but it also allows you to focus on avoiding your puppy becoming excitable.

Make sure you continue your authority when leaving the house. Stop your puppy at every doorway you walk through, make sure you have a loose lead and your puppy is not trying to barge past you. This is particularly important when you exit your front door.

Whoever leaves the house first will dictate the nature of the walk so make sure that is you!

To achieve this, you should avoid putting tension on the lead and collar, your lead should be used only as a backup and not the only means of control. Instead you should use all of the controls you have been building so far:

- Eye contact
- Positive reward
- Body language communication
- Patience and calm energy

Using the door itself to get your puppy to re-focus on you can be a real advantage. It's simple – your door only opens once your puppy is sitting calmly. If they move, then close it and repeat.

Remember you need to stay calm and confident, if you become frustrated during this early stage of the walk you will have lost control by the time you reach the outside world.

If you are travelling by car to the local park, then again be aware of the easy boundaries you can use to check the energy and excitement levels your puppy is displaying. The car door or boot lid can both be used in the same way as the front door to make your puppy stop and pay attention.

The reward is the walk so it shouldn't be necessary to constantly use treats during this process.

Apply your controls throughout and if you are confidently letting your puppy off lead then always make sure the direction of the walk is set by you.

"Puppy runs left = You go right!"

Structuring the Walk

Every walk I do is planned. I choose whether I wish for my dogs to socialise and I choose how much time they spend on and off lead. This is environment led and will be dependent on how busy it is, what my dogs have been doing prior to the walk, how long I want to walk for and whether I am walking to train or just to exercise them physically.

I never walk in the same place or take the same routes, this makes you too predictable and will give your puppy a safe opportunity to stray from you. If you are limited for places to walk and have to exercise your puppy in just one field or area, then make sure you act in an unpredictable fashion, walking or running at different paces, taking a figure of 8 approach to the direction you take and stopping and starting for no reason.

You don't always need to notify your puppy of what you are doing, they need to learn to keep an eye on you at all times. This will keep you in a positive and authoritative position.

Importance of Maintaining Contact with your Puppy

While many owners like to see their walk with their puppy as quality 'down time' for them to relax and for the puppy to run like mad and tire themselves out, I advise the complete opposite.

The dog likes to work and sees most walks as a means of hunting and or releasing and displaying their instinctive primitive and genetic behaviours.

This means it is the wrong time for any dog owner to sit back and relax. In fact, it is the area of dog training that requires the most work and is often the most challenging.

All dogs need some free time and there is nothing more enjoyable than watching your dog running free. This is something that has to be worked for, it doesn't just happen and the more finely bred, excitable or high energy your dog is, the more challenging you may find it.

My advice here is to reach for your long line again as long as it is physically safe to do so. They are not ideal and I have seen many injuries as people use them incorrectly or bring them into their dogs training at a late stage.

I use the long line to help reinforce Hogan's solid down stay practise. There is no harm in having this as back up. It means I can intervene should changes in the direct environment give cause for concern or he is encouraged to break the command as a result of another approaching dog.

**Hogan with the longline attached showing 'sit-stay' practise
4 months old.**

Actively practise all your basic obedience work in as many areas as you can. It is also useful to get other people and their dogs to help you test your puppy in a controlled way.

Having good control of your puppy in public is essential and will ensure you avoid any conflict with humans or other dogs. It is hard and there will be many challenges, but being prepared will ensure you are ready for all eventualities.

Task

Your task for this section is to test your puppy's self-control. Visit a variety of different areas and ask your puppy to sit for a minute without being distracted, keep their gaze on you and don't interact with passers by while doing the exercise. Increase the time slowly as your puppy's ability to stay calm improves.

CHAPTER 21

Socialisation Part 1: Interacting with Siblings and Other Dogs

Socialisation is heavily reinforced by many dog related professionals. However, it should be understood that poor socialisation can be just as detrimental as none at all.

Ensuring you protect your puppy from boisterous or demanding behaviours from other dogs, or negative social experiences is one of the most important things you will do as an owner. If you are not comfortable with an interaction, then stop it!

Likewise, management of your puppy, ensuring he or she does not create high energy or unbalance, is your responsibility.

Take into consideration your puppy's life stages and fear imprinting as this will also have an effect on how your dog responds to social events.

Health Considerations

Bringing any young puppies together will always be challenging and you should always take your puppy's mental and physical welfare into consideration.

If you are socialising your puppy with others of a similar age, then always choose puppies of a physical likeness to yours. Having your pup bowled over physically by a larger puppy puts them at risk of injury and is detrimental to their social learning.

It is also worth considering the **vaccination** status of the dogs and puppies. All should be at least a week clear of their final vaccination in the course.

I strongly recommend you socialise your puppy with other dogs prior to the end of the 12 week critical learning period. This is likely to mean your puppy won't be fully vaccinated so you should approach this with caution and only socialise with adult dogs who are up to date with their vaccinations and in environments of low risk. I have seen many puppies for behaviour who have missed the correct exposure during this important learning period. It is highly detrimental to their social ability and confidence to start socialising later in puppyhood.

NB: *Please be aware I live in a low infectious disease area where regular vaccination of puppies and adult dogs is the norm. There are areas within the UK and particularly internationally that may carry a higher risk and so as a result I have to advise that you contact your local veterinary surgeon for advice on this.*

Managing the Social Time

All handlers/owners should focus on staying in control of their own puppy. Control with the use of a lead is necessary and all parties should be aware that any training will be tested during this moment. Even the most well behaved puppy will become quickly distracted from its owner once fun and games begin!

Always make the walk progressive and never just stand still, this would create an unsettled energy and encourage the puppies to play in an unbalanced way.

The first part of the walk should focus on calming the puppy's initial excitement down. All puppies should stay on a lead. Once you are happily walking well you can then look to letting the puppies off one at a time, or not at all if you feel you will lose control.

Remember puppies don't have to be forced into 'making friends'. Your puppy may just be content to be in the company of other puppies but ignore their interactions, this is fine as every puppy is different.

Overly boisterous behaviour or consistent vocalisation is unbalancing and needs to be stopped. Put the offending puppy on a lead and walk in another direction until they calm down, then slowly re-introduce.

Your checklist of considerations for positive socialisation are:

- Make it positive through good management
- Self-control exercises should be considered – these are great for teaching manners

- Avoid or prevent all boisterous play, your puppy does not need to be 'taught lessons' by unbalanced dogs!
- Protect your puppy from boisterous play in interactions with other dogs
- Observe fear imprinting stage and socialise before the 12 week cut off
- Seek advice on the infectious disease risk in your area
- Manage all social experiences, never allow the puppies to set the energy level of play

Observation of Canine Communication – 'Hands Off and Observe'

I have seen owners interfere with canine behaviour far too often and create unbalance between dogs without even realising. With this in mind I would urge all new puppy owners to really observe the body language of their puppy and others. It is essential that vocal commands are kept to a minimum or not used at all when a 'meeting' between two dogs is taking place. Many flash points between dogs occur as a result of an anxious owner or a dog being affected by the negative and concerned energy an owner may be showing.

Hogan's holiday buddy, a young male Golden Retriever.

I appreciate that you will always be concerned for your puppy's welfare when you are out walking. However, you should just focus on keeping your puppy calm and manageable and working on a solid recall. Choose low populated areas to walk and ensure you are walking in such a way that you have a purpose. Never wander along or stay static as this will always create an intense situation.

Dogs communicate with their body language and if you stay calm and quiet during your observation you will feel energy changes and observe certain obvious behaviour indicators that mark an approaching dog's intentions.

The conversation is over and the dogs go their separate ways. A perfect social experience.

I advise all my owners to embrace this learning curve as much as they can and trust their gut instinct.

If you are uncomfortable with a dog's behaviour then you should address the situation in a confident manner. As previously stated, never pick your puppy up as you may make them more of a target for an assertive approaching dog. Just create some room by gradually moving away sideways and calling your puppy to you. Encouraging your puppy to remain calm is essential if you are to avoid another dog's negative attention.

I hope you never have to deal with a negative situation but you do need to be prepared. My 'pop up' umbrella was a regular sight when Hogan was very small as I felt this would give me a good means of deflecting an approaching dog's attention. It was easy to activate, simple and non-physical, Hogan could hide behind it while I dealt with the situation and it was obviously an essential item for our great British summers so never looked out of place! Nothing is without risk but being prepared is a necessity.

Task

Practise the training you have learnt throughout this book in open social spaces. Note down any problems and make sure you work within your puppy's ability to cope. If you are in a highly stimulated environment keep the sessions short and positive.

CHAPTER 22

Socialisation Part 2: Children and your Puppy

I took a long time to decide how best to approach this section of the Puppy Coach guidance. I was not overly comfortable with my children, niece and nephew being on camera when we produced the Puppy Coach films, but felt real life portrayal really was the only way to ensure a clear message is delivered in how to manage situations with children and puppies during the development of their relationship.

The fact remained that I have first-hand professional and personal experience of this subject which became the motivation to include a real-life perspective.

I am passionate that this section is understood on every level. As a result, I have addressed the subject in such a way that each and every reader can digest the positive and negatives of allowing dogs and children to grow together under one roof.

Children should be encouraged to help train the puppy and respect its personal space. Puppies should be taught personal space boundaries and self-control.

There should never be an occasion where both these young, developing individuals should be expected to clearly communicate with each other or respect values and needs. Guidance needs to be clear and consistent in order to avoid confrontational situations developing.

Dog Attack Statistics

The dog attack statistics involving children in the UK are at an all-time high and this knowledge serves as one of the motivators for this project. Evidence has been collected suggesting most attacks are on children under 5 years old and occur between 5–7 pm in the evening, the majority of which are preventable.

The early positive meeting we set up with our little boy and Hogan when he was just 4 weeks old has facilitated a relationship based on trust and respect from both parties.

This is not surprising given both parties are over tired and being fed at this time, it is also when parents will be most distracted. As a result, there will be many flash points, all of which can be avoided with knowledge and care.

This is why it is absolutely essential that dogs and children learn to respect and understand each other at a very early stage.

You do not need to make them best friends, you just need to encourage and develop a calm and controlled relationship based on kindness and understanding. This starts as soon as your puppy arrives home.

Understanding why Relationships Deteriorate

The areas for concern are as follows:

- Is a down time area in place?
- Does the child respect the down time place?
- Observe challenges around toys
- Does the dog respect the child's personal space?
- Social media – what influence does it have?
- Education – how much canine knowledge do you have?
- Positive socialisation for the puppy
- Adequate exercise
- Control of high energy in the home

Every relationship requires solid communication and respect if it is to flourish, the relationship between a child and their dog is no different.

It is dangerous to buy into the social opinion that a dog should accept a child and not react no matter what. This is unrealistic and will result in the failure of any relationship. It is a two-way street based on control from an attending adult and the recognition that dogs and children should never be left alone under any circumstances, no matter how tolerant the dog.

I have been privy to some serious, and on occasions, life changing incidents between dogs and children and in many cases most of these incidents could have been avoided.

The majority of injuries affect the face and hands, suggesting the child has been in too close a proximity to the dog. This is not to blame the child but merely to point out that a dog will generally avoid a bite if it is able to do so, but if backed into a corner, made to feel threatened or it has breached its coping ability, then a bite will be inevitable. This will be the dogs only means of communicating its discomfort.

The path of social media makes light of pictures of children laying all over a dog, videos of an energetic toddler bouncing on the back of extremely tolerant dog and dogs being goaded into high energy behaviour around a child, all because adults may find it cute or funny. For what gain? Attracting attention to their page and gaining popularity? To show what great dogs they have? Or just because they innocently don't realise the severity of what they may be doing to their dog?

I like to think it is the latter. That they are unaware of the potential severity of their actions, hence the detailed advice I provide. Understanding why it is not acceptable and providing knowledge on what the dog may be communicating will generate a different thought process and hopefully make people stop and think before picking up their camera.

Ultimately, mistakes are made on a daily basis. Building a solid and safe relationship is hard work and takes time.

There are important points to consider to make sure you never find your dog in a vulnerable position, or your child is injured by your dog or any other.

Teach your child to respect the dogs personal space. It is not enough just to check with an owner to ask whether their dog is comfortable with children when outside. When passing an unknown dog on a lead I generally encourage my children to leave them alone.

We have plenty of opportunities to socialise with dogs in our house but if you don't, it really is best that you try and get to know a friend or family members dog rather than allowing your child to approach a strange dog.

It is not acceptable to allow any dog to invade your child's space, lick them or jump up, no matter how nice they seem. These behaviours are unbalanced and should be prevented.

Every dog or puppy should have their own place to go to for some down time away from children and when they are there then they should be left alone. My own dogs spend a great deal of social time with our children but they are conditioned to their beds and so I instruct them to go there when I am distracted.

If other children visit, my dogs are removed to their down time space in my office for the short period they are present. It allows me to relax and avoids my dogs becoming the focus of entertainment. While no child ever means any harm and my dogs are generally safe, it only takes something minor to occur for a serious outcome to result.

Often toys can become a flash point as there may be confusion for the dog over what toys are theirs and what toys belong to children. Any object that gets human attention is high prize and so will interest the dog, unless you teach them otherwise.

This can become a battle of who has the most possessions if you are not careful. My advice is always to keep the dog's toys away and only bring them out for short periods of play and teach the dog not to steal the children's toys, as discussed in Chapter 13.

Always remember to exercise your puppy mentally and physically. This will mean you can comfortably remove them from contact with a child and not fall into the trap of letting them tire each other out, which won't work and will result in your puppy learning behaviours around your child that will be undesirable later on.

Many owners allow the puppy to spend more and more time in a child's social space the older they get and once toilet training is complete. This is the worst thing you can do when trying to create positivity and respect in their relationship. You have to empower your child and give your puppy time away.

Finally, poor social experiences around children is the number one reason for a dog reacting negatively towards a child. Work hard to make sure your puppy is able to get away if they feel threatened and pay attention to your puppy's body language when they are interacting. Remove your puppy if you see signs of stress.

Building a Positive Relationship

Give yourself a break! You will need to have time alone with your child and your puppy to ensure they are both kept entertained and focused. Use the time wisely and ideally involve the child in the puppy's exercise, feeding and training regime when they do come together.

This is my little girl at 2 years of age practising a calm 'down stay' with Marley.

In my consults I always find children are brilliant when I give them a little job to do. They generally find it exciting to watch their puppy do what they ask. When directed, children are very 'black and white' so the dog will recognise their communication quickly if its right.

Little and often is important as you never want them to be in each other's space without clear direction for too long. As long as the contact is positive and calm then things will progress well.

Considering the Autistic Child

I don't consider myself to be an expert on this subject but I have been privileged to work with a number of families who have acquired a dog to help a child with autism.

I am aware that the autistic spectrum is huge and so will only point out advice to provide a thought process on how to approach this successfully, rather than trying to give exact direction.

Many of the problems in families occur if the dog has been introduced too quickly. The child is encouraged to interact on an emotional level and often becomes frustrated as they haven't been able to develop the basics of a relationship first. Additionally, you will always have the initial hurdle of communication.

Autistic children are quite direct in their vocal and physical language which is generally well accepted by the dog as they don't process 'grey' areas or hesitation well. This can become tricky if the child is unpredictable in their interactions, so the dog needs to be encouraged in how to behave when this occurs. Having a positive relationship with a dog can really create an amazing experience for an autistic child, providing a distraction and new focus during periods of sensory overload and providing an avenue to create enough calm for the child to achieve an understanding of their environment.

However, it should be recognised that the dog requires support in this process as well. If high energy, physical situations do occur the dog needs to be trained to understand they must remove themselves, rather than become reactive or try and correct the child.

Dogs are generally very sensitive to human emotion and will always try and rectify unbalance in the only way they know how and this may be physical or vocal. Any anxiety in the dog will prevent them from reading situations well and they may begin to display behaviour concerns themselves in line with the child, rather than acting as a stabling influence.

With this in mind each puppy or dog needs to go through a slow integration process whereby the child is educated, empowered and encouraged to be involved in the dog's development in a positive way. The parents need to understand and recognise the dogs body language and stress indicators to ensure all interaction is positive and communication is developed with understanding.

Above all the dog will require a solid down time area where they are able to be left alone during this early integration period.

I have met many dogs who sleep with autistic children and have developed an amazing bond, but this is not something that just happens and in the majority of cases the result is the dog having to be re-homed resulting in absolute devastation for the child. This occurs as an ill prepared dog in close physical contact with a human is most likely to become confused or affected by unpredictable behaviour and so become reactive towards it.

As I say, I am not an expert in this field and my role is very much to support a family and educate them in ways to provide the dog with positive direction and build on the relationship safely, rather than to train the dog to be an assistance dog or offer help with the child. You should look to source a recognised reputable company for this.

There are a variety of helpful support agencies accessed online so it is worth researching this subject well if an assistance dog is something you have considered.

Setting the Boundaries

Setting boundaries between children and dogs is often almost impossible, but this level of training and understanding for both parties should be your focus and should be something you as an owner and parent take responsibility for.

A boundary can be set anywhere once your dog recognises the leadership skills you have read about in earlier chapters. This is down to an individual having a limit on what they are prepared to accept and in children this tolerance can be very low.

Wherever you set your boundary you should ensure you do so with clarity. If your puppy is creeping closer, even if they are in a 'down' position, you should still remove them to your threshold line.

If I put Hogan on a boundary line during his training I would stand in the doorway of the room and ask the children to police his behaviour! If he moved, they had to come and get me!

They loved to tell tales on the puppy! It was great learning for both them and Hogan and provided a fantastic opportunity for me to explain why and how boundaries were set for him and them!

Fun in the woods. Here are my intrepid explorers with their calm canine counterparts.

Making it Fun

My general attitude towards this relationship is serious and clear and I am aware it doesn't sound like either party will have much fun, but this is far from the case. I have two children who are empowered in their canine knowledge and recognise the dogs are not there for their entertainment.

They look out for their welfare, are careful they don't stand on them when playing around and will always alert me if they think one of the dogs need letting in or out from the garden.

They hang out with the dogs in many scenarios and love to play ball and have them join us on their weekend bike rides.

Our dogs are very much a healthy addition to the children's lives but this is never taken for granted. I will never over-look the fact that our dogs require understanding, direction and positivity in our relationship to remain successful in a domestic environment.

To add value to the fun in the relationship I teach the children to interact through games they understand. Using a bubble blowing machine is great for getting the kids excited, they love blowing the bubbles for the dogs to catch.

This allows the children to feel connected to Hogan and Marley through their own toys and provides a positive game for the dogs to associate with them. It also avoids interaction becoming physical and high energy.

Bubble blowing machine action!

Seek and find games are also excellent as they love to hide the objects and are always delighted when one of the dogs uses its nose to find them.

Involving Children in Training

The best time to build on the relationship between a child and the family dog is during every day activities such as feeding, walking, games and general obedience. Use this opportunity to watch their relationship develop, just make sure you are always present and the periods are kept short with minimal noise distraction.

My kids loved the 'wait' command as we used to practise this with Hogan and see who would move first! I always rewarded Hogan's down stay and released him so the children could compete with each other! The game 'dead lions' is one of my personal favourites, I think I get the most pleasure from this one!

The crate training was also made fun as they each chose to sit in it to get an idea what it was like for Hogan. Having this perception ensured they never bothered him in the crate, banged the crate door or stuck their fingers through the bars.

Whatever you choose to do, always adopt the same concept. Balance the puppy and calm them through short exercises or a series of commands after high energy interaction with children.

Your focus will be to restore balance and become the individual your puppy looks to for guidance. When children are present there will be lots of vocal noise which may be high pitched and excitable. If your puppy is used to following your body language cues and clear direction from you, they will learn to accept the behaviour of children as normal and not be reactive to their energy.

Follow this simple guidance during this process:

- Always structure a training session so you know how to approach it
- Give the child some clear responsibility
- Always manage the contact between the child and puppy
- Focus on teaching both parties 'wait' and recognising boundaries
- Make associations positive
- Periods of interaction should be short and positive
- Focus interaction on a toy not direct contact
- Point out to the child when and how they should stop play
- Direct the dog to its down time area once the interaction has finished

Task

Your task for this section is to establish a positive association with children for your puppy, using the training techniques and games I have advised.

If you don't have children at home you can still facilitate this learning outdoors in controlled circumstances, making sure you are the focus for reward when children are present.

CHAPTER 23

Socialisation Part 3: Visiting the Breeder, Interacting with the Mother and Livestock Training

Hogan had an amazing early start to his life and his breeder's home was an excellent environment to begin his early socialisation around cats, livestock, chickens and other dogs.

In this chapter we will look at my observations of Hogan when we paid a visit to his breeder and his mother. We also took the opportunity for some livestock interaction so will offer guidance on how to manage your puppy safely in a similar environment.

We will also look at using all the tools of control you have been developing since your puppy arrived with you so that you can manage them in every social environment you wish to enter.

During my search for a good breeder I had several important factors for consideration. My knowledge has taught me that a puppy's early social learning is immensely important for grounding a balanced dog so as you can imagine I was immensely happy to see the array of open space, wildlife, livestock and other resident animals all present at Derrie's home on my first visit. Knowing this would be giving him the very best start, I was respectful of the fact this placed me in a fortunate position.

Spending the time to plan for your puppy is always best practice, but if you have rescued or acquired your puppy from another source, they may not have had this exposure. That said it is still possible for you to actively put time aside to seek out these controlled situations as soon as your puppy arrives with you and I strongly advise that you do so.

Do Dogs Recognise their Parents?

The first scenario I wanted to observe was whether Hogan would remember his mum and vice versa. The dog's memory is not developed in the same way as ours.

It develops by a biochemical process known as imprinting which is stimulated by sight and smell and the first socialisation phase begins between 3 and 7 weeks, a time when most puppies are still firmly within their litter and with the mother.

Some observations have been carried out on this subject by other behaviourists, including Stephen Lindsay and Stanley Coren.

We should therefore consider that there will be an element of recognition between Hogan and his mother especially as he is re-visiting the environment of his birth and so will be exposed to many sights and smells all triggering this memory process.

During the observation of his behaviour I saw that a level of comfort and reduction in his normal exuberant greeting was evident. He was calm and respectful throughout. This was fitting with his mum's command of respect and general authority and so my opinion is that he definitely knew his place!

Whether he will retain this memory on subsequent visits remains to be seen but given it is sensory triggered my feeling is that he probably will.

Hogan and his mum Blossom October 2015.

Livestock Social Skills

Dogs are 'prey drive' or 'hunting' animals so they like to chase and many livestock animals will run. This is a recipe for disaster. To avoid this behaviour becoming a fun game with potentially disastrous consequences, you should associate all the self-control disciplines and obedience techniques in the presence of these gentle herd animals. This is known as 'impulse control' and is something we have visited in various capacities in earlier chapters.

There are some simple instructions to follow to ensure early social interactions with such animals go well.

NB: *Don't practise this exercise in the field – make sure you have a perimeter fence to work behind, cattle in particular can become challenging if threatened.*

Firstly, you are looking to inhibit your puppy's excitable response which will definitely occur if these animals move, especially if they spook at your presence.

- Have a lead attached at all times and don't be tempted to remove it too early
- Keep engaged with your puppy, using all the eye contact exercises you have been practising
- Make sure you have a positive motivator such as a toy, treats or be ready with calm praise
- Stand quietly and wait for your puppy to look at the livestock
- If your puppy reacts then put some more distance between you and the livestock
- If your puppy doesn't react then just wait until they look back at you and reward
- Repeat the process
- Add walking into the equation and walk the perimeter of the fence
- Use a long line to increase the distance between you and your puppy safely, repeating the reward for good behaviour
- Practise recalling your puppy away from the livestock using your reward
- Build on your control until you are confident your puppy is responding every time

This level of training in the first year really reinforces the power of positive and appropriate socialisation. It is all part of raising a non-reactive manageable dog in all scenarios, no matter what they experience in later life. Keep in mind that the earlier you expose your puppy under controlled conditions the more chance you have of creating a positive association.

We can further simplify the guidance in line with what you have already learnt:

- Ensure you have solid leadership and good communication
- Use a long line to avoid failure
- Keep the exposure short and positive
- Use high prize rewards but deliver calmly

Throughout this process I started with the use of a food reward to initially 'mark' the positive response but then switched to using my trigger word 'good' to reinforce my approval. Until you have control at this point you should never consider the response to be embedded.

If your puppy is displaying distress, is challenging or vocal then it is important that you slow the training down. Take your puppy away and find a safe coping distance where the reactivity can subside. Perform some simple obedience tasks, reward and finish the exposure. Repeat at a later interval and decrease the distance once your puppy is settling.

If they are reacting, then you are asking too much and you need to remove some of the pressure. Ignoring or being physically or verbally harsh will result in poor learning and is likely to give rise to more serious problems later on.

Finally, always remember your puppy will go through different fear phases and reproductive development so you will need to revisit this area of control periodically to see if the reactivity has changed.

Observation of Puppy Behaviour in the Presence of Balanced Adult Dogs

It is always interesting to observe a puppy's behaviour around other balanced adult dogs. I noticed when reintroducing Hogan to his mum at the age of 4 months he was both deferential and respectful.

Hogan is a particularly busy high energy puppy but I have worked tirelessly on his self-control and leadership. This means he has respect for personal space, isn't territorial and doesn't think that life revolves around him. He is a pleasure to take anywhere and accepted direction from Derrie's resident dogs without issue.

That said, I could not have predicted how this visit would go and if I'm honest part of me was concerned he would be over excited and difficult to keep focused. I think if he had visited dogs with a different energy then this could well have been the case, despite my hard work.

I have always stood by the fact that no human will ever communicate to a dog as well as another dog would and I feel that this was particularly evident here. Derrie's dogs are well exercised and have good manners and control. However, they are also well loved and so cope well with human emotion, plus the experience both dogs have in bringing up a litter for 8 weeks has provided them with a huge amount of tolerance and the ability to give clear and calm direction.

Why Socialise Your Puppy?

Puppies are not born with an understanding of human behaviour or the behaviour of other species. They begin to learn their own language as soon as they are born and so they will already have a means of communicating with other dogs before they arrive with you.

However, while dogs use the same platform of scent and body language to communicate, they still have to learn the variety of different signals dogs use in different circumstances to project their intentions.

They should learn early on to respect an individual's personal space and to recognise when another dog doesn't want to interact with them. For this reason, it is important that you expose your puppy to a variety of dogs in different social environments.

In doing so you will allow them to develop, mature and work out for themselves how well received they are.

During this early socialisation journey it is important to recognise that not all socialisation is good and you should never let another dog correct your puppy's overzealous behaviour. Not only are you setting your puppy up for failure you are also allowing another dog to become distressed and this may trigger a volatile situation.

You should take a sensible approach to your puppy's interaction with other dogs. Focus on keeping your puppy calm and teaching them self-control as I have directed throughout. A calm, balanced puppy will be much more amenable to an approaching dog.

Another piece of invaluable advice is to practise keeping all the attention on you in the presence of other dogs. I was always very strict with this. Hogan was never allowed to play while on the lead and all the rewards came from me. He didn't have free off lead time (without the long line) until I was ultra-confident his recall was perfect. Returning to me always resulted in a high prize food reward.

Although the long line remained attached, Hogan did have lots of free time. This is an important means of energy release. My walks were always progressive and other dogs and their owners joined me to avoid standing still and increasing the energy.

Finally, dogs have several stages in their development known as 'fear phases'. These will occur for isolated periods and your puppy will show caution to a variety of different objects and situations.

These periods are relevant during the following stages of development:

- 8–11 weeks
- 6–14 months

It is important that you **do not** respond to this overly cautious, or frightened behaviour with emotion and apply sympathy. Your puppy will need you to give guidance and be strong. Delivering a clear means of management and applying authority and leadership should be your goal.

These periods will not necessarily occur as detailed as they are dependent upon the puppy's learning and breeding so be prepared and have all your controls in place.

If you have spent time socialising your puppy with objects and other animal's they regularly see you may be shocked when they are suddenly frightened or show challenging behaviour. This will pass without concern if you have addressed the social exposure well. However, new associations during this time could link your puppy's early learning to a negative experience and you may find their negativity continues as a learnt behaviour despite the passing of the fear phase.

Task

Your task for this section is to source two avenues to socialise your puppy independently, taking note of their responses and whether you have had to step in to remove them.

Remember high energy play with another dog should be short lived and you should feel totally in control if you are to allow it.

CHAPTER 24

Socialisation Part 4: Interacting with Horses

Horses are popular animals and many puppies will come into contact with one at some stage in their life. It is far better to have managed the first meeting in a controlled way with training and education in mind, rather than leaving the initial introduction to chance.

Similar to livestock, horses are flight animals and are prone to making sudden movements which could trigger your puppy's natural chase or prey drive instinct. You should teach your puppy self-control exercises such as, loose lead walking and distance 'sit', 'stays'.

I spent alot of time teaching my puppy valuable self-control around my horse George. It has provided the basis for a positive relationship to develop.

To achieve this, you should follow these points:

- Set your puppy up to succeed by controlling any excitable behaviour
- Give calm, clear direction at a safe distance
- Use your trigger word – 'Good' – to reinforce calm behaviour
- Remind the puppy how you expect them to behave by using simple obedience commands
- Remove your puppy further away if they are showing any stress indicators

If it is not possible for you to socialise your puppy safely in the presence of horses or livestock you can still work on your puppy's self-control around other strong triggers such as, people running or cycling, fast traffic or children playing. All will add a level of energy to the environment that will excite or frighten your puppy allowing you an opportunity to offer support and guidance.

Avoid attempts to make the experience 'fun'. I purposefully kept my body language calm. If Hogan was a little over stimulated I threw a toy away from George to provide him with an avenue to let off some anxiety, without it being focused on George.

The early learning we practised meant the game became focused on me. George soon became irrelevant. Whenever you practise this element of your puppy's training ensure you do so safely and with full physical control.

If your puppy displays negative behaviour during the training this is their way of communicating the failure of their ability to cope. You should recognise it as such rather than thinking the dog is just choosing to be badly behaved.

Many behaviours can be attributed to stress signals for this reason. These will be displayed in the following ways:

- Vocalisation
- Running away (flight)
- Lunging (fight)
- Avoidance
- Panting
- Shaking
- Aggression (fight)
- Urination/defaecation

These stress signals are significant and could mark the start of an anxiety response. If you see this situation developing take your puppy's social exposure much slower, begin by putting some distance between your puppy and the trigger. In this instance, the horse.

Once calmness is restored you should reward your puppy and slowly approach again. Never push your puppy to the point of reactivity, this is detrimental to their learning and your relationship.

Building Lifestyle Behaviours

Horses are a prominent part of my life and so any dog sharing this with me has to be able to respect my control and authority and not succumb to fear, panic or instinctive behaviours.

Here Hogan is training to walk out with my horse George.

I took a very calm and consistent approach to socialising George and Hogan. I witnessed some occasional 'jumping up' behaviour signifying Hogan's concern and insecurities.

This shot was taken during the filming of the PuppyCoach.com videos.
A calm, quiet moment of bonding between George and Hogan.

As a result of the solid leadership I have in place in all areas of our lives he looks to me for the guidance to help him cope. If negative behaviour occurs you should always avoid engaging, or giving support until a calmer energy is delivered.

As I write Hogan is approaching his first birthday. He is a strong dog who is balanced, educated and sociable. However, he has started to find his time with George exciting as it is now attached to lovely runs through field's. This has brought with it new challenges as his excitement has opened up some vocalisation and high energy at the start of the ride.

Although frustrating given the level of work he has had, I totally understand why it is occurring and have begun to take things much slower. This means he has to be in a 'sit-stay' while I mount and if he breaks it then I get off and replace him. He then has to 'heel' as we set off. It's hard work and repetitive but we are making good progress, certainly enough for me to be confident he is calming down.

No dog will make things easy for you even if you are an experienced dog handler. You will never be alone when facing problems.

Whenever you are entering any social environment with horses you must ensure you have full control of your puppy at all times. Horses are highly unpredictable and if they are being ridden then your noisy puppy could create a catastrophic consequence for a rider.

Never test your puppy's recall around horses without prior consent from the horse's owner. Aside from causing injury to a human, horses commonly injure themselves charging around fields. If your puppy spooks a horse or pony in any situation accidents and injury are likely.

Conducted effectively you will start to see how your early work around eye contact and leadership has set your puppy up to accept positive socialisation. Hogan naturally engages with me to receive support and direction allowing me the opportunity to make the whole experience positive.

Task

Your task for this section is to set up this form of socialisation.

If you don't have safe access to horses or livestock then you should work your puppy around wildlife or high energy situations such as lots of dogs playing, footballs being kicked.

CHAPTER 25

Observing a Live Puppy Consult: Part 1

I am aware that my training with Hogan wasn't completely perfect, family life often makes things challenging and this has to be accepted. However, I did feel that I had focused heavily on all the guidance I have delivered in this book, plus I had a great start and a very balanced puppy to work with.

As a result, I have a lovely, respectful dog. It would be naive of me to consider that all puppies are the same, especially as I have Marley to provide me with a contrast!

You may be stumbling across issues I haven't experienced with Hogan so I have also included a case study. Nick, Kerry and their three young children were about to collect their puppy Rottweiler 'Willis' when I met them. They have a busy work and social life and provided a perfect real-life opportunity to document the issues faced by a family when introducing and raising a powerful dog.

The family had owned a Rottweiler and other dogs before, Kerry is based from home and they had the time, knowledge and ability to integrate and educate a new puppy. Filming one of my puppy consultations provided an enlightening view of owner interpretation and behaviour and more importantly for me to reflect on my approach and observations as I guided this family through the early months of their puppy's development.

The Assessment

Before I began assessing Willis it was important to understand life with a new puppy from the owner's perspective. Just because I may perceive a potential problem, it doesn't necessarily mean an owner would agree.

Meet Willis

'Willis' the Rottweiler who began his journey with Puppy Coach at just 10 weeks of age.

You should always observe your puppy's character. Watch their behaviour in particular social environments and how they respond to your guidance. It is always good to imagine your puppy performing the behaviour once they are a fully grown adult dog. You will see many situations where puppy behaviour isn't acceptable in the adult dog and more worryingly it could be deemed dangerous.

I would be assisting Willis with his owners and offering support for them as they raise and educate him. For this to be successful they need to recognise areas of concern and also take note of positive progress. Listening to their comments would provide me with a starting point to advise them.

My questioning resulted in some key issues being raised over a number of areas. We will address these individually during this chapter.

My physical assessment of Willis covers a variety of different aspects of his character, personality, confidence, level of understanding of his role and what communicators he uses and understands. It also considers his breed character traits, determination and whether any anxiety related behaviours are present.

This is a comprehensive evaluation that provides me with a solid understanding of how to manage him effectively and offer guidance to his owners of what they may expect of him as he develops.

There is a serious side to working with dogs and always the potential for mistakes to be made. It is important that I look for potential flashpoint areas and make sure Willis isn't resorting to a high energy response to make himself understood, especially as there are children in the house.

1. My arrival

Willis was already conditioned to the utility area of the house prior to my first visit. He was comfortable in there and recognised it as his 'down time area'. I asked Kerry to place him in there a few minutes prior to my arrival so that I could assess his ability to cope when new people entered the house.

It was immediately apparent that he found the lack of integration and attention from me upon my arrival distressing. He initially reacted to the front door and didn't easily settle even after I had entered the house. He spent a great deal of time vocalising, predominantly whining, during the early part of my visit as he wasn't used to being removed from the front door during a guest arrival.

Kerry and Nick allowed Willis to integrate with guests soon after their arrival. This had become a habit and therefore something he would expect to do. However, not all guests would appreciate being welcomed by a 50kg Rottweiler as he developed. Inconsistencies in human behaviour create confusion and anxiety in the dog.

The front door is also an extremely high energy area in most homes and could trigger reactive responses in your puppy.

Willis had an expectation, this was to take an active role around the front door. This behaviour was already beginning to be embedded. It was evident that changing this dynamic had caused some anxiety and this would need to be addressed.

The entrance to your home is an extremely unpredictable area for the dog and allowing free access to it leaves them vulnerable to failure. It isn't advisable for any breed but especially one with guard dog instincts.

2. Stranger Approach

My approach to the utility room resulted in him jumping up at the gate. If he were an adult dog this would put him at eye level with most people and so should be discouraged. It did however reinforce that Willis was a happy, confident little puppy, keen to be involved and behaving completely normally.

Instead of continuing my approach, I just took a step back and didn't engage with him in any way. As soon as all four paws touched the ground I continued towards him and opened the gate. Acceptance is a high reward for such a social animal and so attention should be managed and controlled as any high prize resource would be.

Willis showed no overly dominant behaviour traits, nor was he submissive. Some puppies are prone to displaying overly submissive behaviours, particularly if they become excited in anticipation of human greeting. This should be discouraged and is simply done by moving away and retracting the attention. I would approach a puppy from the side and crouch down quietly if this was evident.

Willis tolerated human touch and handling well, he allowed me to pick up his paws and let me look in his mouth and ears. This level of interaction from a stranger should to be rewarded and as a result he received a food reward and praise.

Prolonged interaction triggered some excitable behaviour and so Willis was then left alone to calm for a few minutes before he was invited out into the garden.

You should always avoid engaging with a puppy during an excitable phase, often this allows high level, unbalanced behaviours to be reinforced and sends the puppy the wrong message regarding appropriate behaviour during socialisation.

While the confident behaviour Willis displayed was encouraging it also raised the importance of ensuring he was well managed and followed leadership from the family. Allowing a confident dog of this breed and nature to take an empowered role in a domestic home would not be conducive to a happy dog-owner relationship.

3. Boundaries and Territory

Kerry highlighted that she didn't want Willis free roaming in some areas of the garden. In order to build on this understanding it would be necessary to show Willis where he can go and correct him using a lead and simple hand signals followed by a reward when he remains in the correct place.

I am a huge advocate of controlling the puppy in an enclosed outdoor shared space, free running should be encouraged on walks and not around human social spaces. Teaching Willis a level of calm in this space is important for his safe management around the children.

4. Toilet training

Toilet training was going well for Kerry. Willis was already aware of toileting outside. The 'down time' area had facilitated this learning. Kerry had chosen not to use newspaper and instead was working hard to take Willis outdoors regularly and at key times.

The family had allocated him a 'dog toileting area' separate from the garden but conditioning him to this area was proving tricky. I reassured them that this would take time as they would have to build a solid association, plus Willis wouldn't have full conscious control over his bladder and colon until 14–16 weeks. In this situation they just need to keep doing what they are doing and be patient. The foundations are being laid so hard wiring of the behaviour will follow with repetition.

5. Coprophagia (eating his own faeces)

This is a common problem and can be motivated by a variety of different factors. In a young puppy you should prevent this act by being strict with the removal of the faeces.

This is straightforward to do with a puppy, you should be with them to reward positive toilet training and can therefore remove the faeces immediately. If, like Kerry, you can't always be there then make sure you never tell them off. Just focus on preventing a habit forming as much as you can.

Understanding and addressing the reasons for Coprophagia will provide you with a checklist of things to rule out before resigning yourself to prevention, as follows:

- Dietary deficiency
- Digestive enzyme deficiency
- Curiosity
- Copying another dog
- Negative management (telling the puppy off if it soils in your home)

Most of the above are easily dealt with by ensuring you manage your own behaviour in response to your puppy. Provide them with adequate mental and physical stimulation, feed a balanced diet and rule out digestive problems. If the behaviour continues to be persistent then you should contact an appropriately qualified behaviourist to help you with a treatment program to break the habit. This should be bespoke to your dog.

6. Outdoor Socialisation

One of the challenges Kerry faced on a daily basis was taking Willis on the school run. Her motivation for this was not only to avoid leaving him alone first thing in the morning but also to address some of his socialisation around people and in particular children.

Managing these two adolescent males in a public environment was challenging, even for me.

Managing the school run, as Kerry was to find out, is way too challenging for both you and your puppy. You will be distracted and your puppy will not receive the correct exposure. If you have someone to manage the children and you can observe your puppy's behaviour then it is achievable, otherwise my advice is to avoid this experience and look elsewhere to address your check list of social exposure situations. Taking this important part of your puppy's development in small stages is necessary if you are to ensure it remains positive.

7. Feeding

Although Willis was being fed dry food, I advised on the variety of dog food choices and research into canine nutrition so Kerry was informed. Kerry stated that Willis didn't always eat his food and asked how long she should leave it in place for as she had read that it should be removed after 10 minutes.

This is something all owners need to be aware of. It is not acceptable to leave food down for your puppy for any length of time. Food is your most valuable resource and allows you a direct level of control and ability to train your puppy. Losing control over this is not an option.

The food should be delivered in a consistent manner and if the puppy chooses to walk away then the food is removed until the next mealtime. If the puppy is very young (less than 4.5 months) then repeat the regime after a couple of hours.

If you are leaving food down, then this may contribute to the development of the following problems:

- A lack of human control
- Grazing behaviours to develop
- Poor weight control
- Encourages resource guarding behaviours
- Poor feeding habits

Nutrition is a complex subject and is dealt with in greater depth in Chapter 10. If you have serious concerns regarding your puppy's feeding habits or weight you should seek veterinary advice.

8. Play

Kerry needed solid and clear advice around introducing play with Willis as this can be tricky with children in the house.

Toys are seen by the dog as possessions and the more attention a possession gets the more the dog will want it. This is the reason many children's toys end up being stolen or destroyed by a dog and the behaviour nearly always begins to be a problem when the dog is still a puppy.

Also, if the children only interact with the puppy physically the play would become extremely unbalanced and potentially dangerous within a short space of time. Mouthing behaviour can very quickly escalate to biting if the puppy only learns to play physically with an individual and the play is focused on direct contact rather than on a specific toy.

Puppies play using their mouths and teeth unless they learn otherwise. You should be cautious with this level of interaction and educate children to control their own energy ensuring they get the best behaviour from their puppy and avoid painful nips.

I always manage the interaction safely and positively, encouraging children to focus on an object through play rather than using their hands. Teaching them to "stand tall and quiet, like a tree" if the puppy becomes challenging is a great way of calming a situation down and empowering the child.

I also teach them to understand that loud vocal noise and running away will encourage the puppy to chase. Learning a more effective means of distracting the puppy onto something positive such as a toy can provide a child with a confident means of interacting with their puppy safely.

I have had some amazing consultations with children and find they do well with responsibility and education. They need as much guidance as your puppy if they are to learn respect for the canine species.

Kerry and Nick's children embraced everything I did with them and enjoyed having their moment with Willis.

Whenever children are present you will need to work on your controlled exposure, little and often to build on your puppy's tolerance of high energy social environments. Begin with lead control, your puppy should be at a distance where they are calm. Move on by encouraging them to 'stay' while you interact with your child.

Encouraging play to be focused on a toy provides an avenue for owner control and avoids mouth to skin contact. This training pattern carried on as Willis developed into adolescence.

Remember to reward good behaviour often, keep sessions short and only replace your puppy twice. If they move a third time, then you should remove them to their area or a quieter place to calm down.

Ensuring you are present and under control during these social periods is achieved with the attachment of a flat collar and plain lead. This is especially relevant when dealing with food.

Kerry displaying calm control during lead attachment.

9. Health Check

After handling Willis briefly during my assessment I asked Kerry if she had focused on any handling exercises to prepare Willis for a veterinary visit. This wasn't something she had considered at this point as he had only been with her a short while.

As a result, I chose to postpone Willis's actual health check until my follow up visit. I asked Kerry to prepare him for this first by allowing him to receive positive rewards from her during handling. This would mean he would cope much better with me.

Her instructions were to leave his collar and lead in place and encourage him to focus on an object or food reward while she gently felt all over his body, picked up each paw, and looked under his tail. Periodically she delivered a treat reward before continuing onto the next stage. Care was taken around his head as I instructed her to look in his eyes, ears and lift his lips to check his mouth.

The mouth may be particularly tricky at this time as teething creates sensitivity and pain. You may find your puppy is intolerant of facial handling so take this process slowly.

This is such an important part of your puppy's learning if they are to tolerate a veterinary visit, ensure you put time aside for this training.

The process should be performed as calmly and slowly as possible with a huge emphasis on positive reinforcement. It is useful if someone else is available to help you, especially if you have a lively puppy. Ideally make sure they have had some physical exercise before you start and choose a time when your puppy is naturally calmer.

This preparation facilitated a positive response when I re-visited and Willis was accepting of handling, albeit a little wiggly as you would expect.

10.   Lead Attachment and Control

Finally, during the outdoor observation Kerry informed me that she had some problems managing Willis on the lead. The lead is your direct link to your puppy so take time establishing this invaluable piece of equipment positively.

Willis was routinely picking the lead up in his mouth. This can be seen as amusing when a cute puppy appears to want to take itself for a walk. However, I have treated many adult dogs displaying severe lead aggression as this learnt behaviour becomes motivated by anxiety. If this occurs, use immediate distraction and reward when it is dropped. Do not create tension on the lead or you will set up a challenge.

Your touch on the lead needs to be light and positive but also assertive and your puppy needs to see this as a means of following guidance rather than something they need to get away from. (Chapter 15 deals with this subject in more depth.)

Task

Your task for this section is to find another dog to observe. If possible discuss with the owner how the dog was during the puppy period and what behaviours they displayed. Ask if any of those behaviours are still evident now and if they are problem.

Try to recognise where you may be rewarding behaviours that could become undesirable. Put in place changes to correct them. It is useful to document your observations.

CHAPTER 26

Observing a Live Puppy Consult: Part 2

My return visit to Willis and his family took place 4 weeks later. In my first visit I requested that his owners put in place all of the direction you have been following throughout this book. I also provided them with the knowledge and physical tools to set leadership in place, enabling them to provide social guidance to Willis as he integrated into the family.

I wanted to document their progress during his development through puppyhood. I also wanted to involve the rest of the family in his training and understand from their perspective if the arrival of this new addition had changed the social dynamics.

In this chapter we will look at family relationships and the effects of human emotion on the dog, highlighting areas of concern and recognising why some dogs fail to behave in a positive way during human social interaction.

Kerry had described some problems she was facing with Willis such as stealing, vocalisation and pulling on the lead. Although these are common and fit with his current life stage there are many contributory factors she will need to be aware of and manage as he develops if she is to avoid negative learning.

While certain behaviours are expected and associated with the puppy period, I often find a client's expectation is that they should grow out of these behaviours early on. The trigger for poor behaviours such as chewing, jumping up, physical challenges and resource guarding may have a number of affecting factors and invariably the behaviour continues to deteriorate rather than improve with age.

Before assuming the behaviour is a 'problem', you should consider ruling out the following factors:

- Teething
- Pain
- Anxiety
- Food intolerances
- Medical conditions
- Leadership challenges
- Testosterone flooding

As your puppy develops and becomes more settled in your environment it will be straightforward to isolate the presence of any of the above.

Improvements

I was pleasantly surprised to see the doorway routine was established and Willis was calm and relaxed when I arrived at Kerry and Nick's home. Willis was able to see the comings and goings but was kept behind a baby gate in the utility room. The 'down time' area was definitely viewed as his positive place to be and he was accepting of his solitary time.

Kerry had been working hard on the social aspect of her relationship with Willis but was starting to feel a little overwhelmed with the responsibility of managing the children alongside this rapidly growing puppy.

This was to be expected and a short conversation with her husband Nick revealed that he was at work all day so Kerry had taken on most of the training herself. He wanted to help but didn't feel he could offer Willis the same level of direction and knowledge Kerry delivered given he was out of the house.

This is normal for most households as you generally find one individual will do most of the primary care for the dog. However, the dog responds socially to a clear hierarchy so it is important all individuals share the responsibility of leadership regardless. This can be achieved even if one family member is away from home more than another.

The dog will adapt to different personalities providing the same level of leadership is maintained so it was important to ensure Nick felt he could still be effective in managing Willis even though he didn't have the same amount of physical time available to be with him.

The dog retains primitive instincts so I advised Nick to focus his attention on maintaining control of Willis around resources that are important for survival: food, territory, possessions and attention. We also highlighted areas where Nick could reinforce the importance of Kerry and the children by ensuring he interacted with them first when he arrived home, before engaging with Willis.

We discussed how Nick could allocate time to spend with Willis, ensuring quality interaction rather than leaving it to chance and allowing Willis opportunities to fight for his attention at inappropriate times.

Leadership can even be applied in play as Kerry demonstrates with control of the toy around Willis.

A rota to document detail on your puppy's management is a really effective means of ensuring everyone who enjoys spending time with the puppy is able to deliver a valuable means of positive social interaction.

Your Puppy Rota Example

This also helps structure your puppy's day and ensures they are fed and walked appropriately.

	Monday (example)	Tuesday	Wednesday	Thursday	Friday	Saturday	Sunday
AM Toilet	Garden: urine						
AM Feed	Eaten all						
AM Walk	Met 2 other dogs, all OK						
AM Toilet	Garden: urine and faeces						
AM Training	Retrieve game						
AM Play	Ball						
Noon Toilet	Garden: urine						
Noon Play/Walk	Practised recall						
Noon Feed	Ate all						
PM Walk	Traffic socialisation						
PM Play	5 mins with rope toy						
PM Toilet	Garden: urine and faeces						
PM Feed	Ate all						
PM Toilet / Bed	Urine and faeces						

Taking a Look at Resources

Kerry reported that she had a problem with Willis stealing the children's toys and items of clothing. Often this begins as simple curiosity and interest in an object. An owner subsequently reacts at a high level to prevent the contact and this has the adverse effect of raising the items importance and making it more interesting.

Fast forward a few days and several objects later and very quickly you find your puppy is seeking out objects to steal, firstly to raise a response and secondly to set up a game or challenge. This behaviour inevitably means the puppy is the centre of attention and inappropriate behaviour begins to become habitual.

This is a situation that rapidly escalates into the puppy learning to swallow said object to avoid conflict, hiding, chasing or becoming defensive. All undesirable behaviours that should be discouraged.

A resource is the term given to anything the dog perceives as high prize. If you just apply some logic to most canine behaviour problems, you can solve them simply by doing the opposite to your instinctive response.

This flow chart highlights the progression and development of a common behaviour problem:

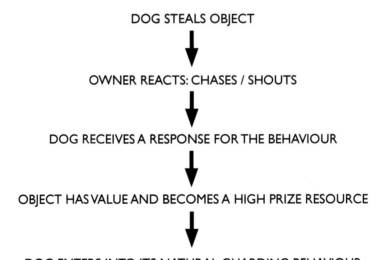

DOG STEALS OBJECT

↓

OWNER REACTS: CHASES / SHOUTS

↓

DOG RECEIVES A RESPONSE FOR THE BEHAVIOUR

↓

OBJECT HAS VALUE AND BECOMES A HIGH PRIZE RESOURCE

↓

**DOG ENTERS INTO ITS NATURAL GUARDING BEHAVIOUR
IN DEFENCE OF OBJECT LEADING TO POOR BEHAVIOUR DEVELOPING
AND BEING REWARDED**

AGGRESSION / SWALLOWING / HIDING / CHASING

Instead of reacting negatively to your puppy you should either use distraction such as creating high energy elsewhere away from the object or encourage the puppy to bring the object to you and trade for something much more exciting. Either way, you are looking at maintaining a positive approach.

Remember your puppy is a little sponge and it is easy to embed the correct responses if you consider the outcome early enough. Dogs are not born to behave badly, they are just dogs and will display dog behaviour so we should recognise their instinctive communication and use it to our advantage by re-enforcing it in the correct way. Teaching your puppy to retrieve an object to you and return it was discussed in more detail in Chapter 13.

Family Dynamics and Emotional Relationships

Integrating a dog into a family environment can be one of the most enjoyable things you will ever do. Getting it right is hard work and if it goes wrong it can do so with catastrophic consequences.

I spend a great deal of time rehabilitating dogs who have just innocently developed the wrong understanding of social situations. Either through negative experiences, poor or insufficient socialisation or a lack of leadership and solid communication.

To ensure Kerry, Nick and the family wouldn't run into problems it was important that they viewed Willis from a dog's perspective rather than applying human emotion to his behaviour.

I recognise, the longer these problems develop the more they become led by anxiety and stress in both the dog and owner and the more volatile a problem becomes. Owner understanding is invaluable if they are to have an awareness of problems early.

I have spent my life working with dogs. My academic pathway and opinions of others has facilitated my professional career but I attribute much of my learning to just being around dogs in different capacities. I came to recognise early on that I could control a dogs behaviour merely by controlling the level of energy I used when interacting with them.

You can do a simple experiment at home with your puppy to understand this, as follows.

Understanding how to communicate with dogs from a young age
facilitates the human-canine relationship and bond.

Energy Experiment

I designed this experiment to help clients understand their puppy and learn
ways to communicate. As a result of the research I developed during my
master's degree.

My study involved observing dogs with and without human guidance
during the entry of a guest to their home. The results were conclusive that
dogs coped in social environments regardless of their background providing
human guidance was delivered prior to the event. Without this guidance all of
the dogs displayed stress indicators and general discomfort for the duration
of the observation.

Attach a lead to your puppy's collar, stand in a room with your puppy with
the doors closed, stay still, fold your arms and stay quiet, observe how you can
create calm in your puppy with your energy.

Follow this with a period of rapid high energy, jumping, clapping, running around, don't direct this at your puppy just do it in the same room, observe your puppy's response.

Finally, stop and repeat step 2. Your puppy is likely to have entered into the same energy level as you and immediately responded with an interest.

You can now repeat the exercise, but before starting place your dog quietly on their bed and repeat if they move during any of the exercise. When you replace them do so calmly and with no voice, just use a lead to direct them.

Your aim is to provide some direction and create an invisible boundary between your behaviour and the puppy's personal space. The ability to direct your dog in this way is the difference between educating a balanced social animal or an interactive nuisance who is persistently banished to their down time area.

Dogs are totally receptive and reactive to the energy around them, your touch, vocal tones, body language and environmental stimulation.

These will all affect their ability to learn and develop. If you are really struggling to integrate your puppy, you should slow the process down and address one social area at a time.

If you have lots of children set them up individually to take responsibility for the puppy, rather than allowing high level interaction all at once which will create an undesirable learning experience for them all.

Separation Anxiety/Over-Bonding

Kerry and Nick reported that Willis was content to stay in his 'down time' area when requested to do so, but they had noticed during busy times (getting ready in the mornings), he was persistently vocal and this could be extreme. He was often whining and jumping up and chewing, indicative of a stress related response.

This reinforces how susceptible the dog is to environmental energy, but it was important for the family to understand how to help Willis cope during these times.

In this instance Willis was being reactive to the social environment, but this behaviour can be common in a puppy suffering from separation anxiety and/or over-bonding. These terms are confusing and both can be tricky to deal with. True separation anxiety cases are problematic and my clients require a high level of support.

So let's put things in perspective and understand how such a behaviour problem develops.

Ultimately a puppy is born into a world where the expectation is to remain within a consistent social hierarchy within a group. Dogs work well in this way and this is the primary reason for the need to engage with your puppy with leadership and direction.

However, solitary time is not something they find easy to accept and certainly not on the scale that today's social culture with dogs dictates.

While I routinely tell clients they should comfortably be able to leave the adult dog for around 4 hours, I often find I'm reeling with discomfort at the thought of educating on this level of solitary confinement. It doesn't sit well with me but unfortunately its very much a rock and a hard place problem. If guidance isn't given the dog may be left much longer or a client becomes stressed and returns early displaying an emotional response of guilt, which is also detrimental to the dog!

To address this social problem, it is absolutely essential that you begin to train your puppy to accept solitary time as soon as you bring them home. Crate training was discussed in detail in Chapter 8 and this is something that will facilitate a positive experience if you set it up correctly.

Your goal is to ensure your puppy doesn't leave the comfort and security of the litter and immediately transfer the same level of physical contact to you. You are not the mother or sibling and your puppy needs to learn from you how human beings behave. Likewise, nor should you put your puppy through a sudden detachment and expect them to cope on their own from the first evening. I make the transition very slow, structured and firm.

Your puppy should spend clear quality time bonding with you, but they should also be put into the crate and conditioned to this area at key times when you are still present in the home. Don't make the mistake of only using it when you go out or overnight.

Some puppies are tough and not at all needy but you won't necessarily know the character of your puppy for a while so be cautious and do the training well.

Your aim is to establish contact on your terms and build on your puppy's confidence levels at being left while also creating a trusting relationship that shows your puppy you are still around and will return regularly.

Transition Periods

Don't allow your puppy to constantly follow you around the house and encourage them to tolerate the odd door being closed. You need to imagine you have left the house around 10-15 minutes before you actually remove yourself from your puppy. Whether this is to go to bed or leave.

This is important as it helps dissociate you and your puppy prior to the leaving experience. During this 10-15-minute period your puppy should be placed in their area.

You should use this time to gradually detach yourself while you prepare to leave. Do not engage vocally with your puppy during this time and ignore any attention seeking behaviour.

Why does it occur?

If you have ever had a busy house and then everybody leaves at once you will feel the silence immediately and begin to appreciate how this may feel to your puppy, who is a highly social animal.

The loss of social energy can be catastrophic for a puppy who would normally be the centre of attention.

The resulting behaviour quickly escalates from sudden detachment, to feelings of abandonment, to panic and subsequent survival behaviours. For a puppy locked in a home the behaviours can range from vocalisation and chewing to complete destruction, self-harm, urination and defaecation.

Your puppy has now become a chemical reaction focused solely on getting back the level of contact they had before you walked out. The longer this goes on the more conditioned the puppy becomes to its feeling of panic when you leave, they begin to learn your associated behaviours and start their poor behaviour earlier.

Treatment

Treating such cases is hard at best and at worst can be life changing for some owners. Often the emotional bond that triggered the problem becomes so embedded in both the owner and dog it is impossible to rectify.

Hopefully this will give you as a new puppy owner the motivation to put the difficult and sometimes emotionally challenging work in early to avoid ever being in this position. After all, prevention is better than cure.

Fortunately for Kerry and Nick they had gone through a detailed detachment program and Willis was comfortable with his solitary time, this meant I could focus on the problem from a different angle.

As soon as Kerry took the children upstairs for a bath Willis would begin whining. I asked her to quietly return to him, walk firmly into the utility, place him back on his bed, show him the flat palm of her hand and then quietly leave. She should repeat this 3 times and if it continued she should close the utility room door in front of the gate.

Willis was quiet after 2 bed commands so it was never necessary to close the door. This is obviously highly dependent on your puppy's social understanding and what works for one will not necessarily work for all. In this instance Willis just needed a bit of help to achieve some self-control when the energy of the house was taken away from him. This focused on re-assurance from his owner as she delivered the usual basic self-control command before retreating.

It is important that you recognise this behaviour as a failure of your puppy's ability to cope. Not as poor behaviour requiring a consequence. This would be an inappropriate response and is likely to make the problem worse. Seek professional help if your puppy remains in an anxious reactive state despite calm consistent control and leadership.

Maintaining a Boundary

The final point Kerry raised was how to integrate Willis into their living room of an evening. I refer to this area as 'prime living space'. This means it is an area where the family relax socially and it will be considered a high prize area for Willis.

As the children play here it is important that Willis is controlled and sees his presence as a privilege, not a right.

With this in mind I showed Kerry and Nick how to safely integrate Willis and used the following direction:

- Attach a collar and lead to your puppy
- Place a mat or bed in the living room (in a corner or at least out of the doorway)
- Walk your puppy to the doorway/entrance to the room and use the flat palm of your hand to signal stop

- Once your puppy is calm, direct them into the room and onto the bed
- Stand quietly while they settle on the bed
- Drop the lead and walk away once your puppy has relaxed
- Use a distraction such as a kong toy stuffed with something tasty when you begin this process
- If your puppy moves just replace them (no more than twice)
- If they move a third time just take them back to their down time area for a few minutes
- Repeat until your puppy settles for around 15-20 minutes
- Build on this time until your puppy is entering calmly

As your puppy's behaviour improves there is a temptation to drop boundaries and allow more freedom around resources (territory, attention, food and possessions). Especially once the toilet training is under control. Following this temptation will result in a reduction in your ability to lead and guide the puppy and an increase in the potential for negative behaviours to develop through adolescence. You should view the early puppy period as a practise run for adolescence. You will need to ramp up your control during the next stage of your puppy's development, sexual maturity can bring a variety of new challenges.

Dogs are opportunists and will always attempt to take a more established position in the home if the opportunity arises. Be aware of this and ensure your puppy is still working with your guidance during close contact time.

Task

Your task for this section is to practise some detachment exercises to test if your puppy is able to cope with all areas of owner detachment, note the response from your puppy to the following:

- Walk out of the room and close the door on your puppy
- Place your puppy in its down time area and close the gate/door
- Place your puppy on its bed and sit somewhere else in the same room
- Walk out of the front door, close it and walk straight back in
- Walk out of the front door and listen before returning

You should be calmly greeted with a wagging tail. If your puppy is displaying stress indicators or is hyper-excitable on your return you will need to re-visit this area of their learning.

CHAPTER 27

Positively Associating Home Appliances

Surprisingly, one of the common problems I am called out by clients to address is high level reactivity towards a variety of household appliances.

This may manifest itself in different ways from fearful/avoidance-type behaviour to vocalisation and aggression. All behaviours are motivated by the same trigger – anxiety. This is usually as a result of fear, insecurity or poor early learning.

Either way, having a puppy or adult dog displaying poor behaviour when you are trying to vacuum or stack the dishwasher is at best irritating and at worst dangerous.

Several of my clients have reported sustaining bites to their hands or legs as a result of trying to remove their dog and get on with their chores. This is not acceptable and it certainly isn't something an owner needs to put up with or make allowances for.

Problems occur early on in the puppy's development. Many owners do not perceive a problem when a cute puppy is barking at, or running away from a vacuum cleaner. Moreover, it is often considered funny to begin with. This emotional reaction from a human will highlight the behaviour with a response and ultimately encourage it.

Your puppy is not born to recognise and adapt to all areas of human domestic life. Everything they meet for the first time is alien and potentially a threat unless you teach them otherwise. Again, it comes back to a common sense approach of introducing new objects and ensuring your puppy is comfortable around them before making them move or creating noise.

Hogan starting his household appliances training.

If you consider an appliance such as a dishwasher from the dog's perspective, you can understand why it may create a response. They are always dealt with in a speedy, loud manner, the crashing and banging alone is enough to alert even the calmest dog. There is a huge food and scent reward, owners often don't have the time or patience for a dog to be sticking its nose in, so the dog is pushed away or verbally controlled, all of which adds more fuel to the fire!

Here Hogan is having his early training to positively associate the dishwasher. It was filmed for the Puppy Coach project (www.PuppyCoach.com).

Associating the Appliances

As with all your social training, you need to spend time associating home appliances positively. It is always best to do this in controlled circumstances. If you have not had the time to condition your puppy before you use the appliance, then just remove your puppy to their safe area before you begin and address the training at another time.

To create a positive association, you will be using some of the control tools you have learnt so far, as follows:

- **Leadership** – your puppy needs to trust that you will look after them
- **Obedience** – it is useful to have some basic vocal commands in place
- **Guidance** – your puppy should be used to following your direction
- **Eye contact** – we will use this to condition your puppy during the 'mat training'
- **Patience** – as always, required in abundance

Mat Conditioning

You should begin by conditioning your puppy to remain in one place while you move around the house. Do not introduce the appliance until you are successful with this training first as this will be your means of control.

I used a square carpet tile on my floor as Hogan's point of contact. I chose to use this rather than confusing things by moving his bed around the house.

Follow this direction to encourage your puppy to sit on the mat and stay:

- Place the carpet tile on the floor
- Have your puppy in the same room and ready to work with you
- Have some treats (or favourite toy) in your hand
- Look at the mat and wait… (patience)
- As soon as your puppy puts one paw on the mat, say your trigger word 'Good' and offer a treat (you can also mark the behaviour with a clicker here if you have one)
- Repeat until your puppy is looking for the mat by following your gaze

- Ask for more by waiting or encouraging the 'sit' (hand signals only)
- Use the flat palm of your hand to signal 'wait'
- Walk around the room and then go back and reward the 'wait'
- Release your puppy with 'OK' and drop a treat on the floor away from the mat
- Repeat
- Once your puppy is routinely looking for the mat you can then add in the word 'Mat'
- If your puppy moves, don't deliver the reward, encourage them back onto the mat
- Once your puppy is happily looking for the mat whenever you direct them, you can then start to add in your domestic chores at a low level.

Early positive reward association around appliances, prior to their use.

If your puppy is bolting from the mat when you start an appliance you are going too fast. Always stay within your puppy's ability to cope to ensure a successful outcome. If your puppy will only accept a vacuum cleaner when it is off to begin with, then that's fine. End on a good note and remove your puppy before you continue with the chore/activity.

The more accepting your puppy becomes, the more you can gradually increase the activity of the appliances and continue with positive rewards. If there are any signs of stress the exercise should be stopped immediately.

Always set the puppy up for success by addressing and managing any changes within their social space, especially if there is an increase in environmental stimulation. Just because they have accepted a particular noise once or twice doesn't mean they are entirely comfortable with it. They may just have been distracted. With this in mind you should get into the habit of communicating your activity to your puppy by 'switching them off' (placing them in a calm 'down stay' on their bed and using the flat palm of your hand to indicate for them to remain in a relaxed state).

They should see that you are in control of what you are doing, accept it for what it is and remain relaxed.

Hogan is starting to study the appliances in front of him.

Tips:

- Keep your vocal communication simple (Good/OK)
- Be patient
- Keep the timing of your reward sharp
- Practise little and often, it may take some puppies longer than others

Before you start an exercise of this nature you should always take into account other affecting factors, of which there are a variety. Testosterone, teething, tiredness, poor concentration and distractions will all play a part in the success or failure of this exercise.

If your puppy is quite reactive, you may find a lead helps to keep them calmer, having a second person to perform the activity while you train your puppy is also useful if you are struggling.

Never overload your puppy. You may find they are more accepting if the appliance is closer. If this is the case but your puppy is still reactive when it's at a distance, then you will be overloading them and encouraging them to shut down. This is not healthy and not advisable. Always check your puppy's response from a distance first.

First and foremost, use your body language to communicate with your puppy. It isn't useful to shout commands over the noise of an appliance and this will only add to your puppy's level of stimulation.

Conditioning to the Vacuum Cleaner

My own conditioning experience with Hogan and the vacuum cleaner wasn't straightforward. Hogan began very well but he is a high energy puppy and so is quite reactive to environmental stimulation. As a result, we had periods where Hogan would run away from the vacuum cleaner.

This wasn't unexpected as the vacuum cleaner is really noisy and causes alot of vibration. This means Hogan was triggered to respond but he didn't know what response to use so avoidance was the easiest option for him. Other dogs may well attempt to make the noise stop and go away and I have commonly seen this in terriers displaying aggression. If this is the case, leave the vacuum cleaner running and remove your puppy. If you stop and turn it off when they are barking, you are rewarding the poor behaviour as the behaviour has received the desired outcome. Ideally, intercept this early and turn the vacuum cleaner off prior to the barking.

Make sure you always take your puppy's character and energy levels into account. I have given you the basic outline to associate any appliance, but follow your puppy's lead with how quickly you perform the exercise.

To slow the process down significantly you can also introduce a high prize reward. For Hogan I used his stuffed Kong to keep him distracted and bring positivity into the exercise.

Building positive associations and balanced behaviour takes time and patience. Make sure you put time aside for these exercises in your early weeks of puppy hood. You do not need to involve your puppy every time, just enough for them to understand the activity doesn't concern them and that the situation is non-threatening.

- Build positive associations
- Time and patience
- Start as soon as possible

Apply Mat Training to Other Objects

Your early positive conditioning to the mat area with the Kong toy is applicable training for all areas of social activity. Being consistent in what you are trying to achieve makes it easier for your puppy to understand what you expect of them.

Using the mat to control Hogan physically allowed me to create a boundary between him and the appliance helping to create confidence and prevent negative behaviour.

Whether you are dusting the house, mopping the floor, answering the door or stacking a dishwasher, having this level of training in place will allow your puppy to see that you are in control of these social activities and encourage them to stay detached and relaxed.

Remember, you are working to embed your control rather than drawing your puppy's attention to the object or appliance you are using. Always deliver your reward while your puppy is on the mat. NEVER deliver a reward if your puppy chooses to come over and investigate what you are doing. Remember you will want them to ignore what you are doing when you try to whizz the vacuum cleaner around before leaving the house for the day!

What to Do if Things Go Wrong

It may be that you perform all this early training successfully when your puppy is young and you find that they are reactive later on in life for no obvious reason.

Each and every dog will want to establish themselves within their family environment. They will take on an attachment to the human owner and be susceptible to emotional stresses and anxieties. Any changes in your life that affect you will indirectly affect your dog's behaviour too. Plus, the dog will have fear phases that occur at stages of their development and they may suddenly become reactive to a stimulus that was previously accepted.

I have treated dogs who never had issues with any of the normal household domestic chores, but suddenly develop reactivity towards an owner using the telephone or stacking the dishwasher. Almost as if they are no longer able to tolerate this behaviour.

This all comes back to understanding the dog's ability to cope with human domestic life. Often a serious behaviour problem isn't always what it seems. Many of my reactive dogs have no issue with the object they are reacting to, it is merely a focal point for a release of anxiety. In simple terms this high energy activity was the final straw and pushed the dog over its coping threshold.

If you feel this may be the case, then remind yourself of all of the important areas of your relationship with your puppy and answer honestly the following questions:

- Does your puppy have a safe area to go to?
- Do you actively encourage your puppy to go there for no reason?

- Do you stop your puppy meeting your guests at the front door?
- Do you prevent your puppy from going upstairs or on sofas?
- Can you keep your puppy calm at home?
- Do you protect your puppy from the high emotional energy in your home?
- Does your puppy cope without you?

If you have answered 'NO' to any or all of the above, then your puppy may be becoming over-attached to you and/or taking on an empowered role in your home. This will lead to anxieties and you need to re-address your leadership skills at your earliest opportunity.

Take time to factor this training into your everyday life, it is not necessary to structure it on top of daily chores. You will have to control your puppy when you perform all of these activities, so use this to your advantage.

It is very easy just to put them in a crate but this is damaging for their social learning and should be avoided. You will be thankful that you have addressed this area once the puppy is a fully grown determined adult.

Task

Your task for this section is to consider what areas of your home your puppy may find challenging. You can apply the same training to your washing machine, kettle and any other appliances that create a stimulus in your home environment.

Remember to take things slowly and use your mat control in advance of any activity. Remove your puppy and finish on a good note if they are struggling.

CHAPTER 28

Addressing Training and Social Skills in Busy Public Places

When entering any busy environment, you cannot expect your puppy to stay focused on you when distractions are overpowering.

Your focus should be totally on your puppy, working towards keeping them engaged on you. Use eye contact to encourage them and deliver praise to make every scenario positive.

Intense situations will give rise to high energy behaviours in your puppy, even if you have taught them to stay calm and follow your direction. Don't be hard on yourself or your puppy, just take things slowly. You will find your first experience of this is challenging.

Just be prepared to utilise everything you have learnt so far.

Importance of Early Training

I cannot stress enough the importance of setting up your puppy properly before they encounter a busy social environment. If you have not developed a positive relationship with your puppy prior to such an event you will find it difficult to control them. Teach them how to behave and provide them with solid guidance to prevent fear and reactivity.

You will require the following:

- Leadership
- Positive relationship
- Obedience skills
- Training aids
- Treats/toys

- An area to remove your puppy to if they are uncomfortable
- Knowledge of the environment you have chosen (are dogs allowed?)

You should keep your expectations low. Each puppy will behave differently based on their prior learning, breed motivation, energy level and physical ability. Having physical control and maintaining a calm energy throughout is essential if you are to be successful with this activity.

Interaction with Members of the Public

Interaction with the general public can be either, your best means of educating your puppy socially or the most challenging situation you will face! Humans will be humans, full of ideas, opinions and advice. It is all subjective to their learning and experiences and may not be relevant to your situation.

Ultimately your puppy is led by you and trusts you to protect them from negative social exposure. With this in mind you should be confident and proactive when you are out with your puppy, set them up for success by keeping them calm around people and other dogs.

Don't allow every person you see to give your puppy attention, make your puppy sit and watch while three people walk past, then deliver a positive reward as the fourth person walks by.

Your self-control exercises will be a useful asset during these encounters. Don't be afraid to ask people with dogs if their dog is ok with a puppy, or to state 'Please could you ignore my puppy'! While you may be a little embarrassed at being so direct it is with the intention of protecting the new member of your family in their early experience of the human world.

Your cute little puppy will always be the centre of attention when you step out in public for the first time. My advice is to consider your puppy as impressionable and delicate as a newborn baby.

Don't under any circumstances allow a stranger to approach your puppy and give them attention. This is why you see many dogs dragging their owners to every person on the street or charging off to greet someone as soon as they leave the house or enter the park.

Allowing your puppy to associate with a stranger with high level praise or, even worse, a food reward will mean you have lost control and your puppy will forever more see strangers as individuals they should approach. This may just be an over exuberant greeting in excitement and anticipation or it could mean more serious behaviours are allowed to develop if the response is not well received by the stranger.

You need to teach your puppy to ignore people and children, focus on you and listen to your direction. This is an easy way to teach them how to act appropriately and safely in public.

You can still make the approach of an individual positive. This is achieved by providing calm direction and delivering a reward to reinforce your delight at the puppy's level of self-control when they are successful.

People can be intrusive and demanding and some can be persistent. If you keep your puppy moving and just be polite then you can avoid most interactions successfully.

Having an overly sociable Labrador was something I wanted to avoid. Hogan is a busy, strong and high energy dog. As a result of his early training he doesn't see anything exciting about people when they approach so I have absolute control. He now weighs 32kgs, so it is essential that I have full physical control of him.

I achieved this by simply keeping him focused on me and rewarding all his good behaviour while explaining to the person that he was in training and would they mind just walking past.

Here Hogan is walking perfectly while I engage these lovely ladies in a conversation all about puppies!

If you are polite and clear most people will respect your wishes and if they don't then just move on and say you're in a hurry or ask the person to join you on your walk so you can explain what you're doing and why.

My management of this social exposure has meant Hogan is not over stimulated or encouraged to focus his attention on anyone we meet outside. I regularly asked approaching people if I could just walk with them for a while until Hogan settled. Building some low key 'chit chat' time can really help keep everybody more relaxed and it provides an opportunity for an introduction to occur between the dogs with little interference from the human owners.

Finding a Positive Motivator

To ensure you are able to make the whole experience positive it is essential that you have a positive motivator with you such as a toy, ball or food reward. These are controlled and delivered by you, only deliver the reward when your puppy responds well and only for brief periods.

You must also recognise that positive motivation will occur naturally if you manage things well. Puppies are social and if you make the experience generally enjoyable and individuals respect their personal space and body language communication then they will get lots of positivity from the actual event.

Sheba, Hogan and Marley having some free time in the woods after a particularly busy day at work.

Puppies also like exercise so the walk itself can be stopped and started dependent on the puppy delivering positive behaviours. This can also be followed by some off lead time in the nearest place of safe open space. This will provide a great opportunity for your puppy to release some of the excitable energy they may have retained from their experience.

Finally, a confident, upbeat and happy owner is everything. Your puppy should be totally in tune with you and your emotion by now and you will be able to control their responses just by staying engaged and delivering praise appropriately. Try to enjoy the experience and so will your puppy.

The Impact of a Simple High Street Visit

This is not a task I would advise that you do too early in your puppy's development. I advise that you socialise as soon as possible but I have treated many dogs who have been over stimulated at a young age as a result of this kind of exposure when they are poorly prepared.

Obviously if you live somewhere busy with lots of environmental noise you will have no option but to expose your puppy every time they leave the house. If this is the case, focus on making sure your puppy doesn't arrive in the environment and immediately become high energy or unbalanced.

You should still focus on all the training tips I have provided throughout the book, especially encouraging your puppy to focus on you for direction.

If not, build up to this level of social interaction gradually. I advise that your puppy is comfortable listening to your basic commands, connects with you through eye contact and is happy to walk past traffic and people. If you have tackled all of these things, then you will only have to introduce the increased noise and social energy.

Just observe your puppy, recognise their communication and provide regular breaks from the environment in quieter areas during the exercise. Above all, be assertive and confident in how you handle the occasion.

Jumping Up

I observed Hogan's behaviour continuously during one of his early visits to a local high street. He coped well but I noticed the extra energy around him affected his level of calm and as a result he was quite bouncy. Although he never jumps up around normal social contact, this is something he was doing to release some energy and seek re-assurance from me.

An alternative behaviour, and one that is commonly seen, is for the puppy to pull on the lead. You should expect these negative behaviours to creep in if you are distracted and not rewarding the desirable behaviour consistently. It is important to try and maintain intermittent, consistent eye contact and praise to avoid poor learning.

Coping with Traffic

During your 'high street' or busy environment exercise it is important to try and make relevant positive connections with all social encounters, covering all aspects of human life. You should be aware that some living environments will be quite isolating for the social development of the puppy. Although this isn't necessarily negative, it will mean that if the puppy meets more intense environments as an adult dog they may struggle to cope.

Plan ahead and seek out high energy environments if you are living in a rural area. If you are in an urban area, then you should seek out livestock and wildlife populated areas.

If a common 'high street' training exercise provides you with the ability to introduce traffic, crowds or loud children then use this to your advantage. It may be the only opportunity you have during this critical learning puppy period.

Provide Time Out from Highly Stimulated Environments

As I mentioned earlier it is important to find a quiet area to accommodate your puppy during this exercise. It is essential if they are to learn what behaviour is acceptable and it will also allow them to remain focused and avoid any anxiety developing.

This doesn't have to be open land, it can just be a carpark or somewhere away from the general hustle and bustle of human activity.

If your puppy is happy to go to the toilet and take treats from you while they are out, then these are good pointers for a positive result. If your puppy is suffering from stress, feeling threatened or under pressure they are unlikely to do either of these two things.

Recognising your Puppy's Ability to Cope

It is important for you to recognise your puppy's coping ability. This will be obvious if they are reactive but if they are struggling and internalising their fear or worry your puppy may appear unusually quiet.

Connecting through eye contact in this way will really help you understand your puppy in every situation.

Pay attention to all the stress indicator's your puppy may deliver. If any are present it will give you the ability to gauge your puppy's perception of the events that they have encountered.

Stress indicators are recognised as follows:

Focal Point On Body	Indicator
Eyes	Dilated / wide-eyed / squinting / staring
Head	Furrowed brow / lack of focus
Mouth	Corners pinned back / lip licking / yawning / panting / jaw snapping at air / refusal of food / whiskers shaking or stiff / biting or chewing / vocalisation
Nose	Clear liquid from nose / sniffing air or ground erratically
Ears	Erect / pinned back
Body	Avoidance / shivering / leaning backwards / hackles up / excessive moulting / repetitive behaviours / excessive self-grooming / very quiet
Paws	Sweaty
Tail	Low tail carriage

Despite what it may look like, this level of stimulation is tiring for any young puppy. Some will appear to be excited and enjoying the experience when actually they are finding it totally overwhelming. Keep the social exposure short.

Task

Your task for this section is to prepare for a high street walk. Make sure you know the area well and find somewhere appropriate on your journey to ensure your puppy has regular breaks and some free time before continuing with your training.

Practise all of the obedience commands you have been learning.

CHAPTER 29

First Aid

*"The practice of delivering assistance to any individual deemed to be suffering a
sudden injury or medical illness, aiming to preserve life, prevent deterioration of the
condition and/or promote recovery, until a suitably
qualified individual arrives."*

To complete your dog-owner knowledge it is essential that you are able to physically manage and assist your puppy in a medical crisis. This chapter will provide you with all the necessary information to ensure you are prepared.

One of the most important things to consider in canine first aid are methods of handling. This subject is the fundamental difference between canine and human first aid.

While I am sure human first aiders would agree that many human patients are unpredictable, they would be no match for a wounded dog. This coupled with a lack of easy communication, means you should consider safe handling techniques to be an invaluable part of learning in canine first aid.

To provide you with a clear contrast of the differences, listed below are important considerations:

1. Differences Between Human and Canine First Aid

Human First Aid	Vs	Canine First Aid
- Anatomical consistency		- Breed variations: size and shape
- Communication pathway		- Communication barriers
- Handling: mostly patient compliance		- Handling: patient unpredictability
- CPR technique consistency		- CPR Different to human & breed variations

2. Parameters of Control for Canine First Aiders

In order for an individual to carry out the practice of First Aid on a dog they should ensure they are aware of the guidelines set by the Veterinary Surgeons Act 1966:

> *"An Act to make fresh provision for the management of the Veterinary profession, for the registration of Veterinary Surgeons and Veterinary practitioners, for regulating their professional education and professional conduct and for cancelling or suspending registration in cases of misconduct; and for connected purposes."*

Schedule 3 Part 1 of this Act dictates the exemptions from restrictions and goes some way to regulate those individuals delivering advice and practical courses on canine First Aid. It should be understood that the only persons permitted to make a diagnosis, deliver medicines and practice surgery are those recognised as qualified veterinary surgeons registered with the Royal College of Veterinary Surgeons.

The detail of this Act has been considered throughout the development of advice delivered in this chapter.

3. Aims of First Aid

You can ensure you stay within the parameters set by the Veterinary Surgeons Act by adhering to the simple structure of first aid practice beginning with the 3 aims:

- Preservation of life
- Prevention of suffering
- Prevent deterioration

You should always focus on dealing with the problem as it is presented rather than looking to make a diagnosis, this is not within the remit of a first aider. Your goals to achieve the above should focus on stabilising the patient, relieving the symptoms of acute conditions and promoting recovery.

If you are faced with more than one injured dog, then it is important that you consider a **triage** system. This procedure should prioritise the most urgent cases and rate them from 'life-threatening, urgent, non-urgent to acceptable to wait'. This will ensure you work effectively and are as successful as possible.

This can be a difficult task and sometimes the category the patient is placed in may change if their condition deteriorates. It often requires a skill beyond the average pet owner but it is worth making yourself aware of as many first aid scenarios as possible so you are able to be prepared and avoid panic.

4. Handling and Restraint

To be successful in delivering first aid, it is essential that you are aware of effective handling techniques to ensure the safety of yourself and your patient.

You will often find that the more severely injured patients will require the least amount of restraint and this observation will provide you with a level of understanding of your patient's medical status before you begin.

Ideally it would be useful to have the following:

- Slip lead (or something similar)
- Muzzle
- Emergency muzzle equipment (e.g. shoe lace, spare lead, cord from a hoodie sweatshirt)
- Blanket

Conscious dog, suffering minor or major injury

Remember the dog will be frightened and so its behaviour will be unpredictable. Even if this is your dog and they know you, you should still expect a poor reaction. Approach in a calm, cautious manner. Your focus should be to control the dog's head as this will give you the safest and most effective management.

Place a slip-lead over the dog's head from a distance ensuring you are as non-invasive as possible, do not make any sudden movements just maintain a reassuring, calm attitude.

If possible and their injuries allow, it is always advisable to place a muzzle if you have one. Alternatively, an **emergency muzzle** can be made from anything you have to hand, such as a shoe lace, belt, second lead or something similar. Simply place over the dog's nose and tie under the chin, cross over the two ends and tie them again behind the dog's head and ears.

Never leave this in place for longer than absolutely necessary and continuously monitor the dog's tolerance of it.

Before doing this it is essential that the airway is clear, there are no head or facial injuries and the dog is not vomiting or panting excessively.

Handle the animal carefully but confidently, ensuring control of the head at all times. Avoid movement until an assessment has been carried out unless it is environmentally unsafe to do so.

Wrapping the dog in a blanket can help them calm down and if the dog is small it will allow you to maintain better control.

Unconscious Dogs

Although your unconscious dog won't appear able to show aggression you should still have a secure collar and lead in place in the event the dog wakes and immediately reacts. The collar should not be impinging on the airway and the lead should be trailing away from the dog for ease of access.

I have seen several dogs appear unconscious after an epileptic seizure and then suddenly awake in a panic and snap at fresh air so expect the unexpected. It is not advisable to place a muzzle on the unconscious dog but you should still secure the head and have a muzzle ready in case you need it.

It is important that you keep the dog's airway clear, gently lengthening the head and neck and pulling the tongue forward is advisable (again if safe to do so).

5. Observation of your Environment

Paying attention to your location is an important factor. This will give you information on what has happened if you weren't present. It will also allow you to assess if first aid can be carried out on the spot or if it is necessary to move the patient to safety.

If you are dealing with a severely injured animal and a worried owner, then being able to tell the vet what was present around you could be the difference between life and death. For instance, walking in open countryside on a warm day with plenty of tall grasses and a dog in pain, and unable to weight-bear, with limb swelling, could indicate an adder snake bite. An antidote would be necessary and time is of the essence if the limb is to be saved.

Likewise, if a dog has been hit by a car it is likely you will need to move the dog to a place of safety away from the road before beginning your assessment.

6. Moving the Patient

In some instances, it may be necessary to drive the dog to the vet as soon as possible. If this is the case, then you should ensure the patient travels securely. A box is ideal if the dog is small enough. Alternatively, wrapping them in a large blanket or towel will help keep control of them and make it easier to prevent them trying to stand. This is may be detrimental to their welfare. Again you should practice this safely and use a muzzle as necessary.

Once you are comfortable with the surroundings and confident that your patient needs treatment in the field then you can begin.

7. Conducting a Patient Assessment

NB: *Before beginning your assessment you should ensure a Veterinary Professional has been contacted.*

Your role is to gather as much information about the cause of the injury or condition as possible.

This information could be vital when a veterinary examination is carried out. Some examples of the observations you could make concern the following:

Road Traffic Accident
- What vehicle was involved?
- Was the dog trapped?
- Roughly what speed was the vehicle doing?

Choking/Breathing Difficulties
- What objects may be responsible, e.g. child's toy, stick, dog toy?
- How long has the dog been struggling to breathe for?
- What methods have been used to remove the object?

Bleeding
- What may have caused the bleeding?
- How long ago was the injury sustained?
- Has the bleeding stopped and started again?
- Is the blood bright red or dark?

Sudden Collapse
- Was the dog exercising?
- Are the weather conditions extremes of heat or cold?
- Does the dog have a pre-existing medical condition?
- How long has the dog been in a collapsed state for?

Some conditions will require immediate veterinary attention and a first aider should prioritise where possible. These are:

- Consistent profuse vomiting and diarrhoea
- Obstructions of the urethra
- Severe burns
- Gaping open wounds
- Gastric dilatation (Bloat/ GDV)
- Any prolapse of organs (rectal/vaginal/penis/eye)

Vital Statistics (Dog)
It is important you are aware of the normal vital statistics of a dog so you can observe for abnormalities, as follows:

Pulse Rate:
- Small breeds = 100-160 BPM
- Medium breeds = 60-100 BPM
- Puppies = 110-200 BPM (up to 10 months)

Respiratory Rate: 10-30 breaths per minute
Temperature: 37.9 -39.9 (100.2–103.8) *(Merck, Sharp & Dohme, 2015)*
Capillary Refill Time: 1-2 seconds

An effective patient assessment is your first task, before considering any form of treatment. This is basic so you can make fast and effective judgements on the welfare of your patient. It focuses on the primary survival factors, or the A.B.C of life:

- **A**irway
- **B**reathing
- **C**irculation

Flow Chart for First Aid Patient Assessment

In order to perform this assessment logically you can follow this flowchart:

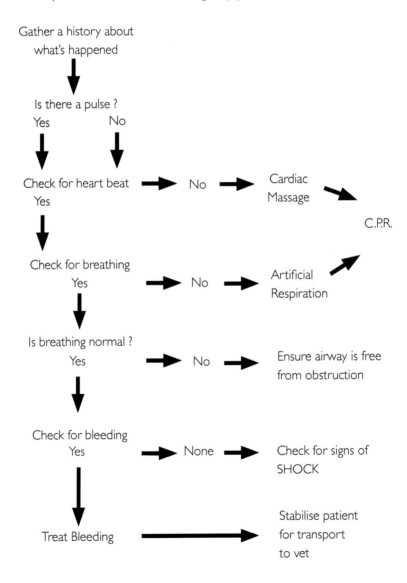

Gather a history about what's happened

Is there a pulse ?
Yes   No

Check for heart beat → No → Cardiac Massage
Yes

C.P.R.

Check for breathing
Yes → No → Artificial Respiration

Is breathing normal ?
Yes → No → Ensure airway is free from obstruction

Check for bleeding
Yes → None → Check for signs of SHOCK

Treat Bleeding → Stabilise patient for transport to vet

Airway

Is the airway clear?

Check for and remove any blockages. During your check you should straighten the head and neck gently. Be aware that you must consider the dog may bite even if they are unconscious so take care if you are attempting to remove an obstruction.

Make sure the dog's collar is loosened if one is present.

Breathing

Observe the patient's breathing, use all your senses for this, so look, listen and place your hand over the chest wall to feel for it rising and falling.

Circulation

Check for the patient's pulse and blood perfusion to the body and limbs. Control any bleeding.

8. Cardiopulmonary Resuscitation (C.P.R.)

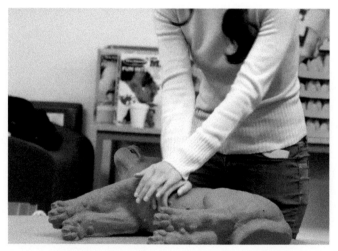

C.P.R. can be fatal if practised on a live dog so it is useful to find a first aid course to understand this technique fully.

Cardiopulmonary resuscitation should only be performed in the absence of a heartbeat, pulse and breathing. This is a hazardous procedure and may cause fatality if performed on a live dog. You should only use it if you are confident it is necessary and any practise should be performed on a dummy dog.

The patient will display the following signs during a cardiac arrest:

- Collapse
- Blue mucous membranes (gums and eye conjunctiva)
- Eyes open and pupils dilated
- Non-detectable heart beat
- Non-detectable pulse
- Absence of breathing

CPR Method (2016)

- Lay the dog on its right side on a flat surface
- Extend the head and neck to open the airway
- Deliver 3 x rescue breaths into the dog's nose, holding its mouth closed
- Place the palm of one hand over the dog's heart (located over ribs 3-4 at the point where the dogs elbow meets its chest in a flexed position)
- Place your other hand over the top
- Deliver 30 x chest compressions
- Follow with 2 x breaths
- Repeat compressions
- Repeat breaths (x2)
- And so on…

In the case of small dogs (less than 15kgs) you should use two fingers for the compressions and observe the pressure you are applying by watching the movement in the rib cage.

It is advisable to familiarise yourself with this procedure as the dog's brain may be damaged within 3–4 minutes of respiratory failure, you will need to act quickly and efficiently.

9. Haemorrhage

Blood loss/bleeding, occurring internally and/or externally as a result of injury or disease of one or more blood vessels.

Types of Haemorrhage

Arterial: The most serious type of haemorrhage. Blood will be spurting and bright red in colour as it is oxygenated blood. The spurting will be to the rhythm of the heart-beat.

Venous: This will have various degrees of intensity depending on the vessel/s involved. The blood is darker in colour than arterial and will be a constant ooze. You will see an exact point of injury.

Capillary: Capillary blood is also bright red and will constantly ooze. There will be multi pin points at the site of injury making bleeding difficult to stop.

You may also have a *mixed bleed* involving all 3 types of vessel.

Controlling Haemorrhage

Haemorrhage or blood loss could result in a serious outcome for the patient, it is essential that you are able to get it under control as soon as possible. You have a variety of different methods you can use to achieve this.

Elevation: As it suggests, elevate the area.

Direct digital pressure: Apply pressure directly to the wound site and over the point of the bleed. Ensure there are no foreign bodies and take care that you do not displace bone if fractures are present. Ideally use a sterile swab/dressing otherwise clean hands will have to suffice.

Pressure points (indirect pressure): This method can be used to stem bleeding from an arterial injury. There are certain areas of the body where it is possible to apply pressure to a vessel by pressing it against a bone. These areas refer to the following arteries:

- Brachial – above the elbow on the inside of the humerus (front leg)
- Femoral – high up on the inside aspect of the thigh (back leg)
- Coccygeal – on the upper aspect of the inside of the tail

Pressure bandage: Direct pressure is applied to the area by using a securely placed dressing and bandage. Usually a dressing with a thick pad of cotton wool is applied and then a firm bandage used to secure it. If blood seeps through dressings bandages should be applied on top to avoid dislodging any clots.

Tourniquet: You should only consider using this if all other methods have failed as it will stop all circulation to the area below the tourniquet and may cause tissue death. Tourniquets are useful for severe limb and tail injuries. You can use a strong bandage, string, rope or shoe lace. Fix it a few inches above the wound and tie it until bleeding stops, it is essential that you note the time of a tourniquet application so it can be removed before tissue damage occurs. Never leave in place for longer than 15 minutes.

10. Shock

This is a life threatening medical condition caused by an acute fall in blood pressure and therefore inadequate perfusion of body tissues 'circulatory collapse'. It leads to a lack of oxygen and ultimately cell death if left untreated. It should be a major consideration of your first aid assessment.

There are several different types of shock and it is important that you have an understanding of them to ensure you are able to stabilise the patient and monitor for potential deterioration.

Types of Shock

- Hypovolaemic: caused by blood or fluid loss
- Cardiogenic: caused by pulmonary embolism or heart damage
- Vasculogenic: caused by anaphylaxis/sepsis
- Neurogenic: condition resulting from spinal injury

Signs of Shock

Shock is classified by the presence of the following signs:

- Low body temperature
- Cold extremities
- Increased respiratory rate (rapid and shallow)

- Decreased pulse strength
- Increased pulse rate
- Pale gums/eye conjunctiva
- Collapse/weakness

First Aid Treatment of Shock

- Call the vet
- Assess for obvious injury
- Deliver C.P.R. if necessary
- Stem any bleeding
- Lay the dog on its right side with head and neck extended
- Cover with a blanket

Shock is the number one cause of fatalities in emergency situations. It will be present where any dog has sustained a major injury, physical or mental trauma and it will require immediate veterinary attention.

11. Wounds

Wounds can be classified by their appearance. Are they open to the air or closed and potentially non-visible? The table below provides you with an outline of injury and treatment.

Outline of injury and treatment for wounds

Wound Type	Description	Treatment
Open		
Incised	caused by a sharp edge, glass, knife, surgical blade	stem bleeding, clean only if bleeding is ceased, dress
Laceration	caused by a blunt or jagged object or tear	as above
Abrasion	superficial scrape	clean the area to prevent infection, dress only if necessary
Avulsion	body part has sustained a ripping force, such as limb detachment	stem bleeding, keep pressure applied

Puncture	caused by a sharp object puncturing the skin seen in stick injuries and dog fights	high risk of deep infection cleaning and flushing with sterile saline is essential
Penetration	sharp object entering and retracting from the skin	assess severity, clean and cover
Gunshot	caused by a bullet or pellet	as above
Closed		
Crushing	body has sustained a great weight or force for a lengthy period of time	veterinary assessment asap
Haematoma	damage to the blood vessels under the skin causing large swelling or bruising	no first aid treatment

12. Anaphylaxis

Anaphylaxis is a life threatening allergic reaction to an allergen ingested, injected, inhaled or in general contact. It causes shock and ultimately cardiac and respiratory failure and death if untreated.

Allergens can be anything the dog's immune system reacts to but common ones are:

- Bee stings
- Wasp stings
- Detergents
- Some foods
- Drugs

Signs of anaphylaxis:

- Respiratory distress
- Lethargy
- Collapse
- Seizures
- Pale gums/lips

- Vomiting
- Diarrhoea

Ultimately the treatment for anaphylaxis requires immediate veterinary attention and would be the same action as shock. However, there are specific treatments you can apply in the field for certain allergens as outlined below.

Bee and Wasp Stings
For the treatment of bee stings you should bathe the area with a bicarbonate solution, wasp stings can be neutralised with vinegar and both areas can be treated with ice.

Snake Bites
Snake bites can cause major body tissue damage and commonly affect the limbs, antidotes are available but you will need to call the vet ahead of your arrival as they are not always kept in practice. You should immobilise the affected area as much as possible to slow the progression of the poison, clean the area and keep the patient calm.

The extent to which an animal reacts to any potential allergen is hugely variable as are the variety of allergens that may cause problems. We have only touched on a few here but symptoms to others will be similar and will always require a fast assessment and treatment program.

13. Poisoning

We should consider when assessing the dog whether we are dealing with an allergic response or if poisoning is a consideration. (See pages 288-289.)

14. Inducing Vomiting

You will always require a veterinary opinion for suspected poisoning cases and time is of the essence so your vet is your first point of contact. They will direct you as to whether inducing vomiting is necessary. In the instances where fast action requires you to do this, you should be aware of how to do so safely.

Types of poisoning

Poison Classification	Active Ingredient	Signs	Treatment
Pesticides	Metaldehyde (slug pellets)	Panting, drooling, muscle tremors, seizures, collapse, major organ death (within 15 minutes of ingestion)	Veterinary attention ASAP, give milk, induce vomiting under direction
	Warfarin (rat bait)	Anticoagulant interferes with blood clotting causes animal to bleed out	Veterinary attention ASAP as the animal will require an injection of Vitamin K. Induce vomiting under direction
Coolant	Antifreeze (Ethylene glycol)	Patient may appear drunk, elevated heart rate, dehydration, congestive heart failure, kidney failure	Veterinary attention ASAP
Medicines	Aspirin	Depression, abdominal pain, vomiting, increased respiratory rate, kidney failure, death	Veterinary attention ASAP, induce vomiting
	Ibuprofen (NSAID)	Vomiting, diarrhoea, bloody faeces, blood in vomit, nausea, lack of appetite, weight loss, gastric (stomach) ulcers and perforation, Increased thirst, Increased urination, decreased or lack of urine, seizures, Incoordination, coma, death	Veterinary attention ASAP, induce vomiting
	Tramadol (NSAID)	Behaviour changes, gastric upset (should be no need for concern if your dog has ingested less than 4mg per 2.2kg bodyweight)	Veterinary attention ASAP, induce vomiting

Detergents	Washing powder	Gastric upset: Vomiting and diarrhoea	Veterinary attention but you may administer water or milk
Plants	Various	Various	Seek veterinary advice and try to identify the plant
Food	Various	Various	See list in Chapter 10
Peanut Butter Chewing gum	Xylitol (sugar substitute)	Causes a potent release of insulin from the pancreas causing profound hypoglycaemia Vomiting Weakness Incoordination or difficulty walking or standing (walking like drunk) Depression or lethargy Tremors Seizures Coma	Veterinary attention ASAP
Theobromine / Caffeine Methylxanthine	Methylxanthine found in tea, chocolate and coca cola **NB:** *100mg/kg of chocolate is enough to cause toxicity*	Nausea, vomiting, diarrhoea, increased urination, seizures, coma, death	Veterinary attention ASAP, induce vomiting under direction

Firstly, there are substances that make vomiting a potentially life-threatening treatment, these are:

- Anything corrosive – batteries, drain chemicals, lime scale removing liquid
- Hydrocarbons or anything to do with fuel – petrol, diesel, motor oil

You should also be aware of when the substance was ingested, if hours have passed then vomiting is not advised. Your patient should be in good general health prior to the event.

Method
Use a syringe to deliver 0.5–1 ml per kg body weight of **3% hydrogen peroxide** and walk the patient around to encourage peristalsis. If your patient has not vomited with 15 minutes you can deliver a second dose but you should then be on the way to the vet if this doesn't work.

The vet can administer an injectable vomiting drug so if you are within 5–10 minutes of a practice it is advisable to go straight there.

15. Epilepsy

First aid can be applied in a variety of circumstances so we should consider this common medical condition which delivers different outcomes.

You should recognise that the seizures and or abnormal behaviour observed in an epileptic patient are just a symptom of a disorder of the brain and therefore there will be an underlying brain disorder. With this in mind you may experience different responses from the dog.

Ensure you observe your own personal safety during your management of these patients as they can be highly unpredictable.

Symptoms

- Sudden behaviour changes
- Muscle rigidity
- Muscle spasms/twitching
- Salivation/foaming at the mouth
- Vocalisation
- Urination/defaecation

- Collapse
- Loss of consciousness

Be aware that some patients may jump from one fit to the next, this is known as 'status epileptics' or cluster fits. If this occurs or if a fit continues for longer than 5 minutes, then the patient is in danger of internally overheating. This is a very serious situation requiring immediate veterinary attention.

Treatment

You will be unable to bring the patient out of the seizure. It has to run its course but the majority of them will be fairly short lived. However, it is important that you do what you can to reduce the environmental stimulation and allow the brain activity to calm.

Follow these steps to ensure patient welfare until veterinary help arrives:

- Phone the vet
- Darken the room
- Keep the immediate surroundings quiet
- Try to safely stabilise the patient
- Remove all objects that they patient could harm themselves on
- Remove collars and leads
- Do not put your hands near the dog's mouth

16. Bandaging

A first aider's responsibility is to stop bleeding so it is important that you are able to apply measures to facilitate this. Your attempt at bandaging does not need to look pretty but it does need to be functional, paying attention to the focus of the task will ensure you are effective.

It is useful to have a supply of bandaging products in your first aid kit as follows:

- Gauze
- Cotton wool/absorbent bandage
- Conform bandage (stretchy)
- Cohesive bandage (vetwrap/co-flex etc.)

- White surgical tape
- Scissors

Bandages should always be checked and changed regularly, your dressing should only be applied to cease blood flow and so should be removed as soon as deemed appropriate. I have seen dressings cause long term and irreparable damage if left on too long so ensure you make provisions for a veterinary examination before leaving your patient.

The aim of a bandage is to:

- Stabilise the affected area
- Stem blood flow
- Provide comfort and support
- Prevent contamination
- Hold a dressing in place

Method

You should follow a simple stacking method when applying your bandage. Your first layer should be in close contact with the wound and should ideally be a **sterile dressing**. Your second layer provides the padding (cotton wool) and acts as an absorbent layer, always apply firmly but not too tightly. Your third layer consists of a stretchy bandage and final covering (conform and cohesive layers).

NB: *If you are bandaging a potentially fractured limb then ensure you include the joints both above and below the fracture site to provide stability and reduce pain.*

Paw bandages should be applied to cease bleeding and the dog should be taken to a veterinary surgeon immediately.

Ear Bandaging

Ear bandages are an absolute necessity if you are to stem blood loss from an ear flap. They bleed profusely and often bleeding will start and stop regardless of treatment. I have treated many cases where second and even third bandages have had to be applied to create enough pressure. Don't be alarmed, this is normal for these injuries.

Whenever you approach a dog who has been injured and requires some form of treatment you should always ensure you are working safely and with the dog's welfare in mind.

Your handling techniques will be tested, dogs may bite, especially if they are in pain. Securing their head carefully and using a blanket or towel to wrap them in can be really beneficial. Consider this before you address the first aid requirement.

You should always seek veterinary attention as soon as possible.

Ear bandages can be tricky to apply. It is worth making sure your puppy
is used to having their ears handled in the event they may need one of
these bandages.

17. Fractures

The most common fracture you may see are those affecting the limbs (femur, radius, ulna, tibia, fibula) pelvis, tail (coccygeal) and mandible (jaw).

As a first aider you should be aware of complicating factors such as treating an 'open' fracture (where the fracture site is open to the air and at serious risk of infection) and ultimately you need to stabilise the affected area.

Signs

Your patient will be in extreme pain. There will be swelling, redness and possibly visible skin injury with loss of function, deformity and noise from the area during patient movement (crepitus).

Treatment

Your primary action is to contact the vet, conduct a thorough patient assessment and immobilise the area and patient as a whole where possible.

Applying a bandage to support the affected area will provide comfort and some pain control. As previously mentioned it is essential to ensure you immobilise the joint above and below the fracture site.

Classification of fractures

Fracture	Description
Complete Fracture	Complete loss of bony continuity
Incomplete Fracture	Some portion of the bone remains intact
Greenstick Fracture	Usually occurring in young animals, bone looks like a tree branch when it splits
Fissure Fracture	Cracks occur within the bone but the bone itself is intact
Transverse Fracture	Fracture is transverse to the long axis of the bone
Depression Fracture	Fracture consists of a large piece of bone that has depressed inwards, seen in head injuries
Oblique Fracture	Fracture line is oblique to the long axis of the bone
Spiral Fracture	Fracture that spirals along the axis of the bone
Comminuted Fracture	3 fracture fragments affecting the same area of the bone
Multiple Fracture	3 or more fracture fragments in a single bone, usually affecting different parts of the bone
Impaction Fracture	Bones impact into one another, commonly seen in long bones
Compression Fracture	Commonly seen within the vertebrae looks like a crushing injury

18. Eye Injuries

Signs of eye injury are usually pretty clear. The dog will be squinting, the eye will be watery, swelling and redness will be present. The dog will be pawing at the area and agitated. Eyes are extremely painful so the dog will also be displaying signs of pain and discomfort as well.

Make sure you contact the vet immediately and prevent the dog making the situation worse.

Prolapsed Eyeball

The most frightening eye injury is a prolapse of an eye ball. I will never forget my first experience of this as a 16 year old girl spending my first week of work experience in veterinary practice. When someone tells you not to panic when you are looking at this situation you are unlikely to want to do anything else.

The dog will be really distressed, but it is important you offer them comfort and stay calm. Remember they don't understand what has happened and they will react to your body language if you panic.

You will commonly see this injury in dogs with protruding eyes such as the Pekinese, Shih Tzu or Lhasa Apso.

Do NOT try to put the eyeball back this will require care and is a veterinary procedure. You should however, keep the eye moist. Sterile saline or salt water solution and a damp cloth will help to preserve the eye. Prevent the dog doing further damage to itself by minimising movement and controlling the front paws. Remember a muzzle may be necessary here as the dog will be distressed and you will be working close to its mouth.

19. Choking

Choking is caused by a foreign body blocking the upper airway. You will see the dog pawing at its face, rubbing its face along the ground, wide eyed, panicking, salivating, coughing and struggling to breathe. If there is no first aid intervention the dog will collapse and die.

Treatment

The type of object involved will govern your choice of treatment.

Direct retrieval – you may be able to dislodge the object with tweezers. Do not put your fingers into the dogs throat if you can't see the object as you may damage tissue or push it further down.

Heimlich Manoeuvre *(only if the dog is collapsed and cannot breathe)*

- Small dogs: hold their back against your stomach (head up, paws down), find the soft area under the ribs. Make a fist with your hand and pull upwards and inwards two or three times, in a thrusting motion.
- Medium or large dogs: place them on their side and kneel behind their back. Place a closed fist again in the area under the rib cage, and push upward and inward sharply, in the direction of your dog's head and your knees.

Regardless of whether you are able to dislodge the object or not you should still seek veterinary attention.

20. Hypothermia

This is an extremely low body temperature (below 100°F). Patients may also be suffering from shock.

Signs

- Thermometer won't register a temperature or it registers extremely low
- Cold extremities
- Respiratory depression
- Collapse
- Disorientation
- Pale gums and eye conjunctiva
- Muscle weakness

Treatment

You should warm the patient slowly. Minimise movement, cover in blankets and warm coats, move to a place of warm ambient temperature, deliver warm water orally if the patient is conscious and swallowing.

21. Hyperthermia

Hyperthermia cases have to be the most prevalent in my mind. Sadly, I have treated an excessive number of overheated dogs, some who have survived but many have died. The most traumatic case concerned a young Labrador who had been left at home shut in the conservatory on a summer's day. There is no need for me to go in to detail about the horrific death that dog suffered, suffice to say this was an oversight by an owner with catastrophic consequences.

Never leave a dog shut in, even on a cold day when the sun is shining in the following places:

- Cars
- Caravans
- Sheds
- Conservatories
- Anywhere metal without temperature control

There are too many instances of hyperthermic death every year as people don't see the danger. Your dog will overheat in minutes if they are left in this way. Never feel uncomfortable reporting a dog locked in a car in a car park, it may save their life! The signs are as follows:

- Above 103.2°F body temperature
- Panting
- Dehydration
- Drooling
- Reddened gums
- Increased heart rate
- Increased respiratory rate
- Vomiting
- Diarrhoea
- Collapse
- Seizures
- Death

Treatment

- Call the vet

- Cool the dog slowly with wet blankets or towels
- Provide shade
- Offer cool water
- Place cool towels around the bottom and belly where there is less fur
- NEVER hose the dog or use freezing water or ice this will cause vasoconstriction of the vessels and could send the dog into shock

Be aware when you exercise your dog that they are wearing a fur coat! Playing ball with the children on a hot summers day or running with an owner are classic examples of cases I have treated aside from the hundreds shut in cars!

You should also consider short nosed (brachiocephalic) breeds as they are unable to dissipate the heat as well as other breeds so their breathing will be compromised much sooner. Likewise, those animals who are suffering with medical conditions, are old or have extremely heavy coats will all succumb to heat exhaustion earlier and should never be exercised during the hottest part of the day.

22. Drowning

Drowning is a complex incident as there are various degrees of outcome. Water aspiration into the lungs is responsible for the demise of the patient and removal of this as soon as possible is necessary. Veterinary attention will be required at the earliest opportunity.

Dogs who have succumbed to the effects of drowning are likely to require C.P.R. so be prepared to deliver this.

You should also consider a process known as 'secondary drowning' which can occur up to 3 days after the original event even if the dog appears to have recovered at the time. Dogs can die from this inflammatory lung tissue process.

Signs

- Bluish tinge to gums
- Coughing
- Vomiting
- Salivating

- Respiratory distress
- Collapse
- Death

Treatment

Treat these animals as you would a patient in Shock and seek immediate veterinary attention. Be prepared to deliver C.P.R.

23. Electrocution

This is always a huge risk to young puppies as they are curious and will often explore and chew whatever they come across. In the event that this is an electrical appliance you should always turn off the supply before touching the dog.

If you are unable to get to the switch, then using something wooden to move the dog away is a possibility providing there is no metal on the object you choose. Never put yourself at risk.

You will need to perform immediate C.P.R. if the dog has gone in to cardiac arrest but veterinary attention is required as soon as possible.

24. Gastric Dilatation Volvulus (Bloat)

This condition is also commonly referred to as a gastric torsion. It occurs more often in 'deep chested' breeds such as the Great Dane, German Shepherd, Weimaraner, Setters, Old English Sheepdogs etc. Basically this is any breed with a large chest cavity allowing lots of space for the stomach to move around. Although it is not exclusive to these breeds and some puppies have been known to have the condition.

It occurs when the stomach dilates, rotates and twists on its short axis blocking the entry of food and exit of gas. It may also involve the spleen.

Signs

- Abdominal pain and distension
- Unproductive vomiting

- Anxiety
- Depression
- Collapse
- Excessive drooling

Treatment

This is a life threatening situation that requires immediate veterinary attention. The fatality rate is extremely high, even after surgical intervention. Your role as a first aider is to take a diagnostic history and make the right decision to seek veterinary help.

Task

I have provided below the contents of an animal first aid kit. Your task is to source your own kit. Make sure it is packed securely and easy to transport.
(Pre-packed kits available for purchase at www.PuppyCoach.com)

First Aid Kit Contents:
- Gloves (non-latex disposable)
- Sterile saline
- Surgical tape
- Scissors
- Tweezers
- Fairy liquid (great for removing tar and toxins from fur)
- Blanket/towel
- Conform bandages
- Cohesive bandages
- Gauze
- Cotton wool
- Tick remover
- Syringes (for flushing)
- Torch
- Foil blanket
- Thermometer
- Hydrogen peroxide 3%

CHAPTER 30

Introduction to Adolescence and Final Guidance

Our final chapter provides a whistlestop tour of one of the most challenging life stages faced during the development of the dog. Adolescence!

Puppyhood will feel like a distant memory by the time your puppy reaches adolescence. Development changes are inevitable whatever sex or breed of dog you have. It is important to recognise and understand this transition and be prepared to consistently embed your leadership and direction. Now is NOT the time to back off and think your work is done!

Hogan sitting patiently with Jake, Sheba and Marley demonstrating how positive leadership during the puppy period is essential for maintaining good control through adolescence.

You can rest assured that all the hard work you have put in during your puppy's early life stage will still be present. It may just be masked in the short term by more challenging and boisterous behaviour patterns, especially if you have a male dog adjusting to testosterone!

Influence of Testosterone

It is important to consider the specific behaviour traits associated with this hormone. This means you should be able to recognise where you may be heading into trouble and more importantly, how you should be addressing the behaviour.

The message this hormone sends is ultimately concerned with empowering the dog to deliver behaviours associated with survival, as detailed in this table.

Behaviour Associated with Testosterone Production	Observed Physical Response
Increase impulse response	Dog becomes overly reactive to a variety of stimulus
Sexual motivation (reproductive status)	Competitive aggression to other male dogs in the presence of a female, mounting
Intense threat of aggression	A reactive response becomes threatening and dangerous
Lack of focus	Deterioration in recall and ability to concentrate during training
Irritability	Pacing, unable to settle, poor tolerance of social environments
Displays of strength	Barging, poor personal space awareness
Reduction in fear	Previous fearful response, replaced by confident reactive behaviour
Risk taking	Less cautious, more invasive
Roaming	Loss of recall and attempting to escape perimeters
Scent marking (territorial)	Indoor urination, persistent leg cocking outdoors

Considering Castration

This topic is consistently discussed by veterinary and behaviour professionals alike. I insist that every dog is judged individually as there are many affecting factors to be considered when assessing a dog's behaviour, not just its reproductive status.

For the purpose of this book and the advice I give, we will focus on the facts as we know them.

Firstly, I am convinced that no behaviour problem will be eradicated by castration alone. Even if testosterone is recognised as the original motivator for the behaviour. There will still be a learnt association that will need breaking down. There may be a reduction in the intensity of the behaviour but it will remain, unless a solid means of management is in place to break habits and reward positive outcomes.

I recommend castration of the dog for a variety of social and health reasons. However, once you have made the decision to have this elective procedure performed you can never go back. It is important that you take into consideration the timing and observe your dog's behaviours throughout.

The decision to castrate should be made after considering the following factors:

What is testosterone?

Testosterone is a steroid hormone produced primarily in the testis but also in the ovaries and adrenal cortex (small amount). It is responsible for the regulation of growth and moods, muscle and bone density and a variety of other physical and mental developmental factors. Early removal of this hormone could deny the dog reaching full adult maturity and have serious health implications.

Age of your dog

It is well documented that you should wait until your dog has reached sexual maturity before opting for castration. Testosterone begins to rise in puppies between 4–5 months of age and peaks at around 10 months with adult levels remaining consistent around 18 months. (Dunbar, 1999).

You will almost certainly witness a change in your dog's behaviour between 10–24 months as most will experience a surge in this hormone before it begins to settle.

Breed of your dog

While there is a general age range for the effects of testosterone, you should keep in mind that there will still be a breed variation and many large breeds will take much longer to mature than smaller ones.

Behaviours

I generally advise that you observe your puppy for obvious testosterone related behaviours and monitor these to decide when would be the best time to castrate. If you are experiencing severe male dog to dog aggression consistently and/or persistent mounting of other dogs/objects and/or humans then you will be required to prevent this exclusively until your dog has reached one year and then consider castrating soon after.

Health implication of early castration

Listing all the available studies on this subject is beyond the scope of this text. Suffice to say there is substantial evidence to suggest neutering a dog prior to one year may increase the risk of bone cancer, hypothyroidism and obesity. It may also delay the closure of bone growth plates resulting in joint disorders, such as hip and elbow dysplasia (Torres de la Riva et al., 2013).

Positive reasons for castration at the appropriate time

It can be an overwhelming decision to put your beloved puppy through an elective procedure but you can rest assured that there are many positive reasons for castration. The risk of testicular cancer is eradicated, you will observe a decrease in testosterone related behaviours which are mostly negative and evidence suggests a reduction in prostate related problems.

Fundamentally you will be removing your dog's ability to reproduce. Dog rescue centres are flooded with unwanted dogs so this control can only be a good thing in the long term.

Once you have decided to opt for castration I usually advise it is performed between 18 months and 2.5 years of age (depending on the dog and circumstance).

From a behaviour perspective you should ideally wait until your puppy is routinely cocking his leg. If you are considering neutering earlier then please seek professional advice as it may not produce the result you are looking for and could make some behaviour problems worse.

Considering the Bitch and Whether to Spay (Neuter)

You should not neuter your bitch as a treatment for any behaviour problem. On the contrary, removing the ovaries means you will strip your dog of not only oestrogen but also progesterone. Progesterone is known to have a calming affect over moods and is responsible for activating the release of serotonin 'the happy hormone'. This is in contrast to advice commonly given about male dogs.

You should apply the same principles to your decision as you would the male dog in respect of health implications. All the sex hormones play a part in the physical wellbeing and mental health and maturity of the dog. This means your focus should be to allow at least one season prior to neutering.

Understanding the process of the dogs oestrous cycle will help you recognise related behaviours and work out the most appropriate time to neuter.

The Oestrus Cycle

The oestrus cycle follows the same path in all dogs, although there may be variations in the length of each stage so observing your own dog is essential.

- PROESTRUS: Lasts 9 days (approx) – swollen vulva/bloody discharge/ will not mate
- OESTRUS: Lasts 7 days (approx) – as above but the bitch is ready ("in heat") to accept a mate
- DIOESTRUS: Lasts 60 days (approx) – period of sexual inactivity
- ANOESTRUS: Last 5 months (approx) – uterus prepares for the next proestrus

To avoid a sudden contrast between the presence of progesterone and its absence you should try to ensure the dog is in the Anoestrus period. This will also avoid the possibility of phantom (false) pregnancies becoming a problem after the procedure.

Your puppy may have their first season anytime from 6 months of age up to and around 12 months. The seasons will occur roughly every 7 months.

If you notice your dog displaying any of the following signs you should keep them on a lead and away from highly dog populated areas:

- Licking their genital area more than usual

- Subdued
- Bed making (nesting)
- Standing still with their tail to the side 'flagging'
- Vulval swelling
- Bleeding

Evidence exists suggesting neutering your puppy prior to a year of age will increase the risk of all of the following conditions:

- Osteosarcoma
- Splenic tumour
- Obesity
- Urinary incontinence
- Vaginal dermatitis
- Orthopaedic disorders

Neutering after this time is recommended and will reduce the incidence of mammary tumour and womb infections 'pyometra'.

General Behaviour

It is important for you to recognise that regardless of your training or your dog's reproductive status you may still experience behaviour changes that could be deemed undesirable. The teenage years will always be the most challenging.

Remember to adhere to your early understanding of what motivates and supports your dog:

Communicate

- Set the dog up to succeed
- Remind them of your direction twice
- Remove them if they are struggling and repeat once the dog has calmed down

All areas of your training will be affected during this rocky period so we will look at them individually.

Heel-work in the adolescent dog

It is important to make sure you are clear with your 'stop' command. This should not involve heavy checking or yanking, merely just to enough to make the dog aware they are at the end of the lead and you are changing direction. The strong contrast is that your dog is rewarded heavily when they do engage with you and you keep their focus.

This differs from the relaxed treat waving behaviour you would have practised in the early puppy weeks. It is now time to get tough and provide a non-physical consequence for rude, bolshy body-language.

Your puppy will be easily distracted and if you own a large breed you may struggle with some of the physical behaviours they display. These can be kept to a minimum if you choose areas of low stimulation, structure the walk and ensure you continue to practise training, keeping your dog engaged and focused on you.

If you feel you are losing control, my advice is to seek professional advice to help you through this period. There are many training leads and head collars available to support you during this tricky period and I would much rather see a dog walked on an appropriate training aid than watch them being dragged, or checked forcefully by a frustrated owner. A qualified professional will assess what is best for your dog at this time, taking age, breed and physical conformation into account. A training aid should do exactly that, aid your training, not just act as an invasive physical restraint.

Eye contact

Your early eye contact training is so important and it is during this period that you will see how invaluable it has been. It allows you a clear embedded connection with your dog that will be the tool you most require to controlling any adverse dog behaviour outside.

Continue to work on this during your normal daily activities. I deliver the command, 'look', before releasing Hogan from the heel position and also before allowing him to approach his food bowl.

Instinctive behaviours

No matter how well trained your puppy has been you should still expect them to give in to instinctive dog behaviours at times and the stronger the breed you have the more difficult this is to manage.

Staying focused on the primary behaviours your dog displays will prevent serious behaviours becoming habitual.

Chewing

Don't think the chewing phase has passed just yet. This problem may deteriorate as your puppy will have higher energy levels and be more difficult to tire. Teething may not be the only motivator for chewing during this life stage. Most adult teeth are all in place as the puppy enters adolescence and instead the motivators are boredom and frustration as they encounter this tricky life stage full of hormones and conflict.

You will need your crate or downtime area to manage your puppy when you are not around so don't pack things away just yet! Also make sure your kong toy isn't just lying around. This is an excellent tool for helping your dog cope with your absence so you should keep it 'high prize' by keeping control of it.

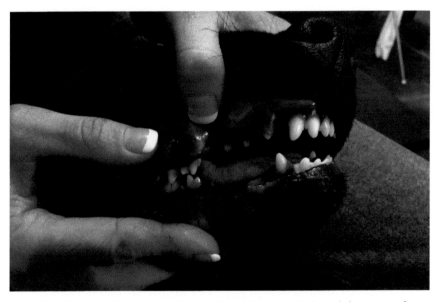

Hogan's mouth. You can see he is still cutting new teeth and disposing of old ones. Chewing is an essential part of the dog's ability to cope with the painful teething period but it does reduce as the puppy develops and the process comes to an end.

Recall

Adolescence is a key marker for a decline in recall so it is important that you have embedded a solid recall command such as a gun dog whistle, but more importantly you need to be aware of keeping your dog engaged or on a long line to manage any behaviour that is undesirable.

Your dog should return to you whenever you ask (and immediately) otherwise you may be considered not in control. If your dog goes on to bully or hassle another dog or involve itself in other social scenarios without consent you may quickly see the situation deteriorate.

If this occurs you should not continue to call your dog, instead, approach calmly and quietly and remove them swiftly. The behaviour is now beyond any level of sensible control. If behaviour escalates your dog is in danger of creating a negative experience for themselves as well as any other dogs involved.

This is invaluable learning for you as a puppy owner. You should recognise how easily things can go wrong even if the dog is fundamentally well behaved.

Stay and wait

Hogan practising one of his many 'down stays'.

I have consistently reiterated and reinforced self-control throughout. This is the most important aspect of your learning. If your puppy can tolerate sitting on the edge of a football pitch without chasing the ball, not charging into a group of dogs to join the play and sit quietly while you have a conversation, then you should be very proud. You will be making 99% of dog owners extremely jealous.

If not, well welcome to dog ownership – it's hard and there is no room for error. However, dogs live 'in the moment' so as soon as you recognise a potential issue, go back to basics, rein in control and consider your options. Start with re-addressing your stay and wait commands. This is easy to do at home and you can gradually build on the level of stimulation you introduce the more comfortable your dog becomes.

Social skills with other dogs

Observe your dog's behaviour with other dogs and correct any high energy or unbalanced behaviour. Keeping your dog close to you is the only way you can continue to encourage successful learning experiences.

You may also see aggressive behaviour patterns during adolescence and you need to monitor these closely and seek help if they are happening often. The earlier you spot a problem the more likely you are to correct it completely.

Make sure you continue to expose your puppy regularly, and under control, to a variety of different social environments. Your socialisation hasn't ended in the puppy period, it should continue throughout your dog's life, including in adulthood. Keep your expectations low, you are likely to find your once happy go lucky puppy is now displaying unbalanced behaviours. These may be defensive such as backing off, lacking in confidence, displaying signs of fear or the opposite, over excitable, jumping up, lunging and highly vocal. Remember this is just another stage and you will come through it, but it may be time to re-visit your leadership skills in the home and exercise a higher level of contact when you are out.

Dog fights

A dog fight has to be one of the most frightening situations any dog owner will encounter. The ferocity, noise and energy involved is horrific and most people panic before thinking rationally.

As I mentioned in an earlier chapter, you can take some comfort in the fact that the majority of fights are literally 'handbags at dawn' and actual damage is unlikely. Male dogs particularly communicate in a dominant fashion. Remember they don't have verbal conversations as we do so the growling, snarling and posturing is them asserting themselves. In many cases it is totally normal dog behaviour, albeit not acceptable in a human social environment!

Bite inhibition is your focus here. This concerns the level of intensity and damage your dog could cause if they bite. Often, dogs that bite regularly use more force every time and react quicker in each scenario. It is essential that you recognise a problem early on and before the behaviour develops.

If your dog has inflicted damage to the abdomen or legs of another dog on its first attack, then you have a very serious problem and should seek immediate professional help. Likewise, a dog attack of this nature should be reported to the authorities. Your dog should be muzzled and on a lead in this instance.

If you are just dealing with noise and no damage, then you have a relatively straightforward problem to fix with some guidance. Breaking the habit is essential and this is simply done by taking back more physical control. Focus on increasing your controlled training in social environments to ensure the focus is kept on you for high prize rewards. Lots of sit and down stays in a variety of different places will all help keep your dogs focus on your leadership rather than becoming distracted with territorial behaviours.

Keep that mouth soft!

Much of a puppy's bite awareness understanding is done during social interactions with the mother and siblings in the early puppy period. However, it makes sense to reinforce it through adolescence. Pay attention to your dog's mouth at home, look in it, lift up their lips and reward if they tolerate your handling.

Teach your dog the 'drop' and 'out' commands to encourage the bite and release on command. Always work with your dog in this way with a calm energy. Remember an overly excitable dog will be unable to learn.

Prey drive

Avoid opening up your dog's prey/chase drive instinctive behaviour at all costs. This natural instinct is more prevalent in particular breeds but is evident in all if their ability to cope socially is breached. Avoid really busy parks, make your walk consistently proactive and don't stop and chat as this creates an unstable environment for your puppy and negative behaviours may result. Likewise, ensure your puppy is on a lead and controlled in areas with livestock and wildlife.

New Behaviours to Consider

Irritable behaviour

This is a common problem in adolescence as the sex hormones are delivered to your dog's brain during this stage. Your puppy is suddenly an unstable teenager trying to understand expectations in a variety of different social encounters, usually involving humans. Be mindful of this and focus on using all the tools for self-control you have learnt from the Puppy Coach guidance. The 'bed' and 'mat' control and 'down- time' periods, 'boundary control' at doorways and leaving a lead on around the home are all excellent techniques for helping your developing dog display appropriate behaviour.

Reactivity

If your puppy is irritable they will naturally be reactive to highly stimulated situations, avoid these where possible and control their environment or remove them.

Do not allow high energy people or dogs to direct themselves towards your youngster, they need calm and balance during this difficult developmental phase.

Hopefully this section has highlighted what to expect from the adolescent period. It can come as a huge shock to some puppy owners when it arrives, especially if you have a large, strong breed. It is important to understand that this period will pass and all of the early training you have done will put you in a good position to manage your dog safely and effectively through this tricky stage of development.

Don't give up and don't get disheartened, you are not alone. Never allow your dog to become over stimulated or take on and empowered position in any environment. Management is easier if you set the boundaries and control early.

Task

Your task for this section is to make a checklist of the areas you are struggling with. Understand why and put an action plan together to deal with them using the advice you have been given.

Don't just make excuses for poor behaviour. It will need addressing.

"Thank you for investing the time and patience to become an intelligent, empowered dog owner. You are now well on your way to a fantastic understanding of canine behaviour, communication and welfare. Be proud of what you have achieved and enjoy a happy, healthy relationship with your puppy and ultimately well mannered adult dog"

with love, Jo x

Visit the www.PuppyCoach.com website for further video guidance and to interact with Jo.

Summary Quote

"You should always remember dogs are dogs, not humans. Applying a human perspective to their behaviour is detrimental to them, you and ultimately the relationship you have."

(Jo Croft, January 2016)

REFERENCES

Dunbar, I. (1999) An Owners Guide to a Happy Healthy Pet. Dog Behaviour. New York. Howell Book House.

Gencon All-in-1: www.puppycoach.com

Veterinary Surgeons Act, 1966. Available at: http://www.legislation.gov.uk/ukpga/1966/36 Accessed: 15/05/16

Goldkamp, C.E & Schaer, M. (2008). Canine Drowning. Available at: s3.amazonaws.com/assets.prod.vetlearn.com/mmah/20/36c72527524f05be65ba11beee8329/filePV_30_06_340.pdf Accessed: 15/05/16

Mullineaux, E & Jones, M. (2007). BSAVA Manual of Practical Veterinary Nursing. BSAVA

Pet MD. (2016) Low Body Temperature in Dogs. Available at:http://www.petmd.com/dog/conditions/cardiovascular/c_multi_hypothermia Accessed: 17/05/16

The Merck Veterinary Manual, 2015. Available at: http://www.merckvetmanual.com/mvm/appendixes/reference_guides/normal_rectal_temperature_ranges.html Accessed: 16/05/16

Torres de la Riva, G, Hart, B.L, Farver, T.B, Oberbauer, A.M, Locksley, L, Messam, Mcv, Willits, N, Hart, L.A (2013) Neutering Dogs: Effects on Joint Disorders and Cancers in Golden Retrievers. Online. Available: http://journals.plos.org/plosone/article?id=10.1371/journal.pone.0055937, Accessed: 28/06/16